Ideologies and the Corruption of Thought

IDEOLOGIES AND THE CORRUPTION OF THOUGHT

Joseph Gabel

EDITED WITH AN
INTRODUCTION BY

Alan Sica

TRANSACTION PUBLISHERS
NEW BRUNSWICK (U.S.A.) AND LONDON (U.K.)

Copyright © 1997 by Transaction Publishers,
New Brunswick, New Jersey 08903

All rights reserved under International and Pan-American Copyright Conventions. No part of this book may be reproduced or transmitted in any form or by any means, electronic or mechanical, including photocopy, recording, or any information storage and retrieval system, without prior permission in writing from the publisher. All inquiries should be addressed to Transaction Publishers, Rutgers—The State University, New Brunswick, New Jersey 08903.

This book is printed on acid-free paper that meets the American National Standard for Permanence of Paper for Printed Library Materials.

Library of Congress Catalog Number: 96-49045
ISBN: 1-56000-287-5
Printed in the United States of America

Library of Congress Cataloging-in-Publication Data

Gabel, Joseph.
  Ideologies and the corruption of thought / Joseph Gabel ; edited and with an introduction by Alan Sica and an epilogue by David F. Allen.
    p. cm.
  Includes bibliographical references and index.
    ISBN 1-56000-287-5 (cloth : alk. paper)
    1. Ideology. 2. Alienation (Social psychology) I. Sica, Alan, 1949– . II. Title.
HM24.G253   1997
302.5'44—dc21   96-49045
                                                                                       CIP

Contents

	Editorial Note	vii
	Introduction: Bridging Pathologies of the Individual and the Collective: Gabel's Contribution to Contemporary Analysis *Alan Sica*	1
1.	Utopian Consciousness and False Consciousness	61
2.	Political Delusion of a Paranoid Patient	71
3.	Axiology and Dialectics	89
4.	Durkheimianism and Political Alienation: Durkheim and Marx	101
5.	Jonathan Swift as Forerunner of the Theory of "Morbid Geometrism"	111
6.	Althusser and Orwell	117
7.	Political Ideologies	129
8.	Stalinism as Ideology	145
9.	McCarthyism: An American Form of Political False Consciousness	157
10.	Eugene Minkowski and the Problem of Alienation	165
11.	*Effet Pervers* and False Consciousness	175
12.	Racist Consciousness as a Form of False Consciousness	185
13.	Anti-Zionism as Ideology	191

vi   Ideologies and the Corruption of Thought

14. The Psychology of De-Stalinization and the
    Problem of Political Alienation   199

    Epilogue: From Schizophrenia to False Consciousness:
    Joseph Gabel and Theories of Psychopathology   211
        David F. Allen

    Name Index   221
    Subject Index   225

Editorial Note

Several years ago Joseph Gabel sent me from Paris a large collection of his essays, a few published in the 1950s, but most written during the last two decades. They treated an array of topics, from the clinically specific and minute to the boldly macropolitical and general. He asked that I select those which might interest today's Anglophone audience the most, which might best cohere as a book, and which were composed in such a way that they could be rewritten more or less into today's academic idiom. Through all this he hoped that his ideas could be presented as useful to contemporary theoretical concerns, yet with minimal distortion. Over time the book came together, but only through the efforts of many hands. A number of translators, working independently of each other over the last twenty years or so, did first drafts of the essays—all of which I have heavily edited—and my own immediate colleagues have also helped in various ways, specifically Samar Farage, Claire Amick, Michael Sauder, and Anne Sica. Samar Farage carried on lengthy transatlantic phone consultations with Joseph Gabel in French, clarifying the project as it developed. She also oversaw the conversion of rough typescripts into more managable word-processed manuscripts. David F. Allen served as intermediary from Paris, assisting Gabel at every turn, and helping considerably in supplying me with the raw materials from which the finished product was fashioned. Claire Amick word-processed one chapter on short notice with her usual skill. As always, Anne Sica efficiently copyedited and proofread, and at very reasonable rates. My colleague Allan Stoekl meticulously checked some thorny problems in French; errors that remain in that department are solely mine.

It is a tribute to the quality of Joseph Gabel's thinking, as well as his personality, that so many harried intellectual laborers have turned their collective goodwill in his direction. One hopes the final result justifies their struggles to get it right.

Introduction

Bridging Pathologies of the Individual and the Collective: Gabel's Contribution to Contemporary Analysis

Alan Sica

> "I dedicate this book, which is written to oppose fanaticism of all kinds, to the memory of my mother who disappeared at Auschwitz in 1945 and my father who died unconsoled in New York in 1968."

In 1975 Joseph Gabel wrote this chilling epigraph for the English language version of his masterpiece, *False Consciousness*. His dialectical joining of the searingly personal with the baldly public has, over the last fifty years, distinguished Gabel's theoretical position from all others within the "Hungaro-Marxist" camp—as he himself named an eclectic group of polymathic scholars. To recall thirty years after the fact that one's mother "disappeared" in Auschwitz—that memory/place about which "everyone" now "knows," and the history of which, as Adorno desperately observed, would invalidate the future's authentic claims to humor or good cheer; further, to record for an anonymous audience that one's father not only died alone in a foreign place twenty years thereafter, but within the harrowing region of "the unconsoled," demands a sort of intellectual character that today's bureaucratization of theoretical imagination makes ever more difficult to sustain. Gabel's consciousness is loftily analytical while, *at the same time*, morally outraged, and therefore assumes a rhetorical shape that is fast disappearing from the Western cultural stage. To brush aside his unique "take" on the world is criminally wasteful, for there remain few others who have shaped a unified vision of the private hell belonging to mental derangement, and, from the other side of the ledger, the gulag-consciousness of the so-called "public sphere" that has embalmed so much of the world since Gabel's mother bore him in 1912. In today's chic jargon, Gabel is the quintessential "micro-macro" theorist *avant le lettre*.

The bulk of my introduction—of my bulky introduction, one might observe—attempts a point-by-point hermeneutic treatment of *False Consciousness*, which played the same key role in Gabel's scholarship that, say, *Truth and Method* did in Gadamer's; both seminal works being published within two years of each other, on opposing sides of the Rhine, as it were. Gabel's book is the theoretical pivot around which the rest of his considerable oeuvre turns. My goal, in writing the introduction in a specific way, is to introduce English-language scholars to a realm of axiological philosophy, Marxism, clinical psychiatry, epistemology, and politics that seems today terra incognita to most students of sociocultural theory—that is, beyond the tight perimeter of Hungarian Marxism and French intellectualism wherein Gabel has labored for many decades.

The collection of essays presented here, however, reveals another side of Gabel's creativity that is less connected to clinical data than was *False Consciousness*, and points more toward a set of cultural totems and patterns which he sought out to suit his particular analytic and political concerns. Though only two of Gabel's books are in English to date, he has published many others in French, including *Sociologie de l'aliénation* (1970), *Idéologies* (1974), *Idéologies II* (1978), *Actualite de la dialectique* (1980), *Reflexions sur l'avenir des Juifs* (1987), and *Etudes dialectiques* (1990). Most of his writing takes the easily recognizable form of the French essay, geared as much to an informed laity as to his professionalized colleagues. This gives his work that special Gallic flavor so distant in form and function from that of his peers (and former enemies) "next door." Whereas German scholars who examine alienation, mental illness, or the ideological corrosion of serious thought normally do so from within a redoubt of exhaustive bibliographical apparatus, Gabel prefers the semi-journalistic essay—in its etymological meaning—in which he can bring together theorizing of a high level with topical events on the global sociopolitical scene. This gives his essays on McCarthyism, Althusserianism, anti-Semitism, and racism an unforbidding depth that does not occur often enough nowadays in similar discussions in the Anglophone world.

There is a price of admission to Gabel's fascinating performance. Without a fairly reliable understanding of works associated with the names and the spirits of Minkowski, Binswanger, Dupréel, Meyerson, Bergson, Lukács, Mannheim, Marx, and a number of others, Gabel's vocabulary might quickly become a mere clanging of the polysyllabic. Just as Marcuse's famous "repressive desublimation" made no sense outside the confines of Freudo-Marxist thought, Gabel's own terminological set (e.g., "morbid dedialectization" or "axiological temporality") soon begin to cloud the mind, not unlike deconstructionist jargon-fests which have recently surfaced among Derrida's American apostles. My introduction is built around forays into Gabel's far-flung sources in order to simplify the patient reader's task, and to show that his neologisms are worth the trouble of comprehension. Or so I hope will prove to be the case.

The Genesis of Gabel's Neglected Achievement

The sociology of scholarly knowledge cannot as yet fully explain why certain new ideas are widely resisted or ignored, for a time, regardless of their manifest power to illuminate, while others are deftly assimilated. This phenomenon becomes most noticeable when theoretical material is reappraised at some remove in time and place from its point of origin. Why, for instance, has this century's social thought witnessed moments of such sharply contrasting enthusiasms (e.g., for Spencer, Durkheim, Pareto, Weber, Freud, Mead, Sorokin, Mannheim, Marx, finally, and those he inspired, like Lukács, Marcuse, and the Frankfurt School), during which each successive figure was hailed as the new and best guide to enlightenment, then allowed temporarily to rule as the favored stimulus for theoretical change and correlated research? (Though most of those named suffered translation into English, all finally received their due in spite of it.)

Two of the oddest cases that illustrate this fleeting centrality were the Hungarian friends, Lukács and Mannheim. The former's major work finally arrived in English in 1971, forty-eight years after its German publication, and thirty-five years after its author had repudiated his most ingenious theorizing in favor of a circumspect Stalinism. His sometime companion, Mannheim, was luckier, for his early fortunes benefitted from the mighty sponsorship of Louis Wirth and the translation energy of Edward Shils (for details, see Kettler and Meja 1994). Yet his major work, *Ideology and Utopia*, now seems somewhat hesitant and theoretically troubled when compared with Lukács'.

Joseph Gabel, strongly influenced by both these theorists (Gabel 1975; 1991) published a work in 1962 that remained unknown in this country until 1975, when its third edition appeared (under a British imprint) as *False Consciousness*. (A paperback version in 1978 did not add to Gabel's renown; both are long out of print.) After receiving several standard reviews, mostly "mixed" in judgment (e.g., Fried 1977; Owen 1978; Swingewood 1977), a single review essay (Tristram 1976), and one appreciative article (Broughton 1976), the book slipped almost entirely from view among its intended audiences: sociologists, Marxists, philosophers, and psychiatrists. The author qualifies as a member of all these groups, and wrote the book for inclusion in their interlaced discourses. (By contrast, there do exist helpful reviews of his other works, e.g., Anctil 1990; Kurzweil 1989.)

In fact, the principal strength of Gabel's book, aside from sheer inventiveness, is the role it serves for the sympathetic reader as a window onto several intellectual and political worlds very seldom amalgamated into theoretically fruitful dialogue. His intentions are vaguely connected with those of Marcuse, Norman O. Brown, R.D. Laing, and writers of those general tendencies. Yet Gabel's project is easily distinguished from theirs. It was not designed to implement "emancipation," aesthetic, political, or personal. Instead, it is the single broadest and most penetrating fusion of clinical psychiatric data, axiology, *Wissenssoziologie*, phenomenological and existential psychiatry, *Kulturkritik*, and Hungarian Marxism yet created. Even the most tepid reviewers saw the great ambition of the book and the sheer novelty of its eclectic, yet coherent, nature. It achieves something rare in social theory: genuine innovation about matters of practical and theoretical importance.

Why has it gone unheeded? The answer partially lies in the text's extraordinary density and unusual style (most of it written for French audiences, whose tolerance for theoretical experimentation is well known), in Gabel's global claims for his theory, and in the fact that no school nor celebrated figure has taken up the book's disturbing central dictum and made it their own. According to *False Consciousness*, schizophrenia is a form of mental distortion whose root processes (reification, morbid rationality, spatio-temporal inversion, etc.) are *identical* to those found in ideologically motivated sociopathologies, such as ethnocentrism, anti-Semitism, and genocidal dehumanization; in short, schizophrenia *is* false consciousness, and vice versa—which is why Gabel is important for social theory, and not only mental health treatment. In his own words: "I have tried to show that some forms of schizophrenia are tantamount to a process of reification of consciousness. In this optic schizophrenia thus appears as an individual form of false consciousness, that is, of the totalitarian mind" (Locher 1981: 170).

This belated essay is offered to rectify in part what ought not to become a permanent slight. In order to provide a worthy hermeneutic of *False Consciousness*, intrinsically as well as contextually helpful, some background is necessary regarding earlier attempts at creating a Marxist theory of psychopathology and personality, and with reference to Gabel's special intellectual debts. Without this understanding, his effort remains impenetrable.

Early Marx/Freud Syntheses: From Reich to Marcuse

Social science journals are no longer filled with serious references to Freud, and use of Jung, Roheim, Reich, Rank, Fenichel, even Fromm remains negligible. Relatedly, social theory texts seldom include Freud and never his lesser followers or opponents in the psychoanalytic and psychiatric traditions. Sociology does not feel pressed to answer the Freudian challenge to its own theories of socialization and sociopathology (i.e., deviance). Those practitioners who do respond become exceptional by definition (e.g., Bocock 1978; Chodorow 1978, 1994; Dollard and Miller 1950; Nelson 1957; Parsons 1964; Wallerstein and Smelser 1969; Weinstein and Platt 1969, 1973; for others, see Kaye 1991: 103–5). And though there is probably a *general* awareness among theorists today of what psychoanalytic ideas mean, there is much less technical expertise than during the fifties and sixties, when Talcott Parsons, David Riesman, Philip Rieff, Benjamim Nelson, and others acquired intimate knowledge of its propositions for both individual and cultural explanation. Interesting exceptions—for example, Alford 1988; Craib 1990; Rabow 1987; Rose 1990; Samuels 1993; Yannis 1983—prove the rule. Also, the sometime ambivalent animus some feminists express toward the Freudian tradition simply adds to its current condition of *ratio non grata* (*inter alia*, Brennan 1992). Freudian, Jungian, and Reichian theories of personality offend sociological sensibility largely because of their fundamental concern with "instinct," however shrewdly defined. Sociologists automatically balk at the "social policy implications" apparently inseparable from doctrines perceived as deterministic (a judgment etched with acid by LaPiere in his little-known but emblematic polemic, *The Freudian Ethic*).

If this is true for most sociologists, it should have been so *a fortiori* for Marxists, for whom "irrational instinct" was always regarded as a theoretical enigma and bourgeois conceit (Lukács 1980; Nahem 1981; Voloshinov 1976). Yet, as is well known, the mutual attraction between Marxism and Freudianism, and subsequently for other varieties of psychiatric thought and practice, was for decades a prominent part of Western intellectual life. (The alliance still inspires substantial theoretical labors, though their frequency has dropped off substantially since its *annus mirabilis* a dozen years ago: Balbus 1982; Cohen 1982; Endleman 1981; Kovel 1982; Lichtman 1982; Wolfenstein 1993.) During the 1920s Marxists assayed the use to be made of psychoanalytic doctrine, an effort which reached its apogee[1] with Reich's "Sex-

Pol" essays (1929–43/1972). Reuben Osborn contributed an early statement in English (1937 [1965]), but the next significant attempt at synthesis (excluding the revisionists) was Marcuse's *Eros and Civilization* (1955), arguably the most important work of the genre.

During the 1960s political events demanded that Marxists within active factions in Europe and the U.S. reconsider Marcuse's and Reich's efforts to incorporate individual consciousness into theories of class struggle and the dynamics of capitalism. The apt quotation was Merleau-Ponty's: "Thus Marxism needs a theory of consciousness which accounts for its mystification without denying its participation in truth" (1973:41), written in the mid-fifties, but used polemically later on.[2] The fruits of this third or fourth generation Freudo-Marxist encounter included Reiche (1970), Bruce Brown (1973), Phil Brown (1974), and Schneider (1975). The strength of these monographs, as different as they were, lay in restating the basic themes of Freudian dogma as sociologized in the fifties by humanist Marxism, but then shifting the debate, as it were, from "behemoth" to the "affirmative culture" of the sixties.

Such efforts had their critics, of course. Lasch, for example, saw such appropriation of Freud by the Left as ill suited to both:

> In other words, they [the New Left] turned to Freud for very good reasons. Unfortunately they brought with them a set of assumptions that owed more to the socialistic theory of the family (as Max Weber once called it) than to the founder of psychoanalysis. Their attempt to base a general theory of culture on psychoanalysis, or to read psychoanalysis itself as a general theory of culture, led them further and further away from the critical core of psychoanalysis: its interpretation of clinical data. What began as a fruitful confrontation between psychoanalysis and Marxism ended in a reassimilation of psychoanalytic ideas to an older socialist critique of the patriarchal family—a critique that is becoming increasingly irrelevant to the conditions of advanced industrial society, misleading at best, downright dangerous at worst (1981: 25–26).

It was precisely this combination of theoretical errors that Gabel completely avoided, but neither Lasch nor the authors he criticized seemed to know of his alternative theory.

In a sense, though, students of Reich, Marcuse, Fromm, and their epigoni found nothing fundamentally original in such works of the New Left, because the basic configuration—Freud deinstinctualized, Marx psychologized—was left unchanged. Terms of the debate were somewhat updated, but Marcuse's notion of repressive desublimation, for instance, was neither transcended nor eliminated. Schneider's German view, emphasizing work and consumption as pathogenic, stands in interesting counterpoint to Brown's American version which turns on individual repression, but both fall well within theoretical limits established decades earlier. Among the basic themes are these: fractionalization of the family due to capitalist social organization; enforcement of excessive psychosexual repression among the proletariat (and their masters, for that matter) to fit industrial and bureaucratic discipline; doctrinal subordination of women and ideological affirmation of their inferiority to men in the social world; more importantly, homologous reconstruction (or decomposition) of the personality along the lines of "commodity fetishism"; finally, critique of the potentially repressive nature of psychotherapy.

In spite of the substantial attention such ideas received on the left, academic, and even mainstream press (e.g., Stillman 1969)—while little noticed in sociology journals—they have failed to stimulate in the U.S. the excitement that greeted the more recent French contribution of Deleuze and Guattari, *Anti-Oedipus* (1977), a sympathetic Lacanian response to R. D. Laing, and their *Thousand Plateaus: Capitalism and Schizophrenia* (1987), both much appreciated among certain circles here and abroad (see Massima, 1992; *Semiotext(e)* 2:3 [1977]; Turkle 1978: 141–53). Even allowing for the jargon and syntax of poststructuralism, the strictly theoretical distance between *Anti-Oedipus* and *Eros and Civilization* seems definitive.[3] It might roughly be likened to the use made of Marx by the Frankfurt school of the 1930s compared to his propagandized image within Communist party ideologies at the same time; that is, another polarizing of "soft" and "hard" Marxism, as in Adorno versus Althusser. For Marcuse a "political-economy of the unconscious" (Gross, 1972)[4] could surely be appealing metaphorically, but would not make for plausible theoretical extension. Yet for more recent French Marxism of several types, a virtually calculable political-economy of psychic processes, linked materialistically from the outset to commodity fetishism—Marx's supreme conceptual inspiration for these writers—is not only promising but essential to their political and psychotherapeutic goals.

But to take *Anti-Oedipus* as the sole expression on these matters within French left thought would be quite wrong. At least two other major statements exist which deserve a reading from theorists resolved to heed Merleau-Ponty's general advice, by bending *Capital*, in spirit and word, into rapprochement with the psychological knowledge (and condition) of the late twentieth century, and to overcome the "triumph of the therapeutic" (Rieff 1966).[5] These two are Lucien Séve's *Marxisme et la théorie de la personnalité* (1969), translated from the third edition as *Man in Marxist Theory and the Psychology of Personality*, and Gabel's *La fausse conscience* (1962).[6] Both works are little known here, even to professional chroniclers of Marxism (e.g., Agger, 1979, who mentioned neither). In France these men are well known (Postel, 1994: 743–52; Poster, 1975:133, 261–63, 308n), but even there those who have enticed Freud and Marx into the same theoretical frame (Sartre, Lacan, some would say Levi-Strauss) do not use Séve or Gabel. On the other hand, both have been known there to the political public, Séve for his leadership in the Communist party, Gabel for his polemical attacks upon conceptual Stalinization in periodicals of wide distribution such as *Masses*, *Esprit*, and *Revue socialiste*. As for translations of their work into English, aside from these *Hauptwerke*, there is little. Séve carried on a famous debate in France with Godelier which was later translated (1972). And Gabel published two small essays in *Telos* (1975; 1976), reprinted and augmented in a small monograph on Mannheim that quickly disappeared from view (Gabel 1991), issued a minor piece on Durkheimianism (Gabel 1982), and one brief chapter in Stehr and Meja (1984).

Curt bibliographical reference to Gabel's *False Consciousness* is typically misleading (e.g., Berger and Luckmann 1967:200), since the book is not about "reification" or "false consciousness" as commonly understood (Berger and Pullberg 1965).[7] Instead, it concerns what Gabel, following Minkowski, calls "morbid rationalism" and the consequences of "de-dialecticization" in the intrapsychic *and* interpersonal worlds. A number of other authors from disparate fields have *cited* Gabel for their own purposes (e.g., Adams 1982: 535, 540; Blankenburg 1980: 101, 106; Bloom 1978: 546; Doerner 1981: 305; Ericson 1991: 235; Eyerman 1981: 314; Frug 1980: 1079; Peter Gabel 1977: 639; Gachnochi and Skurnik 1992: 242; Harris and Shorter 1978: 292; Karapostolis 1985: 694; Kemali 1986: 78; Kettler et al. 1990: 1444n3; Lefebvre 1991b: 22n, as "Jean" Gabel; Mezirow 1985: 150; Reich 1991: 1442; Rogers 1981: 151, 157; Sallnow 1989: 249, 257; Warren 1989: 526, 533). But far fewer have appropriated his ideas with any thoroughness (Broughton 1981a: 18, 25; 1981b: 382, 388, 390, 403; 1983: 629; Broughton and Zahaykevich 1982: 167, 173; Brown 1987: 146; Kafka 1983: 32–38; Hull 1991: 354–55; Warren 1990: 605–7, 616, 618, 623, 631, 633).

For example, Berger and Pullberg's didactic division of reification into four separate concepts (1965: 199ff) is uninspired when compared with Gabel's manifold theoretical display. Indeed, there is a "pre-Gabelian" and "post-Gabelian" reckoning of "reification," and so far as I can tell, very few to date—not even Lukács himself—have crossed the threshold from the former, inferior understanding, to the latter. (The same can be said for Séve's intricate theory of personality.[8] The only extended comment about Séve's book in English came from an Italian Engelsian Marxist who warmly admitted the importance of the contribution, then turned it aside for extratextual reasons [Timpanaro 1975: 212–19].) There are, however, a few bright lights of recognition, especially regarding the stark adumbration of Gabel's ideas regarding time's spatialization and parallel notions that inhabit postmodernist thought (see Maley 1994: 148–49, 160–61, 165–66, who analyzes these similarities, as proposed by Jameson [1984] and "the new political geographers," Brunn and Leinbach [1991]).

If, as I claim, Gabel and Séve are wrongly neglected by social theorists concerned with capitalism and individual life (or by others pursuing personality theory or psychopathology), one wonders why they have been ignored. Sheer textual difficulty is undeniably part of it, but Sartre's analogous work, *Critique de la raison dialectique*, has found numerous commentators among Marxists and non-Marxists, and by comparison is triply prolix and doubly ambiguous, not to say confused (see Lichtheim 1967: 282–315 or Aron 1975). In addition, both Séve and Gabel based their works on empirical data, dear to mainstream methods, while Sartre has not (unless "data" be redefined along Sartrean lines). Examining in detail one of these texts—the one most synthetically ambitious and theoretically creative of all recent attempts—might disclose some sources of resistance, while demonstrating the wastefulness of such dismissal.

Gabel's Points of Departure: Lukács, Mannheim, Minkowski, Binswanger, Lalo, Duprèel, Meyerson

Gabel was born in Budapest on July 12, 1912, and, leaving his homeland due to a racial quota system then controlling higher education, studied medicine, philosophy, and psychiatry at the University of Paris, graduating in 1939 with a medical thesis concerning madness and genius in Maupaussant (Allen 1994:1). His "much missed mentor" (Gabel in Thomas 1977) and friend was Eugene Minkowski, the phenomenological psychiatrist, known in English for *Lived Time*. Gabel taught with false papers in Toulouse during World War II, and then fled to Spain in 1944, continuing to teach and publish about schizophrenia. His return to France gave him time to write his *These d'état, La fausse conscience*. He taught, as a "sociologist of knowledge" (personal communication), in Rabat, Morocco from 1965 through 1971, and then at the University of Picardy in Amiens from 1971 until his retirement. As he explained, "I am particularly interested in questions of ideology, utopia, false consciousness, and reification, and have tried to personalize the school of Hungarian Marxism" (Locher 1981: 170).

Poster (1975:261) identifies him as part of the *Arguments* group (Henri Lefebvre, Edgar Morin, Kostas Axelos, and Pierre Fougeyrollas) which revitalized Marxism in France between 1956 and 1962 by liberating it from Stalinist dogma as embodied in the French CP. It encouraged attention to existentialism, phenomenology, and even bourgeois social science to combat the stultifying party line. *Arguments* sponsored publication of Gabel's second doctoral dissertation. Though hardly a carefree eclecticism, the congeries of sources he used seemed to be assembled within few formal boundaries, and discloses in part an autodidact. Gabel's encyclopedic intellectual imperialism, as we shall see, is in keeping with a cosmopolitan Marxism that needed desperately to shake off Soviet ideological influence, while at the same time illuminating postwar French life ("*la vie quotidienne*" as explored by Lefebvre 1991a [1947/58]), and the psychopathologies that mark late modernity.

False Consciousness describes a new intellectual orbit, as robust and variegated as any put forth in recent decades, whether in psychiatry, social-psychology, or sociology. Though its bibliography lists 502 works (all of which are cited in the text), the critical direction comes from a handful of writers: Mannheim, Lukács, Ludwig Binswanger, Eugene Minkowski, Emile Meyerson, Charles Lalo, and Eugene Dupréel, plus scores of psychiatric and psychoanalytic clinicians.[9] And though Gabel has published in French since 1939, his unique mix of Mannheim's "partial" versus "total" ideology, Lukács' "reification," Minkowski's and Binswanger's phenomenological-existentialist psychiatry, Meyerson's concept of epistemological "identity," and Dupréel's axiology of "precariousness" and "consistency," is the unmistakable hallmark of cheerfully eclectic "Hungarian Marxism" (Gabel 1975). This school, mostly Jewish and from Budapest, included Lukács, Mannheim, B. Fogarasi, E. Szabo, P. Szende, I. Meszaros, even Arthur Koestler, and shared a noted capacity for theoretical synthesis and reconstruction. (Gabel hypothesizes that this intellectual efflorescence in Budapest between 1900 and 1920 was due to "marginality" of the kind Simmel immortalized [1975:187].) Gabel's work epitomizes this tradition of virtuoso amalgamation.

Thus, Gabel's analytical apparatus and its exotic vocabulary are an agglomeration from the works of the principal theorists listed above, given empirical substance by copious reference to clinicians' reports. His mission has been to transform explanations of schizophrenia so that they freshly illuminate disturbances that have collective consequences, that is, behavior anchored in distorted (ideological) thought. He sees ideological consciousness as by definition reified, that is, paralyzed, and temporally frozen, due to the collapse of dialectics. "Dedialecticization"—the refusal or inability of thought and action to partake of life's salutary progression through antipodes and resolution—produces an atmosphere conducive to collective conceptual distortion as well as atomized psychic crises. The question might be asked whether Gabel's confidence in dialectics as "normal," as nonpathogenic, is as much an empirical observation of health as it is a "normative" theoretical axiom, indebted to Hegel, Marx, and Lukács. But before this can be answered, an examination of the works that motivated Gabel is required.

Lukács

The first pages of *False Consciousness* are among the book's most difficult. Gabel's careful reliance on key sources is documented when he introduces the central concept, "reification." In a virtuosic footnote (6–7), Gabel defends Lukács' formulation, does battle with a number of critics (including Lukács himself!), and then turns to Bergson, Binswanger, Minkowski, Roheim, and others in redefining the term: "an existential entity involving mainly phenomena of spatialization and devaluation... whose clinical expression is schizophrenia" (7, n.11). This use of Lukács first appeared in Gabel's writings of 1951 and 1952, "where the Lukácsian point of view is summarized from the viewpoint of its relevance for psychopathology." While admitting to a "personal terminology" (ibid.), he insists that his reading of all these men's works generates an indisputable dictum: *"the world of reification is the center of a decline of dialectical temporalization with a compensating prevalence of spatial functions,"* thus "... the link with the psychiatric conceptions of Minkowski and Binswanger" (8, n.12; emphases always in original unless noted otherwise). And as for creatively corrupting Lukács, Gabel explains:

> My aim has been—all questions of orthodoxy aside—simply to find a formula for *social* alienation which might concretely encompass a sector of *psychiatric* alienation, that is to say for which clinical and phenomenological study of schizophrenia... might provide experimental support. Lukács' view which involves elements as "psychopathological" as the category of totality, reification or anti-dialectical false identification, seems to be able to offer such a formula. (35)

Marx had little to say about spatialization of time and sociotemporal relations. Lukács recalls the famous paragraph from *The Poverty of Philosophy* ("Time is everything, man is nothing; he is, at the most, time's carcass. Quality no longer matters. Quantity alone decides everything . . . " [Marx/Engels 1976: 127; Lukács 1971: 89–90].) Gabel's insight concerning the "indirect Bergsonian influence experienced by Lukács" (149, n.7) seems borne out by Lukács' ensuing remarks:

> Thus time sheds its qualitative, variable, flowing nature [what he later calls "the irrationality of the given world," 118]; it freezes into an exactly delimited, quantifiable continuum filled with quantifiable "things" (the reified, mechanically objectified "performance of the worker [Binswanger would say "the patient"], wholly separated from his total human personality): in short, it becomes space. (1971: 90)

The footnote to this section directs the reader to *Capital*, volume 1, where Marx analyzes heterogeneous versus organic manufacturing. In his least philosophical tone, Marx points out that "different stages of the process [heterogeneous manufacturing] previously successive in time, have become simultaneous and contiguous in space" (1977: 469). Marx does not mean here the phenomenological space of interiority, but simply relations of space among workers and their tasks within the factory. Lukács' *apparently* cogent extrapolation of Marx's term into the sociopsychological (even ontological) realm owes more to Bergson, Husserl, and Weber than to Marx, which, of course, is partly why he later repudiated the book, and wrote *The Destruction of Reason*.

Gabel is always the pragmatist when colonizing others' ideas. Whereas Lukács suffered from his lingering Kantian tendencies, longing for a fuller *Lebensphilosophie* than Marxism could provide, Gabel's driving motive is not ideological purity, but clinical precision and enlarged applicability. He believes that mental illnesses can be interpreted with more verity through dissection of reificatory processes—particularly vis-a-vis space/time relationships—than by means of conventional theories. And yet he acknowledges uncertainty about the Lukács-Binswanger-Minkowski path of the book: " . . . [I]s it legitimate to contrast space and time radically? If I personally tend to contrast them with each other in a rather rigid way, it is because my earlier studies of political alienation seem to justify the value of such a contrast as a working hypothesis" (253).

Gabel then notes both Minkowski's and Binswanger's reservations about "a too absolute confidence in the Bergsonian categories." But even as he explores this difficulty further—"To talk in psychology of space and (or) time is in any case an abstraction; no being exists in pure time or pure space..." (254)—he harks back to Lukács' original theme, that is, "duration... degraded into spatialized time in the... rationalization of the production line worker" (ibid.), because, finally:

> ... time is axiogenic and space devaluing (the basis of the conceptions of Ostwald, Köhler, and Dupréel); but it is a secondary problem to know whether it is time which creates conditions of value or, on the contrary, whether it is the presence of value which structures—and consequently temporalizes—the milieu; both possibilities may be true, according to the chosen perspective, and in psychopathology, according to the pathogenic mechanisms at issue. (255)

He then offers his "triple convergence": "sub-axiology" in the "pre-temporal stage" of childhood, the "axiological void" of schizophrenia, saturated by spatialization, and the crises similar in structure but less chasmic for those in "the world of false consciousness." But what does his central contention really mean, that "time" *creates* value, "space" destroys it? It is here that Lukács is as much responsible for Gabel's key point of departure as any of the French axiologists who figure in *False Consciousness*. By returning briefly to *History and Class Consciousness*, we can see why and how.

"*Die Zeit ist der Raum der menschlichen Entwicklung*" (Time is the space of human development), and whether "*Raum*" is rendered "place" (Lukács 1971: 166), "room" (Marx/Engels 1969: vol. 2: 68), or "space" (Gabel 1978: 149, n.7), the point Marx wanted to make in *Wages, Price, and Profit* is consistent with Lukács' great fructification of the theme sixty years later.[10] What is at stake is a correct understanding of the "total personality" (Lukács 1971: 90) and its susceptibility to distortion: "the personality can do no more than look on helplessly while its own existence is reduced to an isolated particle and fed into an alien system." The "perfectly closed system"—lacking axiogenic "precariousness"—"reduces space and time to a common denominator and degrades time to the dimension of space" (89), and from this arises the "atomization [detotalization] of the individual" (91) and its "reified consciousness" (93).

Perhaps the central antinomy within Lukács' thought, which Gabel does not explicitly challenge, concerns what Fichte christened the *"hiatum irrationalem"* (known to Weber and others as *"hiatus irrationalis"*): "The absolute projection of an object *of the origin of which no account can be given. . . . the space between the projection and the thing projected is dark and void"* (Lukács 1971: 119). This legacy of Weber—an ascetic, even aesthetic, intolerance for "the irrationality of the given world"—affected Lukács profoundly, and what he therefore refused to perceive was the strong possibility that alienated, detotalized, anaxiogenic, reified consciousness—the "place" of anti-dialectics—might very well "live" *beyond* a mode of being-in-the-world into which the saving grace of dialectics can be reintroduced. It might endure within a *schädliche Raum* itself—a "maleficent space"[11]—that is, the mere sorry present, over which, according to Lukács himself, subject and object struggle hopelessly to merge (1971: 204). This possibility Lukács utterly ignored, *assuming* instead that reified consciousness "wished" emancipation into the realm of rational control, of deobjectivization.

Gabel bests Lukács here, because for him the remarkable feature of modern life is not that *schädliche Raum* exists, but that it is not totally in command of all consciousness, that dialectical forces in opposition to schizophrenic/ideological pathologies manage to surface at all—in short, that *Brave New World* has been postponed. Gabel, therefore, has taken the kernel of Lukács' polemic against "The Antinomies of Bourgeois Thought" (Lukács. 1971: 110–49)—*das Irrationalitätsproblem*, as it came to be known—and has shown that thought and social action do not fall into these unsavory, "inorganic" postures principally because of "rationalization," but rather, because the "precariousness" and "irreversability" (150) of dialectical life are *naturally* more prone to degeneration than their opposites—concretized ideologization and reification of living processes: *"the state of being crushed by the World"* (153). It practically becomes a matter of inertia, as unforgettably documented in Binswanger's "Ellen West" case (May 1958: 275ff).

Gabel does not say this, of course, since such an admission would jeopardize his Marxism, but the rudimentary form of such a belief appears beneath his book; which brings us full circle to the question of "normal" versus "normative" dialectics. The tortured beauty of *History and Class Consciousness* lies in its Enlightenment pose taken quite unselfconsciously, in that Reason is held responsible for saving itself and humankind from its own creation—oppressive rationality. Lukács cannot theoretically acknowledge the beneficent influence of *ir*rationality, as could Bergson, because Marx had made no theoretical or practical room for it. But if time—fluid, changing, creative—is related conceptually to the nonrational, and if space is the rational given "form," then Gabel's focus on this dialectic as propitious to the good, nonreified (authentic) existence is indeed "normative"— *but* all the while with a foot in the empirical givenness of untroubled authenticity. The "normal" is given in "blocks" (cf. Minkowski's case of "blocked time," time stopped *and* cut into chunks [Minkowski 1970: 186; May 1958: 133]), which dialectics (temporalization) can animate, *if* social structure allows it to occur—which is where Gabel's Marxism shows. And it is upon this collection of Lukácsian themes and notions that Gabel erects his synthetic method by which a simultaneous Marxist hermeneutic of derangement *and* ideological experience becomes not only integrally feasible, but fairly obvious. Without the seminal passages from *History and Class Consciousness* noted above, Gabel's plan would not have been possible, but for our purposes—even though Lukács is his main inspiration—it is equally important to register his debts to others.

Mannheim

Gabel provides a bridge between Lukács and Mannheim, at the same time compressing many of the former's ideas explored above:

> ... false consciousness and ideology are two aspects of the reificational rejection of the dialectic: false consciousness as a diffused state of mind (*Wahnstimmung* type), ideology as its theoretical crystallization of a generally justificatory nature ([Pareto's] derivation). These are *schizophrenic* phenomena to the extent that this state of mind can be defined as having a reificational structure. The spatio-temporal structure of false consciousness is characterized by the preponderance of static, anti-dialectical spatial experience ... The result (logical and empirical) is a crisis in temporalization ... a process of devaluing ... It is as a crisis in dialectical temporal-

ization—at the level of the dimension of the historical future—that utopian consciousness joins this combination. (22)

Mannheim becomes important for Gabel in exploring the relation between "utopian consciousness" and false consciousness. As with Lukács, Gabel brings Mannheim into his theory early in the book (22–36), again modifying the original to fit his interests. Two of Mannheim's *Hauptideen* explicitly underlie Gabel's scheme: (1) the difference between partial and total ideologies, and (2) the condition of *seinsgebundenes Denken* (thought determined by—"bound up with"—existence) and the "privileged point of view" (*Standorte*) claimed by Mannheim for intellectuals, and for the proletariat by Lukács, who in each case elude the normal constraints of cognition and judgment.

As might be expected, Gabel accepts "total" ideology as a "corollary of false consciousness" (23), but rules out a Marxist use of "partial" ideology because of its intrinsic voluntarism. He concedes that Marx himself—particularly when attacking religion—fell into the "voluntary mystification" that burdens the term. "Utopian consciousness" is partial ideology, since it excludes from itself the "dialectic of the future," and assumes its utopian mantle via denunciations, not analyses. Views that oppose it, that propose alternative historical processes and results, are denigrated as fruits of helpless stupidity. (Marx used this surrogate for dialectical analyses frequently when young, particularly in the less readable portions of *The Holy Family* and *The German Ideology*, which lends to this rhetorical ploy its stylistic currency.)

By contrast, Gabel understands the threefold nature of "total" ideology this way: it takes in an entire *Weltanschauung*, not a fragment; it analyzes an opposing ideology not psychologically, but at the "theoretical or noological[12] level"; it carries out a functional (structural), not merely psychological, analysis. Thus, by adapting Mannheim's "total" conception of ideology, Gabel protects himself from the limitation of "kantianized" Marxism, reducing almost to nil the *analytical* place of individual consciousness, and its distortion. This is especially surprising given his principal interest—the clinical expression of schizophrenia, always a crisis for an individual—but also one of his major Marxist innovations. And hence his preference for "structural" rather than "functional" analysis as the title of this method.

This tack is essential for Gabel in that he wants to protect "science" from an absolute reductionism—to distance it safely from ideology. He does this by acceding to Mannheim's notion of *Standorte*, while realizing that his allegiance to Lukács' epistemology is in jeopardy by doing so. It is folly, Gabel argues, to ignore the determinate nature of (especially) social knowledge. It is bigger folly still to equate scientific praxis with ideological "neostructuration" (an arbitrary, hence undialectical, reconstruction of facticity). Lukács' "solution" to the problem, of how to ground science properly, is tied to his theory of alienation (the subject of "Part One" in *False Consciousness*). According to Gabel's interpretation, scientific truth is distinguishable from "objective error" even though it necessarily functions within an encompassing "reified context," because "one does not ask the scientist for definitive truths but only the maximum *historically possible* congruence with the facts" (30).

This strategy, a *nonrelativizing* historicization of science, stems from Mannheim's youthful "developmental" trichotomy of rationality (aesthetic, dialectical, and progressive types). Following Alfred Weber, Mannheim claimed that it is only with natural science, economics, and law that "progressive rationality" becomes possible (Mannheim 1952: 116ff), and, as before, it is Gabel's innovation to introduce here Lukács' social ontology, for which reification *is* life. What varies, in life and in thought, are the quality and quantity of less reified ingredients. For Gabel, of course, science embodies the conditions for minimal reification, and it is important to his theory of mental illness that scientific judgments be consensually verifiable, that they be credited with nonideological content. "Dialectical rationality" (for Mannheim) is suited only to the *Geisteswissenschaften*, and since psychopathology and sociopathology, joined as they are by Gabel, clearly partake of both natural and human sciences, it is essential that the hindrances of *Standorte*—of radical perspectivism—be held to a minimum. It is not that Gabel favors apotheosis of "dialectic" for its own sake. (He points out, in fact, that while a sociogenic theory of schizophrenia demands dialecticism, it may well be wrong, since "toxic" or organic sources of the disease may have more to do with its etiology, finally, than social relations [1978:315].) Rather, his refinement of Mannheim's various distinctions is a subtle attempt to save the sociology of knowledge from itself—from its own complete relativization—and to do the same for Marxism, tending as it does toward uncritical celebration of dialectics in spite of substantive fact. (He points to the weakness of Pavlovism as an instance; 29, n.59.)

Thus we see that in acknowledging the strangling effect of positioning (*Seinsgebundenheit*) upon analysis of all sorts, even the most dialectical, and relatedly, by discarding the partial (psychologistic) for total (structural) conception of ideology, Gabel manages to preserve the critical thrust of Mannheim's sociology of knowledge, but not at the price of giving up altogether those truth claims lodged by Lukács' theory of alienation and reification. And it must be remembered that reification is at once a universal condition of constraint *and* an invitation for its own dialectical overcoming. It is this double movement that Gabel finds so helpful in seeing schizophrenia with new eyes. And it is by cultivating the tension between Lukács' belief in apodictic, class-related truth and Mannheim's more engulfing skepticism that Gabel constructs

> ...a way of defining alienation capable of: (a) serving as a common denominator for the different forms of ideology; (b) allowing a precise definition and delimitation of the concepts of ideology and false consciousness, and (c) defining a sector common to individual alienation (clinical) and social alienation. (24)

This search for "the common denominator" unifies *False Consciousness*, giving it from the outset the remarkable synthetic quality implied above. In fact, when Gabel uses his theoretical apparatus to explain "empirical" cases of de-dialecticized social phenomena (e.g., McCarthyism [26, n. 55] or ethnocentrism [30, n.6]), the powerful originality of his ideas becomes even more persuasive.

Minkowski

French scholarly books often lack indices, and *La fausse conscience* is no exception. But if either the original or the translation had one, Eugene Minkowski would be revealed as Gabel's most cited source, appearing over forty times throughout the book. Until four years after his death, none of Minkowski's five books was available in English, and although *Lived Time* (1970) mitigates the omission somewhat, his earlier, untranslated *La schizophrenie* (1927) is equally important for Gabel. Though Minkowski published over 240 items (Minkowski 1970: 435–52), only two short essays appeared in English during his life (1926; 1958). Yet his fame rests upon his classic case, translated as a chapter in May's important anthology (1958), the original title of which is literally "A psychological study and phenomenological analysis of a cause of schizophrenic melancholia" (1923). It is Minkowski's special brand of phenomenology (neither Husserlian, nor Heideggerian, but cautiously Schelerian [Gabel 1978: 220; Minkowski 1966: 295ff; Minkowski 1970: xxvii–xxxvi]), enriched by Bergson's portrait of time and space, which made his early studies so important for psychiatry, and ultimately, for Gabel. Minkowski's "morbid geometrism" and "morbid rationalism," both of which cause the "loss of vital contact" symptomatic of schizophrenia, made possible Gabel's "convergence" between Marxism and clinical psychiatry. A clear understanding of these concepts is important, then, in evaluating the plausibility of this convergence.

Unlike Lukács and Mannheim, Minkowski has not received much critical attention by Anglo-American scholars (Laing [1963] and Spiegelberg [1972: 233–47] are unusual), though, indeed, identified by Merleau-Ponty as a pioneer of phenomenology (1964: 47), whose "sensitivity for neglected phenomena ... is unique" (Spiegelberg 1972: 246). More to the point, and still true today, "[h]is carefully documented phenomenological investigations are an important contribution to psychiatry, and one which has by no means yet been adequately assimilated" (Laing 1963: 207).

Minkowski's development itself is fascinating, but cannot be fully pursued here. We know that reading Scheler's early work on sympathy and Bergson's *The Immediate Data of Consciousness* (English translation: *Time and Free Will*) around 1915 (Spiegelberg 1972: 237), coupled with the experience of "dead time" in World War I trenches, gave him his key to a new form of psychiatry. From the former he learned that human life must be apprehended intellectually in terms that are harmonic with life-as-lived (or, congruent with "being-in-the-world," as he would later write, following Binswanger), and not from Olympus—as he felt was the case with Husserl and Heidegger. From Bergson he took the idea that "vital contact"—for its originator a biological given—was the pivot of existence; its disturbance resulted in "disintegration of personality."

Just having assimilated these ideas, "[i]n the year 1922, a stroke of good luck" allowed Minkowski to spend two months with a sixty-six year old man "who presented a depressive psychosis accompanied by delusions of persecution and extensive interpretation" (May 1958: 127), a "patient who remains for me not *a* case but *the* case" (Minkowski 1966: 295). Although it is impossible to position succinctly the findings of this case within Minkowski's entire theory of mental existence (see Minkowski 1970: xvii-xxvii for a summary), he christened the salient clinical feature "blocked time." Minkowski felt that Bergson's polarizing of space and time, with life's positive characteristics owed exclusively to the latter, was too simple. Rather, "lived time"—the setting for the origin of "personal *elan*," for personality itself—had to be set opposite "lived space," the root of consistency, stability, and other features of life that "oppose" pure duration. (In Gabel's terms, temporality is axiogenic because it is played out against "the possible"; space is anaxiogenic—or can be, as in Minkowski's patient—because it is locked into materiality and an incomplete or false causality, an undialectical appraisal of *possible* events.) Minkowski's rejection of Husserl's transcendental reductions sprang from his (perhaps Schelerian) conviction that the analyst/therapist must perceive the patient's life-as-lived in order to treat the disturbance successfully; or, as stated by another, "the aim of the investigation is the reconstruction of the inner world of experience of the subject" (May 1958: 116). (This quasi-Diltheyan strategy, which pointedly rejects psychotherapeutic dogmas, occurred to Minkowski seventy years ago; a later, though theoretically inferior form, can be found in Watzlawick 1978).

For Minkowski, the old man presented data of personality disintegration—fascinating, but too elaborate for explication here—which did not require analysis via Freud's, Jung's, or others' systems, and could instead be hermeneutically explored solely with reference to the ascendancy of spatial over temporal relations. Normally, of course, the two dimensions work together, but often in psychopathologies one or the other triumphs, working its will on the weaker, and thereby extinguishing their crucial life-giving balance. The old man was convinced that he would be humiliated, tortured, and then killed in the most brutal fashion each evening. He lived in terror; his personality was "invaded" by space, and the value-giving hopefulness of future time was "blocked." The fact that he lived till the morning, beyond the dreaded moment of execution, did nothing to diminish his fears each new day. The "syntony" of life (sympathetic social existence) collapsed, and with it went "contemplation" and the source of all personal uniqueness and satisfaction, what Minkowski called "the dimension of depth." From this Minkowski later concluded that the future, composed of "activity, expectation, desire, hope, prayer, and the ethical act" (Minkowski 1970:80), was the most vital modality in life, since the past and the present have more to do with fact and knowing than with progressive existence. For is there any worse fate than being "futureless"?

A thorough understanding of the patient's illness, and the analysis Minkowski made of it, would illustrate the depth of Gabel's debt to him, and also substantiate the convergence Gabel found between Minkowski's phenomenology and Lukács' Marxism. It could also serve as a substitute analysis of *Lived Time*, a compendium of astonishing scope, into the center of which the author placed a condensation of this very case. Lacking sufficient space for that, let me say that the unbearable ordeal that had become this man's life is very plausibly interpreted by means of Minkowski's theory—based on the data he provided—and the fit between his "social ontology," so-called, and Lukács' is uncanny. In fact, one could hardly ask for a more graphic description of reification in Lukács' sense than the story Minkowski tells. Very likely Minkowski did not read *Geschichte und Klassenbewusstsein* when it appeared in 1923. But had he, it would have been difficult not to make the connection between his patient's conflation of objects and human beings, all of which/whom speak the same clear, reified language of oppression and terror, and Lukács' analysis of reified consciousness and communication under conditions peculiar to a society dominated by commodity fetishism. It is this snuffing out, from lived time and lived space, of the "life impetus" that Gabel recognized in Minkowski's work, as the analogue and extension into psychopathology of Lukács' dissection of "normal" social relations under capitalism. From this distance, and after reading Gabel, it seems astonishing that the link was not made before.

Still more telling details of this case, as well as several dozen others in *Lived Time* and *La schizophrenie*, could be added in order to buttress the claims just advanced. But for the moment it might be wiser to proceed with Minkowski's analytical summary of this single case, and a few of his other, general theoretical principles that originated with it, and were refined over the next forty years of practice. First, his own summary, as revised ten years later for inclusion in *Lived Time*:

> The personal *élan* is weakened, the synthesis of the human personality is disintegrated, the elements of which it is composed gain independence and enter into play as such. The notion of time is split up and is reduced to the notion of the succession of monotonous days. The phenomenon of sensorial pain *determines the attitude* with regard to ambience. All that is left is the ego that faces a hostile universe. Between the two are the objects of ambience which intervene and are interpreted as a result of this confrontation. *The intellect translates* this by making men persecutors and things the instruments of torture. The delusionary ideas are no longer seen simply as the products of a morbid imagination or in terms of judgmental disorder; on the contrary, they represent an attempt to express in the language of the prior psyche the unfamiliar situation wherein the personality finds itself disintegrating. (Minkowski 1970: 191–92; emphases added)

The two crucial phrases are "determines the attitude" and "the intellect translates." Both connote an assumption behind Minkowski's entire project—specifically his clinically derived belief that schizophrenia is an *achievement* of a mind seeking vainly to reestablish balance between present and future, space and time, via a new, if slowly deteriorating, personality. For instance, the normal response "when?" routinely becomes, for many schizophrenics, "where?" (Minkowski 1970: 275).

In linking "schizophrenic attitudes" with dread of the "void" beyond sanity, Minkowski alludes to:

> a new form of compensation which, found by means of the extension of the structural analysis of mental disorders [cf. Gabel's use of the same term], limits the importance of the affective compensation. I propose to call this

sort of compensation "phenomenological compensation," since it refers to the essential characteristics of the phenomena of which life is composed and grants only a secondary role to their affective content [highlighted by traditional psychiatry]. (Minkowski 1970: 242–43)

When "the void that opens up in him" threatens to overtake all waking life, the patient, through a "compensatory tendency... attempts to add vivid color to the arid countryside of the autistic life" (ibid.) Why? "It is better to give oneself up to sterile reveries"—to asking questions impossible to answer—"or adopt an attitude of regret or an interrogative attitude than to fall into the void" (244). Put in terms of the old man, it is "better" to practice grueling enumeration, as part of morbid rationalism and geometrism (the obsession for hypersymmetry, for pseudo-identification) than to succumb to pure autism—the final closure into alienation. This war between rational control and irrational (deranged) neostructuration of being-in-the-world occurs in this way because "the human personality dies progressively and because of this substitutes conceptions of a rational order for the weakening dynamism. The sick person replaces the irrational feeling of power ... by an affirmation of imaginary power in the present ... he rationalizes [makes rational] everything ... thus breaks the ties that bind us to the whole of becoming" (1970: 276).

This analytic bias accounts for the ease with which Gabel uses Minkowski's ideas, as opposed, for example, to Freud's antirationalist view of the unconscious. For surely in ideological "thought" and practice, there remains a residue of rational control that cannot be purged by even the most reified political atmosphere. Thus, the homology—Gabel's "convergence"—becomes patent. Just as with racism, a false identity equates each individual with all others of similar hue, and for the old man "every day is the same, nothing changes," thus for many schizophrenics "*the feeling of measures and of nuances* that surrounds all of our precepts ... is lost" (277). Paralyzing spatialization takes over; from one patient: "Everything around me is immobile. Things appear isolated, each one in itself, without suggesting anything.... There is an absolute fixity around me ... the creative power in me is abolished" (276–77). Lukács could have written these words in describing life on the production line; it is what Gabel called "the crime against duration" (1978: 184), the failure to achieve the "permanent conquest" of "vital contact" (1978: 245, n.102), or, for Marxists, simply the loss of "praxis" (1978: 306).

This is where Gabel expands significantly upon Minkowski's conception of the schizophrenic as "a person dominated by spatiality" (1978: 80). Gabel (1951) has shown that Bergson is the common source for the use of dialectics—gaining and losing *durée*—for both Lukács and Minkowski. For Minkowski's schizophrenic, loss of vital contact ends in virtually the same place (space) as does reified existence and the collapse of praxis for subjects within industrial society, as rendered by Lukács. What Gabel does, then, is to push Minkowski further along the road toward Lukács by carrying out a "'materialist-sociologizing' reevaluation of Minkowski's concepts" in three conceptual steps. First, he shows that morbid rationalism is due largely to a "preponderance of the identificatory function" in Meyerson's sense (see below), the undialectical nature of which makes feasible a critique of ideologies based on Minkowski's apolitical theory. Secondly, by allowing "loss of praxis" to stand in for "loss of vital contact," Gabel can define morbid rationalism as a "reificational syndrome" with broader application than originally intended; it becomes "the clinical form of reified existence" (81), just as ideologization becomes, analytically, "a form of alienation" with "a schizophrenic structure" (87). Thus, the third step; for having established this "structural identity" between schizophrenia and political alienation (false consciousness, racism, ideologization, and so on), Gabel can redefine all of them as laboring under the identical mental dysfunction of the schizophrenic: "thought enclosed within itself, dogmatic, detached from reality, unchanged by experience" (81).

Gabel claims (81, n.11) that he was the first to equate false consciousness and schizophrenia in this way, in 1948 and 1949, which puts him in the front rank of Marxist innovators. This dissection of alienated *political* processes equals in importance Lukács' initial foray in the early 1920s. Yet *History and Class Consciousness* enjoyed rebirth, while *False Consciousness* came and went nearly undetected in its English-language version. If scholarship itself suffers from a modicum of reified thought, perhaps

Gabel—though here addressing another topic entirely—can supply an answer for this mystery: "Obviously anti-dialectical existence (and also thought) is convenient; one does not easily abandon such comfort . . . it is easier to think in schemas that to dialectically capture truth" (1978: 207, n.138).

Though Gabel puts Minkowski's ideas and cases to use in a number of other ways, we must proceed to his next important source of ideas and data.

Binswanger

Except for spare theoretical emendations, Gabel steadfastly praises Lukács, Mannheim, and Minkowski, but not so Ludwig Binswanger. Minkowski seems less highly esteemed than Binswanger in histories of phenomenology or psychiatry (Spiegelberg 1972: 193ff; Arieti 1974: 696), but Gabel, perhaps because he knew the former, has reversed this perception by criticizing Binswanger's pronounced "sociologism" as well as his cumbersome terminological innovations (1978: 230ff; 263; 268; 306; 308–9). This is not to say he does not profit substantially from some of Binswanger's ideas. But while his précis of the other men's works are judicious in scope and substance, and his application of their major ideas creatively posed, he deals with a thinner slice of Binswanger's theory, and mostly for comparison with Mannheim and Lukács.

As pointed out earlier, this entire subdivision of theory and therapeutic technique has somehow eluded most general treatments of the field, giving the impression that a phenomenological-existentialist-Marxist synthesis is incapable of making the transatlantic voyage. Perhaps the philosophical background demanded by it reduces possible audiences. And yet Arieti, who informs even Habermas' "distorted communication" (Habermas 1970: 218), found room in his major statement for Minkowski, Binswanger, and even Gabel. He proposed treatment for schizophrenia in the early 1950s by means of what he called the "structural approach" (Gabel's phrase as well), since renamed the "psycho-structural approach." Via this notion, we can quickly locate ourselves vis-a-vis Binswanger, for without expressly saying so, Arieti has identified the central preoccupation of all phenomenological psychiatrists:

> The psychostructural approach . . . makes us enter into the world of schizophrenia. It reveals how the patient feels, thinks, acts, and relates, and how he experiences his own body, the inanimate world, art, work, the passage of time, and the looming of space. It focuses on those parts of the human being that are particularly human: symbolism, as expressed in imagery, language, thinking, interrelations; and volition, as expressed in choice and actions. The schizophrenic deformations will reveal themselves as psychodynamic conflicts that have assumed unusual and yet interpretable forms. . . . the psychostructural approach transcends the field of psychiatry. Excursions into other fields, such as anthropology, sociology, logic, aesthetics, neurology, and general biology, are necessary. (Arieti 1974: 6–7)

Karl Jaspers introduced the Diltheyan impetus (*Verstehen*) into psychiatric theory nearly eighty years ago, so the first sentence of Arieti's description is hardly attributable to Binswanger. But everything that follows could well be a gloss on what he tried to do between the 1920s and the mid-1960s, bringing Husserl's, then Heidegger's, theories of consciousness into psychiatric theory and practice.

Binswanger's psychopathological theory (very unlike Minkowski's) is part of a master project involving a "phenomenology of love." This he set against Heidegger's central concern, *Sorge* (care), and Minkowski's less abstract interpretations of pathology along the lines of Bergson and Scheler. This difference gives Minkowski's interpretations a more immediate plausibility, but allows Binswanger to soar into a philosophical region that the former carefully avoided. Binswanger's overall success is difficult to measure: Freud (his friend), Heidegger (a houseguest), and Jaspers (friendly competitor) all responded unfavorably to his major efforts (Spiegelberg 1972: 230–31). And yet, "[q]uite apart from the fact that Binswanger modified Heidegger's implicit anthropology significantly, he not only applied his *Daseinsanalyse* but put it to the test of more painstaking case studies than any other existential psychologist or psychoanalyst had done, especially in the studies on the flight of ideas, in the five schizophrenia studies on melancholia and mania" (ibid.).

Binswanger is unique in dispensing entirely with organo-genetic theories of schizophrenia and pursuing instead a pure "sociologism," perfectly compatible with Gabel's Marxism. It finds its explanatory power within philosophical and literary reflections upon imbalance, rather than medical models of pathogensis. For example, Binswanger's analysis of Ibsen's *Master Builder* and the pathology of *Verstiegenheit* (having lost one's way while climbing) speaks wisely both to the drama and to many schizophrenic cases (Binswanger in Gras 1973: 185–216). This dual capability—connecting experience with literary expression and recognizing disturbances as principally sociogenetic—makes Binswanger's place in *False Consciousness* essential, even if sometimes only as Minkowski's straw man. And had Gabel attended to Binswanger's "hermeneutics of love" (1942), even this slight may have been softened.

Though Binswanger's main work has not been translated, Needleman's excellent monograph (Needleman in Binswanger 1963: 1–145) begins with the *cogito* and culminates in Binswanger's particular *Daseinsanalyse* of *Daseinstruktur*. It is unnecessary here to unravel the Husserlian and Heideggerian vocabulary melded into Binswanger's own, not to mention his conversion of Freud's *homo natura* into a creature of existential becoming with an *irreducible* consciousness. It is enough to glimpse his five famous case histories—Ellen West, Jürg Zund, Lola Voss, Suzanne Urban, and Ilse—drawing from them the analyses of time, space, motion, modes of being-in-the-world, and so on, which prompted Gabel to observe:

> ... to have established that the psychopathological theories that depend on the *Daseinsanalyse* are generally of a dialectical inspiration and can, through a straightforward materialist re-evaluation be integrated into a general Marxist psychopathology ... I am convinced that the direction of this theory ["a complete Marxist theory of schizophrenia"] lies in the analysis of the subject-object dialectic on the clinical level, and in the materialist integration of theories of existential anthropology. (1978:307)

Analyzing the breakdown of *Daseins* requires understanding the peculiar "rationality" that progressively displaces sanity's self-control. The patient's "rational" attempt to rebuild a disintegrating personality, and to salvage what little "vital contact" is left, Binswanger called the patient's "mode of being-in-the-world." All five patients he described evidenced different modes, and for each a new analytic vocabulary was called for, since their individual struggles to forge a new *Wohnordnung* (life-order) were carried out in sociopathic conditions not subsumable under a general theory (thus Binswanger's repudiation of Freud's *homo natura*). Binswanger sought a nonreductionist view of pathological being that made sense even to the victim, in short, a hermeneutics of emotional crisis ambitiously true to the "text." Following the methodological dictates of "phenomenological empirical" knowledge (and not of "discursive inductive" science), Binswanger charged practitioners to desist from what Flaubert called *"la rage de vouloir conclure,"* to "let the something speak for itself . . . as it is" (May 1958: 192–93). For other theorists, patients' reports and dreams were grist for a generalizing theory, but for Binswanger the mode of being-in-the-world *was* the theory, and recording its self-unfolding became the analyst's task.

Without probing the technicalities of Heidegger's and Husserl's philosophies as they bear on Binswanger (see Needleman in Binswanger 1963: 16–23; 25–31; 59ff; Binswanger in May 1958: 191–213; Spiegelberg, 1972: 217–30), it is important to note a few terms he borrowed and modified. The climbing over, the transcendence (*Ueberstieg*) of both "self" and "world," according to Binswanger, eliminates the "fatal defect" of psychology, the "dichotomy of world into subject and object" (*ibid.*). Through our unique—but socially formed—*Stimmung* (key), we come to know what our self and those of our coexistents are doing in the world (the *Mitwelt*). The world is not over-against, as prior to Heidegger, but is made and perceived through our key, which supports normalcy. Its destruction or modification signals impending trouble. One of the many forms such troubles take is the process of *Verweltlichung*—"mundanization." And it is this term especially that Binswanger expanded to meet the clinical challenges posed by some of his famous patients. Gabel also finds the term indispensable.

Binswanger identified two major forms of psychotic "world" modifications, (1) "leaping" and "whirling" (tied to *Ideenflucht*: flight of ideas) or (2) "a shrinking and simultaneous narrowing of existence" (mundanization) (May 1958: 194). The latter Gabel summarized as "the crushing of *Dasein* by the world" (1978: 86). The crisis is one of freedom. For Heidegger, this freedom, to cultivate *Dasein* and to think about it as the process unfolds, is distinctively human. When this process stops, one possible result is schizophrenia, which according to Binswanger is "a particularly intensive and peculiarly constituted variation of that change of freedom into unfreedom or, as we express it, of existence into world" (Binswanger 1963: 314). The operative word is "world," a crushing, unwanted, even dreaded, weight upon being:

> *Dasein* can no longer freely allow the world to be, but is, rather, increasingly surrendered over to one particular world-design, possessed by it, overwhelmed by it. The technical term for this state of being surrendered over is: "thrownness" (*Geworfenheit*). ... Being overwhelmed in this sense finds its extreme expression in the phenomenon of delusion (*Wahn*). (Binswanger 1963: 284)

Summarizing the empirical detail of Binswanger's two most thoroughly worked out cases, Lola Voss and Ellen West, is impossible in short compass (Binswanger 1963: 266–341 and May 1958: 237–364), and generalizing is risky given Binswanger's doctrinal attention to "the unique aspects of each individual case" (Binswanger 1963: 249). However, in the introduction to *Schizophrenie* (a collection of all five cases), Binswanger isolated several "distinct modes of existence" (Binswanger 1963: 250) which he labeled "basic constitutive concepts." These were hermeneutical tools—and do not comprise a finished theory of psychopathology—since artful interpretation of unique data seems to Binswanger the central point of his undertaking, and the source of his refusal to follow established analytic doctrine. Because Heidegger outlined *Dasein's* proper order or structure, Binswanger is able to chronicle ontological disorder and collapse, by comparing sets of the "sheer, dazzling multitudinous plenum of historical, psychological, psychopathological, and biological data that we bring together clinically under the term 'case.'" The goal is to reveal the "*specific* ontological structure" of each case, without losing the opportunity to compare through constitutive categories.

When the subject begins to lose the calm, unbroken sense of "residing" (Heidegger's *Aufenthalt*) that protects "natural" experience, the beginnings of a schizophrenic episode may be at hand. If this condition worsens, one has entered the "schizophrenic existential pattern" because "of a breakdown in the consistency of natural experience" (252), what Binswanger calls "inconsistency." Properly dialectical social existence calls for an undistorting appraisal of things and people as they are; by contrast, inconsistency "implies precisely that inability to 'let things be' in the immediate encounter with them." "Encounter" is of special import here, since Gabel repeatedly illustrates (antidialectical) false consciousness as, *inter alia*, a failure of genuine encounter, an almost willful destruction of alterity in behalf of power. He calls it the "loss of the valuing encounter" (1978: 270, n.177). But in the case of mental illness, this false encounter is due to fear, not coercion. And, as previously pointed out, the desperate search for a way out of this "inappropriate mode of life," the futile pursuit of order along habitual lines of action, is the mainspring that sets the whirl of psychotic activities and delusions in motion.

Though terrifying for the subject, the first constitutive concept is much weaker in effect than the second, which Binswanger calls "the splitting off of experiential consistency into alternatives, into a rigid either-or" (254). Mutually incompatible "extravagant ideals" are concocted; a "wall" is built around the victim by one of the two antipodal ideals, and the psyche destroys itself pursuing one or the other, oblivious to real life. Yet, "giving up the Extravagant ideal means the bottomless *anxiety* of succumbing to the other side of the alternative" (255). A "perverse imperative" is at work, on the one hand giving *Dasein* something to do as it tries to pick up the broken thread of existence, on the other disallowing any resting place from the tension caused by the inappropriate action the ideals instigate. This, then, is a "deficient existential mode" (257), since temporalization (*Zeitigung*)—the process of retaking a lost future—is restricted to this single mode, mere *Verweltlichung* ("worldification") or mundanization. It is manifested in "the deficiency of those modes in which we encounter conscience, regret, genuine humor, and, above all, love . . . " (ibid.). With such lacunae, inauthenticity and its bitter fruit, permanent anxiety, are assured.

The third concept is the simplest, what Binswanger called "covering": "the sisyphuslike effort to conceal that side of the alternative that is unbearable to the *Dasein* so that the Extravagant ideal might thereby be buttressed" (258). That which is "unbearable to the *Dasein*" will triumph despite all conscious efforts to the contrary.

And lastly the concept of "the existence's being worn away (as though by friction)" (258), during which there is "no longer a way in or out." All avenues have been tried, all failed to lessen the crisis. *Dasein* gives up its autonomous growth, and through "existential retreat," hands itself over to other people or even to objects. This coincides with Gabel's idea that "heteronomous" values and actions stem from immersion in false consciousness, and that loss of authentic autonomy inevitably follows. For the schizophrenic, this is the entrance to catatonia, the helpless slide into the void.

Though Gabel registers many correctives to Binswanger's theory, particularly regarding his underutilization of dialectical analysis, his debt to these case studies and their interpretation is profound. In Gabel's commentary on "The Temporal Structure of the Maniacal Universe" (185–87), it is Binswanger's discovery "that the maniac lives in an eternal present" and that the "maniac's world" is one of "homogeneity and monochrome nature (*Nivelliertheit und Reliefarmut*)" that serve as the base point. Characteristically, Gabel takes Binswanger's clinical discovery and moves it onto new ground:

> Between schizophrenic spatialization and maniacal presentification one always discovers at least one essential element in common: axiogenic incapacity. Whether the axiological void of the reified (schizophrenic) universe is a consequence of the preponderance of the "consistency" factor, whilst maniacal loss of value appears to be more dependent on the preponderance of the "precariousness" factor, it amounts to the same thing as far as the result is concerned. It is in fact the dialectical synthesis of "consistency" and "precariousness" (a synthesis achieved in concrete dialectical totality) which conditions the existence of values; now, maniacal consciousness, like schizophrenic consciousness, is incapable of synthesis. Seen in this perspective, the phenomenon of "maniacal mourning" is not paradoxical, but the expression of a dialectical necessity. (186)

Even without going into the axiological theories of Dupréel and Lalo and their ideas about precariousness and consistency (see below), a sense for Gabel's meaning is available in the text, clearly revealing his reliance upon Binswanger's inspiration. The new ingredient, once again, is dialectics.

Gabel also isolates five features of Binswanger's general approach which are "essential elements for my subject" (229–34): (1) *Daseinsanalyse* is "a concrete analysis of the social conditions of mental illness," at times pushing the perspective far enough to attain "blatant sociologism" (n. 42); (2) again in synchrony with Marxism, *Daseinsanalyse* relies heavily upon "the category of totality"; (3) Binswanger and his students are especially tied to "the notion of the loss of the Subject-Object dialectic (Self-World), otherwise known as praxis." From this Gabel expands: "One is Self only in a dialectical-axiological relationship with the *Mitwelt*; personality is a dialectical conquest" (231); (4) clinical accounts of "authentic reification" and its two mechanisms, "loss of freedom with objectification of the *Dasein*" and "the crushing of the *Dasein* by a power alien to the Self" suggest to Gabel another convergence, this time with psychoanalysis; (5) mundanization, which Gabel correctly links to "the anthropological problem of life-order as Heidegger envisaged it on the philosophical level... and is one aspect... of the Marxist-Lukácsian concept of alienation as a phenomenon of reification" (233). To be sure, Gabel's appropriation of Binswanger's ideas takes a hermeneutic toll on the original intentions and correlated texts, as does any synthesis. Yet his borrowing is generally well mannered, and certainly propitious for his own ultimate goals.

Eugéne Dupréel and Charles Lalo

Lalo (aesthetician) and Dupréel (social theorist) are no longer much known. What was true in 1950 still holds: "Recent French and German writings on esthetics and related subjects have been little read in the United States. Even the long and productive career of Charles Lalo in Paris has been little discussed" (Munro 1950: 657). And in the most exhaustive history of sociology extant, "the eminent Belgian sociologist Eugene Dupréel" receives no more comment than those words (Becker and Barnes 1961:III, 824). Yet for Gabel, their ideas play important roles in his effort to ground a Marxist sociopathology that deals effectively with values, or axiology. He works from Dupréel's *Esquisse d'une philosophie des valeurs* (1939) and Lalo's *l'Art et la morale* (1934). From the first Gabel takes the axiological "dialectic of consistency and precariousness," and from the second (a sociologized aesthetics) the related, though more fundamental idea that values are sources of energy in social and aesthetic life, requiring explicit analysis at both psychological and collective levels. Both sets of ideas are only slightly less important to *False Conscious-*

ness than "reification" and "dialectics."

Axiology, the study of absolute value, has not for a half-century,[14] been widely pursued by American philosophers or social scientists, culturally relativistic for the most part. Meanwhile, theologically inspired discussions of value-theory thrived in France. Though Gabel is sociologically skeptical, he does consider the possibility of transcendentally or transsocietally essential human values, a position borrowed mostly from Dupréel. As Polin, another Gabel source, explained, "Man is originally an axiological consciousness . . . he cannot but think in terms of values" (Polin 1950: 214), a position that in Gabel's intellectual circles seems almost a platitude. Moreover, it makes some sense for Gabel to graft detheologized axiology onto Marxism, since he considers them both *fundamentally* dialectical enterprises. So while it may appear peculiar at first blush that a Marxist concerns himself with what seems at times an effort to enunciate transcendentally applicable values, this enigma softens when Gabel's intellectual environment is taken into account.

Once the role of axiology is recognized, the structure of *False Consciousness* seems odd. Rather than building on clinical works, showing that "[t]he dialectic is the opposite of the way schizophrenics live and think" (Gabel 1978: 62, n.44), and then moving into the antidialectical characteristics of political ideologization, Gabel began with Lukács and Mannheim, and composed a political sociology *before* turning to individual false consciousness. This is perplexing since without the clinically based documentation of schizophrenic processes, Gabel's special political sociology (based on "externalized" dedialectization) must be taken on faith. A hint for the rationale may lie in the book's dedication to his mother lost to Auschwitz, for an unconsoled father, and against fanaticism. So, despite his skillful reinterpretation of clinical data, Gabel wrote the book principally for macroanalysis—of political coercion, terrorism, and "the big lie." And it is through Dupréel, Lalo, and Emile Meyerson that he grounded his own values in a broader axiological vision, one more daring than Marxists usually attempt.

By taking what he needs from these thinkers, and then adding Lukács, he creates a new axiological platform. Its three parts include (1) the relation between totality and value; (2) the spatio-temporal structure of reificational devaluations; (3) reified value (social sacredness), the second of which being most important (1978: 66–77). He connects "totality" (both spatial and temporal) with "value," a motor and justification for social activity. This is inseparable from a "certain formal context; ... dynamic form and *requiredness* of value ... are *one and the same thing*" (67). These are definitive claims, for if "dynamic form" is an indefensible concept, the rest of Gabel's general theory is threatened. It is here that dialectics strain to overcome an apparent empirical contradiction, for surely "form" has about it more of the spatial, the unyielding, than could normally be described as "dynamic" (*pace* Simmel).

Beneath these cryptic notions lies Lalo's theory, which in very truncated form holds that: (1) values are morally energizing "forces" (due to Nietzsche's importing of the term from economics into philosophy; thus the mechanistic imagery); (2) "axiological existence"—presumably the entire sphere of human values—originates in what is intrinsically valueless, "but whose assemblage or *synthesis* has to acquire precisely this [given] value as an essential characteristic" (Lalo 1934: 127). Lalo sees "value" as correlative with "concrete action" and the "conscious imperative" derived from it, owing its origin to valueless entities that are combined axiogenetically: "The genesis of values is the same in the area of knowledge or truth or beauty, serious activity or morality: *each value is always the synthesis of elements without value*, and they differ among themselves through the particular form that this group assumes" (154; 161).

Gabel holds that Dupréel "has shown that every value possesses two essential characteristics: consistency and precariousness," which comprise "axiological bipolarity." The first involves "the autoconservative tendency of forms, the intensity of which acts as a measure of the difference between weak and strong forms" (69). As the limits of a form are approached, "precariousness" sets in, always threatening to destroy a weakened form (reminiscent of the Second Law's entropy). Thus, "concrete totality," the ultimate in consistent "form," is axiogenic, that is, "value-giving" (21), serving as the antipode to reificational processes, which by their nature "devalue," simplify, destroy—and leading toward chronic precariousness. Value itself becomes a "corollary of *dereification*" (69), because of the definitive axiological inferiority, judged by Dupréel's bipolarity, of mere objects to living things. To be alive, to participate in consciousness, *is* to value (as Polin pointed out above), and the more dialectical the consciousness, the more active the interplay between consistency and precariousness; hence, the less thinglike. Ethnocentrism, for example, can be interpreted in this way as a "reificational neglect of the dialectic of the totality" (60), plus a rejection of history dialectically known.

Gabel believes these ideas "prove" that analytic consideration of "totality" is *necessarily* (1) axiogenic, (2) dialectical and, therefore (3) liberating. He does not stop there, however. Pushing Dupréel's axiology further, Gabel argues that "what characterizes value above all is a sort of autotranscendence; value is a perpetual transcendence of self. Likewise, reality organized into a form is in a constant state of autotranscendence" (70). This tendency toward self-*Aufhebung* vitalizes Gabel's dialectic, due to the presence of a "pre-dynamism," a potential source of axiological and virtual form-breaking energy, that is, the fuel of creative precariousness. The trick, existential or analytical, is to understand the unique *axiological* bipolarity of a given historical entity or existent condition, to perceive its limits and possibilities, its real chances of self-transcendence.

Having covered a lot of terrain, Gabel turns to "temporalization and valuation." He needs to establish the anaxiological (valueless or value-destroying) nature of space, especially as experienced schizophrenically. Bergson's distinction between homogeneous (clock) time and heterogeneous (human) time—*durée reelle*—had already been put to good use by Lukács. But Lukács skipped one of Bergson's keenest observations, that in true, flowing duration, development occurs which is irreversible in form or outcome. This is the distinctly human quality of time, of temporalization. Without invoking Bergson, Gabel turns this proposition to axiological ends: "irreversibility is a condition of all valuation: a value situated on a reversible continuum is not a true value" (72). The burden of this claim falls, of course, on "true."

Finally, by combining Minkowski's antipathy for space with this axiological aversion for reversibility, Gabel has all he needs for the micro-macro leap: "Space thus appears as the anaxiological dimension of the spatio-temporal continuum; the psychopathology of schizophrenic states will not contradict this thesis. Complex interrelationships exist between the notions of *space, aggressiveness*, and *devaluation*. Space predisposes to *aggressiveness*" (73). In short, space does not allow for irreversibility (recall Minkowski's patient), and therefore corrupts by its very nature one of the fundamental qualities of any "true" value.

False Consciousness is filled with creative permutations upon these themes, but Gabel saves the most heterodox for last: the possibility of a Marx/Freud synthesis in a previously unknown form. Since Freud, psychiatrists have known of an ailment called WUE (*Weltuntergangserlebniss*), the "deranged experience of the end of the world," which Gabel redefines as "the psychopathological homologue ... of false consciousness" (290). He notes a convergence between the observed misoneism (hatred of the new) that overtakes (reified) victims of WUE, and Lukács' parallel observations regarding the catastrophic quality of immediate perception for radical empiricists, those resisting the Hegelian sensitivity for structural, but not superficial, change: "For anyone who sees things in such immediacy, all effective change must consequently appear incomprehensible. The indisputable fact of change is reflected in the awareness of immediacy as a catastrophe, in other words, it appears in the form of a sudden change coming from outside and excluding all mediations" (Lukács 1971: 154). Gabel concludes:

> The dialectical interpretation of the phenomenon offers one advantage, that of linking two apparently unconnected clinical data into a coherent whole: the syndrome of external action and the deranged experience of the end of the world. In the spatialized universe, the event, as we have seen is doubly proscribed: as act of temporalization and as creation of value. Consequently, when the event forces itself into reified consciousness, the latter makes this evident through a double technique of partial obscuration: from the point of view of causal explanation it interprets it as the act of an external power; on the level of lived experience, it experiences it either as a catastrophe or, on the contrary, as a sudden significant (and always heteronomic) irruption into the axiological void of the world itself: a *divine mission*. In short, like a manic crisis, the WUE is an axiological crisis, a sort of storm of values on the boundaries of two atmospheres of different axiological-dialectical density.

And after reference to germane works of Jaspers, Freud, Binswanger, Trakl, Kafka, Strindberg, and others, Gabel announces his discovery:

> If one takes as a starting point the postulate of axio-dialectical equivalence (axiogenic function of the category of concrete totality) and the axiological nature of the libido, one sees that an interpretation, Marxist in its origins, can without difficulty link up with Freudian conceptions; furthermore, it provides a common (reificational) denominator for the phenomenon of deranged perception—interpreted earlier as anti-dialectical perception—and the WUE, which it thus organically integrates into the general phenomenological structure of derangement. (292–93)

Emile Meyerson

When Gabel reflects on the theoretical "convergence" he's found (reminiscent in its scope of Parsons' in 1937), Meyerson's ideas often appear, as here: "The loss of the dialectic is seen either in the prevalence of the reversible spatial constituent of experience with *anti-dialectical identification* ('false identification') as the logical expression, or in a loss of temporalization with an incapacity to understand the 'event' in any other way than as a miracle or a catastrophe" (116; emphasis added). Meyerson's is probably the strangest of all Gabel's radical appropriations, and therefore requires separate treatment.

Despite published compliments from Einstein and Popper, Meyerson's stature in the philosophy of science[15] now seems weak, though, like Dupréel (judging from Gabel's references), in French intellectual history it is secure. A chemist and administrator without university affiliation, Meyerson published *Identité et realité* in 1908 when nearly fifty, a somewhat Germanic compendium and review of scientific thought which owes its unity to several linked ideas. Gabel refers explicitly to the one idea he chose to use early in the book, and also on the last page:

> E. Meyerson's epistemology reflects . . . the inevitable ambiguity of the act of knowing: on the one hand there is identification, an anti-dialectical, spatializing step, the expression of the inevitable element of reification in the social act of knowing; on the other hand, there is intuition of various matters relating to the concrete specificity of reality as totality . . . identification, an eminently anti-dialectical step, can simultaneously play the role of a legitimate element of the scientific "train of thought" and a constituent of ideologized thought. [Meyerson's] work constitutes the real epistemological basis of my attempt . . . Everything [he]

tells us about the role of identification in the processes of knowledge and on the limits, nay the dangers, of its abuse enter into the frameworks of this *epistemology of reification*. (32, 326)

Meyerson's goal was to overturn rigid philosophies of scientific procedure and knowing (Mach's is the best known: Meyerson 1930: 366), in favor of one which emphasized identity, time, common sense, and what he called "previsions." By listening to Bergson, Helmholtz, Ostwald and other antipositivists, Meyerson created an epistemology "humanized" through an apotheosis of "common sense" *qua* scientific perception (354–83) that could explain scientific innovation in an Einsteinian universe. He called his approach the "*a posteriori* analysis of expressed thought." From Meyerson's encylopedic formulation, Gabel took only two notions: the principle of identification, and the meaning of what Meyerson called the "elimination of time" and "irreversibility" (explored differently than in Dupréel's approach).

For Meyerson knowledge is pursued because of the natural, irrepressible process of reason, which itself is determined by "the principle of identity . . . the eternal framework of the mind" (284). By this he means that the central scientific concept, causality, is reducible to the temporal relation between a phenomenon's antecedents and its current condition. This is the identity Meyerson is after.

Unlike many philosophers of science, Meyerson is willing to acknowledge the unknowable, the irrational, and the human mind's eagerness to shield itself from this everpresent threat to its analytic self-confidence. There is always more reality than reason can handle. The human mind protects itself from directly facing this problem: "[i]t is, moreover, easy to establish the union between the notion of the rational and that of the persistent throughout time. The principle of identity is the true essence of logic, the real mould into which man pours his thought" (43). What prevents Meyerson's identity principle from lapsing into tautology is the injection of time. When "time is added" to any concept, we move from (Kant's) analytic to synthetic judgment, for only the latter can accommodate real objects instead of mere concepts about them or their interrelations: Thus the principle of causality is none other than the principle of identity applied to the existence of objects in time (43). Understanding causality means knowing a phenomenon's "preexistence in time," or applying "the empirical rule determining its change in time."

This brings us to Meyerson's contribution to *False Consciousness* regarding irreversibility. In a chapter on rational mechanics called "The Elimination of Time," Meyerson charges that "science in its effort to become 'rational' tends more and more to suppress variation in time" (230). (In Gabel's terms science approaches a sub-realist, schizophrenic *Wohnordnung* as it "advances.") Meyerson shows that "perfect identity between cause and effect" implies equivalence, of antecedent and consequent (216), and thus the supplanting of space by time since no movement is possible. The key to this sort of hypothetical relation is "reversibility," but this is not the same as "identity": a seven meter beam is equivalent but not identical to two beams of four and three meters each (282). Thus in science "all motions are reversible," but "on the earth...there can be no mechanisms absolutely deprived of friction, and therefore there exists none that is really reversible" (218). In rational mechanics, however, "time is indeed something analogous to space." This, then, is the connection between Gabel's "morbid rationalism" and Meyerson's analogous concern for the vanquishing from physical reality of its dynamism through overly mechanistic models of science: the spatialization of (axiogenic) time.

His objection to scientific analysis is similar to Gabel's: how far can the search for objective identities go before critical distortion, and finally the collapse of time into pure Parmenidian stasis, take over. For Gabel, the question is the same in substance but worded differently: how much reification is too much? When the victim suffers from a "preponderance of the identificatory function," when false identities prevail over justifiable similarities, when causality becomes delusional, then one has become "meyersonized": "obsessed with the identical" (Gabel: 150). What is for Meyerson a natural tendency, toward conversation, inertia, identity ("which leads us to postulate the equality of antecedent and consequent," 219), has becomes for Gabel's patient a grotesque victory of space over time, when time—lost to true identity—is swept away into Eleatic despair. What for the normal scientific mind serves, if Meyerson is heeded, as a healthy limiting concept has become in psychopathology "a universe eternally immutable" (Meyerson: 230).

Gabel took this rarefied epistemology of science and turned it both to clinical use and toward *Ideologiekritik*. *Identitätszwang*, identificatory compulsion, is "the symbolic experience of schizophrenics ... the manifestation of an abnormal prevalence of the identificatory function in epistemology" (Gabel: 284, n.214). But pathological identification can also be located at the macro level. It plays a part in creating a "privileged relationship" (the negative *Standorte* Mannheim tried to neutralize) from which antidialectical social knowledge can be generated (90), that "privileged knowledge" making up "privileged systems" (87) which disseminate artificial political "facts." Moreover, the role of "antidialectical identification" in political life, in ideologization, "should not be underestimated: it is a turn-table between the different aspects of false consciousness. It is the atom of nondialectical logic, the factor of dissociation of concrete totalities." (cf. the Frankfurt School's sustained attack upon Hegelian "identity theory," prompted by similar political and intellectual concerns; see Adorno 1973: 146ff; Horkheimer 1939/1972: 10–46.)

For Gabel, collapse of the totality is the final *axiological* crisis, so identification is transformed in his equation from an epistemological condition (Meyerson's usage) to a primary factor in the destruction or preservation of values: "it is also an agent of spatialization, for space alone lends itself to total identification; objective or subjective time, filled with irreversible events is by definition refractory" (97). These concepts originate in *Identity and Reality*, but their connotations are thoroughly reworked to fit psycho- and sociopathologies. What for Meyerson was a "limiting concept"—the push of reason for identity, the refusal of "Nature" to be rationalized toward this constraining identity—is for Gabel the entire sphere of interest. Gabel begins beyond Meyerson's limit, particularly as he applies the latter's epistemology to macrosocial events—which he does throughout *False Consciousness*, with terms like "collective egocentrism," "sociocentrism" and "ethnocentrism" (88–91; also 88–105; 100ff; 149ff; 224ff). Egocentrism is perception of a privileged type, that ignores reversibility (or reciprocity) in social process.

Gabel explains how this works when expressed ideologically by political parties:

> The presence of the "privileged relationship" appears as a foreign body in the concrete totality of relationships whose combination constitutes the object; it fixes the intellectual process at the analytical level and thereby blocks the dialectic of analysis and synthesis . . . [This is not understandable without remembering Meyerson's theory.] Furthermore, the artificial (heteronomic) primacy of the relationship necessarily involves an obscuration of the non-privileged relationships and also historical data; this results in a preponderance of non-dialectical identificatory functions with dissociation from totalities and an ahistorical spatializing perception of reality. (90)

This means that fully developed (hence, dialectical) perception, for the collectivity and its members, is doubly blocked. The synthetic appraisal Mannheim favored, including in its purview the unique case, cannot be accomplished because its precondition, holistic understanding, is crippled. In addition, historical relationships and pressures, which, if considered honestly, would show the fatuity of "privileged" viewpoints, are likewise absent.

The inevitable result is faulty, massive identification. Gabel's best example of this is in his discussion of "social sacredness," which "lives under the sign of identity" (74). As Yahweh said, "'*Ehje aser ehje*'—I am the one who is ," (or "I am that I am") which crushes "precariousness," exaggerates "identification" and therefore serves a "devaluing function." This sort of *a priori* thinking frequently figures in authoritarian statements; equally independent of any experiential (*a posteriori*) corrective to ideological needs is racism. To the extent such mental forms ignore experience—that is, dialectics—they become carriers of "autistic, anti-dialectical identificatory value" (75). In sum, it could be said that all ideologies operate as part of privileged systems (of nontruth, one could say), which stimulate "anti-dialectical identification at the expense of intuition of differences," betraying a mechanism clearly homologous to the "logic of schizophrenia" (87). Where details matter, ideological portraits will never do; the strokes are too broad, the imagination hobbled.

With enough space, much more could be said about Gabel's creative appropriation of Meyerson's ideas. In the end, it is essential to Gabel's redefinition of schizophrenic process as displaying four principal symptoms: "dissociation from totalities," "devaluation," "predominance of the identificatory function in relation to intution of diversity," and "predominance of the spatial function in relation to the temporal" (Gabel: 103). This analytic symptomology, with macroscopic applications, is as robust as any proposed by other theorists, and has the advantage of a manifold and varied lineage. By combining a reanalysis of Meyerson's "identification" with new observations on disturbed time and space (Bergson and Minkowski), devaluation (Dupréel), cognitive privilege (Mannheim), and reification in general (Lukács), Gabel advances a previously obscured understanding of private mental anguish and its grave collective manifestations.[16]

Gabel's Synthesis: Private and Public False Consciousness

Between 1939 and 1962 Gabel developed a nonsuperficial "sociologism" that explains schizophrenia, without recourse to a fictional philosophical anthropology (Marx's "species-being"), nor to dogmatism of the diamat variety. He therefore extended his model to societal pathologies by carefully bringing clinical data into contact with sociopolitical history *at the analytic level*. As suggested above, he accomplished this by positioning his ideas and theoretical goals in relation to theories and empirical findings that to date have not been seen in Anglophone social science. Even if his explanation for the etiology and operation of mental illness is wrong (perhaps "organogenesis" will prove the superior answer after all), his *Ideologiekritik* remains indispensable in our period of heightened ethnic hatred and decreasing tolerance for "The Other." Thinking dialectically, in his sense, is virtually its own reward, both for the theorist and the citizen. However, Gabel would want his theory appraised by the same scientific standards he applied to the scores of clinicians and theorists who people his book, and not exclusively in terms of its "practical" value. With that in mind, a few closing remarks, mostly of his own making, are in order.

Gabel ends *False Consciousness* with a dense "Conclusion," restating his major points. Allowing him to speak for himself *in extenso* might convey a fair sense of his argument (even though a truly responsible hermeneutic would have to turn on Gabel's interpretation of clinical data, 90 percent of which is untranslated, hence unknown here):

> The concept of *morbid rationalism* has appeared throughout this study, as the essential element of a global theory of alienation: the common denominator of its individual and social forms. In fact the preponderance of the spatializing-reificational aspect of the perception of reality—over its temporalizing-historical aspect—is the common denominator of the various forms of economic and political alienation, including voluntary mystification. Furthermore, a morbid rationalism, the expression *par excellence* of non-dialectical, reified, anaxiological consciousness, appears as the *schizophrenia type*, i.e., as the closest clinical form to a "fundamental disorder." It is the dialectical structure of his involvement in the world which protects man (individual and social) against derangement. The mechanisms of ideologization and the mechanisms of deranged neostructuration should thus be mutually illuminating. (313)[17]

Virtually all Gabel's main ideas are here in "coded" form. There are dozens of lesser, even peripheral notions, that he explores in the book, but "morbid rationalism," "alienation," "spatializing-reificational perception," "temporalizing-historical perception," "non-dialectical, reified, anaxiological consciousness," and the "mechanisms of ideologization and deranged neostructuration" assume pride of place. These phrases, as dissonant and clumsy as they may seem, are not cheer-words, nor mere jargon (*pace* Poster 1975: 263, "Hacking our way through Gabel's jargon . . . "), nor magical incantation.[18] In spite of initial appearances, he does not indulge in gratuitous neologism, but takes great care in defining concepts. He is particularly concerned to show that each is related conceptually and empirically within a unified understanding of anomic and collective "de-dialecticization."

In the preface to the first edition, he summarizes his global vision of micro and macro disturbances:

> "The drama of alienation is dialectical," said H. Lefebvre. An excellent observation, but one which requires concrete content. I have turned to psychopathology for this "concrete content," convinced that a Marxist theory of consciousness . . . is to be found at the intersection of findings from the study of pathological consciousness and false consciousness. *Schizophrenia* . . . in fact clearly represents a form of reified consciousness, characterized on the existential level by a deterioration of dialectical *praxis*, and on the intellectual level by a de-dialecticization of cognitive functions, a phenomenon described long ago by E. Minkowski as *morbid rationalism* [1927]. The appropriate rationality of false consciousness, characterized by a loss of the dialectical quality of thought is therefore clearly a social form

of morbid rationalism; inversely, I consider the onset of schizophrenia as an individual form of false consciousness. The mental state therefore constitutes a real bridge between the areas of social and clinical alienation; it is a form of alienation both in the Marxist sense and in the psychiatric meaning of the term. It is significant in this regard that the writings of young Marx devoted to the alienation of human work, anticipated certain mechanisms that psychiatrists discovered only much later in their own research. This is a phenomenon that—to borrow H. Aubin's expression [1952]—could be described as *socio-pathological parallelism*. (xx-xxi).

It is Aubin's term that Gabel seizes upon in offering a "new nosological unity" (xii) out of the welter of data comprising schizophrenia research, by defining "a rationality of a particular type—a sub-dialectical rationality" (xxii).

Two major subdivisions, "the problem of alienation" and "reified consciousness," give *False Consciousness* its structure. By exploring each in extraordinary detail, particularly the latter, Gabel comes to this conclusion:

> False consciousness and ideology are two forms of non-dialectical (reified) perception of dialectical realities, in other words, two aspects (or better: two degrees) of the rejection [whether voluntary or not] of the dialectic... these are two phenomena of a *schizophrenic* nature. False consciousness is a *diffused state of mind*; ideology is a *theoretical* crystallization. The objective, scientific value of such theoretical crystallization is naturally subject to caution; it is not *ipso facto* worthless. (11)

With this analysis, Gabel demonstrates that certain scientific procedures and discoveries, in being *Seinsadäquat* (corresponding with what exists), enjoy a "superior epistemological fate" (or, following Dupréel, an "axiological privilege of truth") to ideologies, even those which *in form* struggle to imitate science. Anti-semitism is the prime example; it is "doubly false" in reifying the image of Jews around particular mythical concoctions based on a characterology which is *not* recognized for what it is—historical in origin, rather than supernal: "By considering reificationally these historical products as the expression of a natural law, racist *false consciousness* denies history: racist ideology tends to build on false consciousness a pseudo-history which, instead of explaining the Jew through history, claims to explain History through the Jew" (13). The vital nature of such observations, given postcommunist anarchy in Central Europe and apparently endless Middle Eastern strife, cannot be gainsaid.

Still another way of inviting Gabel's thinking into contemporary theoretical concerns is to reflect on his argument that certain mental aberrations, racism, and ideological thought are conditions of *Wahnstimmung* (the delirious state of mind) which, as he notes, is graphically expressed in Kafka's major novels (15n.). This is the state of delirium—"derealist thought" at its most extreme—of which only human beings are capable. It is by practicing a "reifying vision (an actual *delirious perception*) of the racial enemy" (10), for instance, that racist ideology originates and then displaces "normal" (dialectical) perception. It must be emphasized that when Gabel casts racism as a form of delirium, he is not moralizing; rather, he is making a scientifically defensible statement.

As may be clear by now, Gabel's achievements are many, not the least of which has been to open wide a door into a little known chamber in theory's mansion. He summarizes his achievement succinctly:

> The notion of a "reified consciousness" independent of economic reification permits the enlargement of this conception. Collective egocentrism, by dichotomizing the human universe, also dissociates the axiological totality "consistence—precariousness"; the result is a general reduction in the axiological contents of existence, a little like when one cuts a bank-note in two. The privileged system is established as an exclusive value without precariousness; the non-privileged residue is down-graded to a value without consistency: these then are "values." Likewise the logic of alienation—the logic of "false identities"—is heteronomic, the axiology being *external to the person*. It is therefore to the extent that alienated axiological consciousness fails to appreciate or obscures the autonomous axio-dialectical quality of reality that it can be described as *false consciousness*. (77)

All this and a bit more is collapsed into a table halfway through the book in which Gabel dichotomizes schizophrenia and paranoia (except for a few anomalous cases), rendering them basically as "sub-realist" and "sur-realist" tendencies respectively. By the first Gabel means "an excess of reification manifesting itself through anti-dialectical thought, abstract attitudes, spatialism, identification, artificialism, dissociation, devaluation, incomprehension of and destructuration of concrete valuing totalities ('axiogeneous forms')" (155). "Surrealism" includes "insufficient reification of the real world, over-concrete attitudes, temporalization, over-valuation, and an abnormal reinforcement of significant dialectical structures." I have reproduced the table (appended) and added several terms as they are subsequently explained in the remaining parts of the book.

False Consciousness is a masterpiece of synthesis and theoretical daring. In this space I have been able merely to introduce Gabel's theory in part, trying along the way to clear up potential ambiguities, and also to hint at some of the work's limitations. I have not probed the theory itself thoroughly, nor examined his use of clinical data, which occupies two-thirds of the book. But just on the basis of what I did cover, it seems to me perfectly obvious that Gabel—if granted his special form of phenomenological-Lukácsian Marxism—has made a contribution to general theory regarding personality, psychoses, racism, and ideological analysis beside which any other post-World War II work in the same sphere of inquiry, Marxist or otherwise, seems tame. If I have been relatively uncritical, it is because Gabel is autocritical. His footnotes and asides indicate that he has spent many years in conscientious dialogue, refining these notions, and that a reputable hermeneutic with critical intentions could only succeed if done holistically.

I have not, then, tried to render an exhaustive account of Gabel's theory. Much was omitted, for example, his thoughts on Swift's coprophilia or "spatio-temporal structures and oral frustration in *Alice in Wonderland.*" Instead, I have tried to carry out what might be called "an archaeology of Gabel's knowledge." His is not a self-revealing, self-explicating text, freely admitting its specific place within intellectual tradition; nor is it a self-locating text. Through its density and structure, it violates the basic etiquette of scholarly prose. Probably despite the author's wishes, *False Consciousness* is an unfriendly text, never giving an inch, almost begging to be ignored—thus, easily thought of as too outrageous or iconoclastic to deserve careful study. Gabel's lifework teeters throughout toward "precariousness," but its innovative brilliance, so I believe, saves it from mere idiosyncratic self-indulgence and lends it enough "consistency" to make the troublesome journey worthwhile. Perhaps my simplifying map will help others who wish to explore this new terrain *in toto.*

Conforming, however, to Gabel's own sharp style, I dare not end on a saccharine note. It might be useful here to lodge a singular, if major, complaint against Gabel's achievement. The missing element in *False Consciousness*—leaving aside completely the need for a formal political-economics—concerns the type of social setting that might foster a dialectical life that works successfully toward preventing anaxiological, antidialectical thought and social action. Failure to specify or even comment upon this future condition seems odd, since Gabel seems to have had in mind throughout the book a clear notion of the "good"—the rediscovery of which has been preoccupying so many moral philosophers and social theorists for the last decade or so. For Gabel, liberating social structure would seem to call for a private and public life in which dialecticization is given free play, so that "autonomous" values may arise; the kind of structure in which false consciousness is not so much proscribed as simply unnecessary. (Its "necessary" quality today for so many of the afflicted, like creatures in a Kafka tale, goes without saying.) In order for Gabel's theory to illuminate as clearly as it might within its own claimed tradition, it must be fleshed out in the direction of polity, for while the dilemmas of individualized consciousness are exhausted in the book, those of the wider social spaces are not.

While not satisfying this complaint completely, many of the essays that follow do, it seems to me, carry Gabel's analytic energy and imagination into a sphere far removed from the psychiatric clinic. In these shorter sallies, his motivating wish—"to oppose fanaticism of all kinds"—spurs him to attack macro-level problems of bad faith and evil social organization that, when viewed as a whole, add that necessary dimension to the extraordinary achievement of *False Consciousness* which might constitute the conceptual completion of Gabel's lifework.

Outline of a General Psychopathology

Surrealist tendency *	Normal state	Sub-realist tendency **
Lack of identification	Normal identification	Compulsion for identification (*Identitätszwang*)
Asymbolism		Symbolism of identity
Morbid realism		Morbid rationalism
Absence of the notion of the possible		Preponderance of the notion of the possible
Over-structured perception of reality		Insufficiently structured perception of reality
Preponderance of the *temporal* aspect in the perception of the world[1]		Preponderance of the *spatial* aspect in the perception of the world
Preponderance of the experience of the 'Here and Now' (Cassirer)		Loss of the function of the 'Me-Here-Now' (Minkowski)
Preponderance of the category of *being* over *having*[2]		Preponderance of the category of *having* rather than *being*
Incapacity for objectivation		Morbid objectivation[3]
Impossibility of separating 'Me' from the 'internal attitude'[3]		Radical separation of 'Me' from the 'internal attitude'[4]
Morbid authenticity (patients incapable of lying)		Individual false consciousness
Insufficient reification		Excess of reification
*Melancholia; aphasia; derealism; paranoia		**Schizophrenia; compulsive lying; hysteria; manic-depression states; psychasthenia; anonymography; WUE syndrome; hallucinations; deranged perception; weak dialectics

The term 'identification' is used strictly in E. Meyerson's sense.
1. Cf. Binswanger [(54), p. 606]. The notion of 'in front of' and 'behind' have an absolute significance for the aphasic just like 'before' and 'after' in time.
2. Van Der Horst's interpretation (456).
3. Cf. Wyrsch (476), Ey (146) and my critical summary of these views in the following chapter.
4. Zutt's notion of '*innere Haltung*' (483); the application of this notion to the asphasic's 'mode of being-in-the-world' is my own.

Source: Adapted from Joseph Gabel, *False Consciousness*, p. 157.

Notes

1. Other synthesists of the early period included Bernfeld, Fenichel, Sapir, and Fromm (Poster 1978: 211, n.8).
2. Sartre, too, noted early on the need for a "theory of the person" in Marxism; yet for Marxists, Sartre went too far into subjectivity ever to recover the necessary macrostructural dimension they insist upon. See Caveing 1971 (cited in Poster 1975: 133n.).
3. For an unusual comparison of Marcuse's theory versus Deleuze and Guattari's, see Poster 1978: 58–63, 105–9. I find his attack upon Marcuse too unforgiving, however.
4. This is an interesting review of Lacan's *Ecrits* and Deleuze and Guattari's *Capitalisme et Schizophrénie: L'Anti-Oedipe*.
5. Other Marxists have pursued this very goal, but without recourse to psychiatric or psychoanalytic thought or practice. A well-known example is Lukács' student, Agnes Heller, who has published much on the concept of "needs," a quasi-psychiatric or psychotherapeutic matter, as it relates to humanist Marxism (an effort which Gabel does not regard as entirely successful [personal communication]). It is impossible to consider here all recent important Marxist theory on "self and society." I am interested instead only in those that have tried simultaneously to use clinical psychiatric data and Marxist concepts in defining the role of social processes in self-formation and malformation. (For the alternative, see, for example, Heller 1976; 1979.)
6. Séve's *Man in Marxist Theory*, translated by John McGreal (Sussex: Harvester Press, 1978); Gabel's *False Consciousness*, translated by Margaret. A. and Kenneth. A. Thompson (Oxford: Basil Blackwell, 1975) Both translated versions include revisions of and additions to the original editions, especially Séve's.
7. Berger and Pullberg's laudatory but empty reference to the book is representative: "The last work [*La fausse conscience*] is particularly important for the psychological and psychiatric ramifications of the concept, but is beyond our present scope" (199). Gabel has remained beyond nearly everyone's scope, it seems, although his is the keenest elaboration extant of Lukácsian "reification," among other things. Even a more recent monograph (Lewy 1982), expressly given over to a detailed critique of false consciousness qua intellectual and analytic concept, fails to make any mention of Gabel's work.
8. Even an acute student of French social theory like Poster seems prematurely exhausted by Séve: "One other book of note on Marxist psychology by L. Seve ... deals not with the family [Poster's topic] but with the work situation" (Poster 1978: 213, n.50). This is like saying Weber's *Wirtschaft und Gesellschaft* "deals with" money and banking.
9. Among the cases and clinicians Gabel uses are Binswanger's "Jürg Zünd," "Mary," "S. Urban," K. Goldstein's work, that of Klaus Conrad, L. van der Horst, C. A. Pallis, H. Fauré, H. Ey, I. Caruso, A. Hesnard, V. Gebsattel, Medard Boss's "Erika P" and "Rico D," D. Lagache, H. Baruk, H. Mignot, H. Tellenbach, H. Claude, to name a small fraction. Standard sources like Kretschmer and Janet also figure in, as to Blondel, Piaget, and Lacan.

10. The footnote in *History and Class Consciousness* regarding the source of this quote is incorrect; see p. 210, n.26.
11. "Pernicious chasm," the English translation, obscures Lukács' meaning and therefore also Gabel's; cf. *False Consciousness*, p. 149, n. 8 with Lukács, 1971: 204.
12. The English translation reads "nosological" where the original has *"nooligique"* (Gabel 1962b: 27). This (printing?) error might obscure this and related passages. Gabel frequently mentions the need for a "nosological unity" (*nouvelle unité nosologique* [1962b: 111]) vis-a-vis schizophrenia as theoretically expressed. "Nosology" means a category or list of diseases. But in the sentence above, although "nosological unity" makes perfect sense, it could as easily read "noological unity" and still convey Gabel's meaning.

Mannheim's definition of "noology" is "the study of the contents and forms of thought in their purely cognitive interrelations" (1936: 349). He uses it thus: "We touch upon the theoretical or noological level whenever we consider not merely the content but also the form . . . and mode of a thought" (1936:57). In *False Consciousness* where Gabel summarizes these very pages from Mannheim's book, it reads, "the partial concept analyzes the opposing ideology at the psychological level, the total concept at the theoretical or nosological level" (22). To complicate matters even more, Gabel also notes that translating *Wissenssoziologie* into a French adjective can only be rendered *"gnoseo-sociologie,"* which the translators then reproduce throughout the book as "gnoseo-sociological" or "gnoseo-logical" (5, n.5; 19).

I have no way of telling whether Gabel meant to include within his theory this ambiguity—since in many contexts, surprisingly, either word will work, though denoting different things, of course. This initial conflation of terms hints at other conundrums in the book. Some of them, like this one, suggest a philosophy of scientific method which Gabel clearly has in mind but nowhere enunciates for the uninitiated. (The central epistemological category of his theory—"identification"—is similarly problematic, as noted below.)
13. For a concise analysis of the book, along with key translated passages unavailable elsewhere, see Laing 1963.
14. For example, in an issue of *Social Research* entitled "Philosophy: an Assessment" (47:4, Winter 1980), of thirteen articles, none deals with axiology. One article on "ethics" mostly concerns political rights.
15. Einstein complimented Meyerson's "brilliant studies in the theory of knowledge" (*The Times*, February 5, 1929), and Popper called *Identity and Reality* "one of the most interesting philosophical studies of the development of physical theories" (1968: 80n.).
16. As with the other major sources, many applications of Meyerson's ideas—particularly with reference to clinically diagnosed ailments—appear in the book which I have not been able to cover. These include: the temporal structure of dissociated meaning and the phenomenon of "the cauldron" (109, 122, 215); "Lack of identification" in the case of an agnosic (170); the connection between obsessive identification and the "logic of pure identity" (154); very importantly, the relation between Meyerson's principle of identification and the same term as used in psychoanalysis (300 n); the hysterical imitation and the identification compulsion of schizophrenics

(200); the place of identification in Von Domarus' four functions (224ff); and so on.

17. Gabel's emphases are retained in all quotes.
18. I disagree with Broughton's suggestion that Gabel's system might be suffering from an "apparent interchangeability of terms such as 'reified,' 'anti-dialectical,' 'spatialized,' 'de-temporalized,' 'reversible,' 'de-totalized,' 'dissociated,' and 'devalued'" (1976: 235). It is quite true that stylistically Gabel can be faulted for stringing together adjectival phrases which often employ a number of these words, and it is also true that all terms Broughton lists are intimately (and positively) related in Gabel's analysis. Gabel admits as much in referring to "the close correlativity between terms such as 'non-dialectical thought,' 'false consciousness,' 'reification,' and 'alienation'," all of which "concern the same fundamental phenomena seen from different angles" (149). But for the most part he is not, it seems to me, joining a Parsonsian semantic game by slinging bunches of substantively identical modifiers at an object. If he is forgiven stylistic lapses, and if each term is considered as defined in the text, he is remarkably careful and consistent, if inventive, about their application.

References

Adorno, Theodor. 1973. *Negative Dialectics*, translated by E. B. Ashton. New York: Seabury Press.
Adams, Paul L. 1982. "The Influence of New Information from Social Sciences on Concepts, Practice, and Research in Child Psychiatry." *Journal of the American Academy of Child Psychiatry* 21:5 (November): 533–42.
Agger, Ben. 1979. *Western Marxism: An Introduction*. Santa Monica, CA: Goodyear Pub. Co.
Alford, C. Fred. 1988. *Narcissism: Socrates, the Frankfurt School, and Psychoanalytic Theory*. New Haven, CT: Yale University Press.
Allen, David. 1994. "False Consciousness and the History of Psychiatry." Unpub. ms, 18 pp.
Anctil, Pierre. 1990. Review of Joseph Gabel, *Reflexions sur l'avenir des Juifs*. *Contemporary Sociology* 19: 481–82.
Arieti, Silvano. 1974. *Interpretation of Schizophrenia*, second edition, completely revised and expanded. New York: Basic Books.
Aron, Raymond. 1976. *History and the Dialectic of Violence: An Analysis of Sartre's Critique de la Raison Dialectique*, translated by Barry Cooper. New York: Harper and Row.
Aubin, H. 1952. *L'Homme et la Magie*. Paris.
Becker, Howard and Harry Elmer Barnes. 1961. *Social Thought from Lore to Science*, 3rd ed., 3 vols. New York: Dover Pubs.
Berger, Peter and Thomas Luckmann. 1967. *The Social Construction of Reality*. New York: Anchor.
Berger, Peter and Stanley Pullberg. 1965. "Reification and the Sociological Critique of Consciousness." *History and Theory* 4:2, 196–211.
Binswanger, Ludwig. 1942. *Grundformen und Erkenntnis menschlichen Daseins*. Zurich: Niehans.

_____. 1963. *Being-in-the-World: Selected Papers of L. Binswanger*, translated and with a critical intro. by Jacob Needleman. New York: Basic Books. Reprinted, 1968, Harper & Row Torchbook.

Blankenburg, W. 1980. "Anthropological and Ontoanalytical Aspects of Delusion. *Journal of Phenomenological Psychology* 11:1 (Spring): 97–110.

Bloom, Richard W. 1978. Review of Mark Altschule, *The Development of Traditional Psychopathology*. *Journal of Personality Assessment* 42:5, 545–47.

Bocock, Robert. 1978. *Freud and Modern Society: An Outline and Analysis of Freud's Sociology*. New York: Holmes and Meier.

Brennan, Teresa. 1992. *The Interpretation of the Flesh: Freud and Femininity*. New York: Routledge.

Broughton, John. 1976. Review article on Gabel's *False Consciousness*. *Telos* #29 (Fall): 223–38.

_____. 1981a. "The Divided Self in Adolescence." *Human Development* 24: 13–32.

_____. 1981b. "Piaget's Structural Developmental Psychology: V. Ideology-Critique and the Possibility of a Critical Developmental Theory." *Human Development* 24: 382–411.

_____. 1983. "Women's Rationality and Men's Virtues: A Critique of Gender Dualism in Gilligan's Theory of Moral Development." *Social Research* 50:3 (Autumn): 597–642.

Broughton, John and Marta K. Zahaykevich. 1982. "The Peace Movement Threat." *Teachers College Record* 84:1 (Fall): 152–73.

Brown, Bruce. 1973. *Marx, Freud, and the Critique of Everyday Life*. New York: Monthly Review Press.

Brown, Phil. 1974. *Toward a Marxist Psychology*. New York: Harper & Row.

Brown, Richard Harvey. 1987. "Personal Identity and Political Economy: Western Grammars of the Self in Historical Perspective." *Current Perspectives in Social Theory* 8: 123–59.

Brunn, S. and T. Leinbach (eds.). 1991. *Collapsing Space and Time: Geographic Aspects of Communication and Information*. London: HarperCollins.

Caveing, Maurice. 1971. "Le Marxisme et la personnalite humaine" [review of Seve's *Man in Marxist Theory*, in *Psychologie et Marxisme*]. Paris.

Chodorow, Nancy. 1978. *The Reproduction of Mothering: Psychoanalysis and the Sociology of Gender*. Berkeley: University of California Press.

_____. 1994. *Femininities, Masculinities, Sexualities, Freud, and Beyond*. Lexington: University Press of Kentucky.

Cohen, Ira H. 1982. *Ideology and Consciousness: Reich, Freud, and Marx*. New York: New York University Press.

Craib, Ian. 1990. *Psychoanalysis and Social Theory: The Limits of Sociology*. Amherst: University of Massachusetts Press.

Deleuze, Gilles and Felix Guattari. 1977. *Anti-Oedipus: Capitalism and Schizophrenia*, translated by R. Hurley, M. Seem, and H. Lane. New York: Viking.

_____. 1987. *A Thousand Plateaus: Capitalism and Schizophrenia*, translated by Brian Massumi. Minneapolis: University of Minnesota Press.

Doerner, Klaus. 1981. *Madmen and the Bourgeoisie: A Social History of Insanity and Psychiatry*, translated by J. Neugroschel and J. Steinberg. Oxford: Basil Blackwell.

Dollard, John and Neal Miller. 1950. *Personality and Psychotherapy: An Analysis in Terms of Learning, Thinking, and Culture*. New York: McGraw-Hill.

Dupréel, Eugene. 1939. *Esquisse d'une philosphie des valeurs*. Paris: PUF.

Endleman, Robert. 1981. *Psyche and Society: Explorations in Psychoanalytic Sociology*. New York: Columbia University Press.
Foucault, Michel. 1976. *Mental Illness and Psychology*, translated by Alan Sheridan. New York: Harper & Row.
Ericson, Richard V. 1991. "Mass Media, Crime, Law, and Justice: An Institutional Approach. *British Journal of Criminology* 31:3 (Summer): 219–49.
Eyerman, Ron. 1981. *False Consciousness and Ideology in Marxist Theory*. Stockholm: Almqvist and Wiksell Inter'l.
Feuer, Lewis. 1975. *Ideology and the Ideologists*. New York: Harper and Row.
Fried, Yehuda. 1977. "Alienation: Pinel versus Hegel" [review of Gabel's *False Consciousness*]. *Contemporary Psychology* 22:11, 823–24.
Frug, Gerald E. 1980: "The City as a Legal Concept." *Harvard Law Review* 93:6 (April): 1059–1154.
Gabel, Joseph. 1951. "La Réification, essai d'une psychopathologie depensée dialectique." *Esprit*. October.
———. 1962a. "Délire politique chez un paranoïde." *L'Evolution Psychiatrique*. No. 2.
———. 1962b. *La fausse conscience: Essai sur la reification*. Paris: Les Editions de Minuit.
———. 1974. *Ideologies*. Paris.
———. 1975a *False Consciousness: An Essay on Reification*, translated by Margaret A. Thompson, with the assistance of Kenneth A. Thompson; with an introduction by Kenneth A. Thompson. Oxford: Blackwell.
———. 1975b. "Hungarian Marxism." *Telos* 25 (Fall):185–91.
———. 1976. "Utopian and False Consciousness." *Telos* 29 (Fall):181–86.
———. 1978. *False Consciousness: An Essay on Reification*, translated by M.A. and K. A. Thompson. Pb edition. New York: Harper and Row.
———. 1982. "Durkheimianism and Political Alienation." (ed. by Alan Sica). *Canadian Journal of Sociology* 9:2, 179–89.
———. 1984. "Is Nonideological Thought Possible?" Pp. 25–33 in *Society and Knowledge: Contemporary Perspectives in the Sociology of Knowledge*, edited by N. Stehr and V. Meja. New Brunswick, NJ: Transaction Publishers.
———. 1991. *Marxism and Hungarian Marxism*, translated by William Stein and James McCrate. New Brunswick, NJ: Transaction Publishers.
Gabel, Peter. 1977. "Intention and Structure in Contractual Conditions: Outline of a Method for Critical Legal Theory." *Minnesota Law Review* 61: 601–43.
Gachnochi, G. and N. Skurnik. 1992. "The Paradoxical Effects of Hostage-taking." *International Social Science Journal* 22: 235–46.
Gras, Vernon W., ed. 1973. *European Literary Theory and Practice: From Existential Phenomenology to Structuralism*. New York: Delta Books.
Gross, George. 1972. "The Political Economy of the Unconscious." *Cambridge Review* 94 (#2210) Nov. 17, 53–61.
Habermas, Jürgen. 1970. "On Systematically Distorted Communication." *Inquiry* 13: 205–18.
Harris, Adrienne and Edward Shorter. 1978. "Besieging Lasch." *Theory and Society* 6:2 (September): 279–92.
Heller, Agnes. 1976. *The Theory of Need in Marx*. New York: St. Martins.
———. 1979. "Towards an Anthropology of Feeling." *Dialectical Anthropology* 4:1 (March):1–20.

Horkheimer, Max. 1939. "The Relation between Psychology and Sociology in the Work of Wilhelm Dilthey." *Studies in Philosophy and Social Science* 8:3, 430–43.

_____. 1972. *Critical Theory*, translated by M. J. O'Connell. New York: Herder & Herder.

Hull, John M. 1991. "Religion, Education, and Madness: A Modern Trinity." *Education Review* 43: 347–61.

Jameson, Fredric. 1984. "Postmodernism, or the Cultural Logic of Late Capitalism." *New Left Review* No. 146: 53–92.

Kafka, John S. 1983. "Challenge and Confirmation in Ritual Action." *Psychiatry* 46 (February): 31–39.

Karapostolis, Vasilis. 1985. "Thematization in Everyday Life: A Critical Approach." *Sociological Review* 33: 691–707.

Kaye, Howard L. 1991. "A False Convergence: Freud and the Hobbesian Problem of Order." *Sociological Theory* 9:1 (Spring): 87–105.

Kemali, Dargut. 1986. "Research on Schizophrenia in Southern European Countries." *Schizophrenia Bulletin* 12:1, 74–82.

Kettler, David, Volker Meja, and Nico Stehr. 1990. "Rationalizing the Irrational: Karl Mannheim and the Besetting Sin of German Intellectuals." *American Journal of Sociology* 95:6 (May): 1441–73.

Kettler, David and Volker Meja. 1994. "'That Typically German Kind of Sociology Which Verges on Philosophy': The Dispute about *Ideology and Utopia* in the United States." *Sociological Theory* 12:3 (November): 279–303.

Kovel, Joel. 1982. *The Age of Desire: Case Histories of a Radical Psychoanalyst*. New York: Pantheon Books.

Kurzweil, Edith. 1989. Review of Gabel's *Mannheim et le marxisme hongrois*. *Contemporary Sociology* 18: 784–85.

Laing, R. D. 1963. "Minkowski and Schizophrenia." *Review of Existential Psychology and Psychiatry* 3:3 (Sept): 195–207.

Lalo, Charles. 1934. *l'Art et la Morale*. Paris.

LaPiere, Richard. 1960. *The Freudian Ethic*. London: George Allen & Unwin.

Lasch, Christopher. 1981. "The Freudian Left and Cultural Revolution." *New Left Review* 129 (September/October): 23–34.

Lefebvre, Henri. 1991a. *Critique of Everyday Life; Vol 1: Introduction*, translated by John Moore. London: Verso.

_____. 1991b. *The Production of Space*, translated by Donald Nicholson-Smith. Oxford: Blackwell.

LeSenne, Rene. 1972. "Ethics and Metaphysics." Pp. 133–55 in Joseph J. Kockelmans, ed. *Contemporary European Ethics*. New York: Anchor Books.

Lewy, Guenter. 1982. *False Consciousness: An Essay on Mystification*. New Brunswick, NJ: Transaction Publishers.

Lichtheim, George. 1967. *The Concept of Ideology*. New York: Vintage.

Lichtman, Richard. 1982. *The Production of Desire: The Integration of Psychoanalysis into Marxist Theory*. New York: Free Press.

Locher, Frances C. (ed.). 1981. *Contemporary Authors*, vol. 101: 170. Detroit: Gale Research Company.

Lukács, György. 1971. *History and Class Consciousness*, translated by R. Livingstone. London: Merlin Press.

_____. 1980. *The Destruction of Reason*, translated by Peter Palmer. London: Merlin Press.

Maley, Terry. 1994. "The Politics of Time: Subjectivity and Modernity in Max Weber." Pp. 139–66 in *The Barbarism of Reason: Max Weber and the Twilight of Enlightenment*, edited by Asher Horowitz and Terry Maley. Toronto: University of Toronto Press.
Mannheim, Karl. 1936. *Ideology and Utopia*, translated by L. Wirth and E. Shils. New York: Harcourt, Brace and World. (pb ed.: nd)
_____. 1952. *Essays on the Sociology of Knowledge*. Ed. by P. Kecskemeti. London: Routledge & Kegan Paul.
Marcuse, Herbert. 1955. *Eros & Civilization: A Philosophical Inquiry into Freud*. Boston: Beacon Press.
Marx, Karl. 1977. *Capital*, vol. 1, translated by B. Fowkes. New York: Vintage Books.
Marx, Karl and Friedrich Engels. 1956. *Selected Correspondence*. Moscow: Progress Pubs.
_____. 1969. *Selected Works*, 3 vols. Moscow: Progress Pubs.
_____. 1976. *Collected Works*, vol. 6. New York: International Pubs.
Massumi, Brian. 1992. *A Use's Guide to Capitalism and Schizophrenia: Deviations from Deleuze and Guattari*. Cambridge, MA: MIT Press.
May, Rollo, Ernest Angel, and Henri F. Ellenberger, eds. 1958. *Existence: A New Dimension in Psychiatry and Psychology*. New York: Basic Books.
Merleau-Ponty, Maurice. 1964. *The Primacy of Perception*, translated by J. Wild. Evanston, IL: Northwestern University Press.
_____. 1973. *Adventures of the Dialectic*, translated by Joseph Bien. Evanston, IL: Northwestern University Press.
Meszaros, Istvan. 1971. "Contingent and Necessary Class Consciousness." Pp. 85–127 in Meszaros, ed., *Aspects of History and Class Consciousness*. London: Routledge & Kegan Paul.
Mezirow, Jack. 1985. "Concept and Action in Adult Education." *Adult Education Quarterly* 35:3 (Spring): 142–51.
Meyerson, Emile. 1930. *Identity and Reality*, translated by Kate Loewenberg. New York: Macmillan. Reprinted, New York: Dover Pubs., 1962.
Minkowski, Eugene. 1926. "Bergson's Conceptions as Applied to Psychopathology," translated by F. J. Farnel. *Journal of Nervous and Mental Diseases* 63:6 (June): 553–68.
_____. 1927. *La Schizophrenie*. Paris: Payot.
_____. 1958. "Multiple Approaches to Treatment in Schizophrenia and Discussion of Indications." *American Journal of Psychiatry* 114, no. 7: 577–82.
_____. 1966. "Phenomenological Approaches to Existence." *The International Forum for Existential Psychiatry* I: 292–315.
_____. 1970. *Lived Time: Phenomenology and Psychopathological Studies*, translated by N. Metzel. Evanston, IL: Northwestern University Press.
Munro, Thomas. 1950. "Present Tendencies in American Esthetics." Pp. 613–27 in *Philosophic Thought in France and the United States*, edited by Marvin Farber. Buffalo, NY: University of Buffalo Publications in Philosophy.
Nahem, Joseph. 1981. *Psychology and Psychiatry: A Marxist View*. New York: International Pubs.
Nelson, Benjamin (ed). 1957. *Freud and the 20th Century*. Cleveland, OH: World Pub. Co.
Osborn, Reuben. 1965 [1937]. *Marxism and Psychoanalysis*. New York: Delta. [First published as *Freud and Marx*.]

Owen, John E. 1978. Review of Gabel's *False Consciousness*. *Contemporary Sociology* 7:1 (January): 97–98.
Parsons, Talcott. 1964. *Social Structure and Personality*. New York: Free Press.
Polin, Raymond. 1950. "The Philosophy of Values in France." Pp. 203–18 in *Philosophic Thought in France and the United States*, edited by Marvin Farber. Buffalo, NY: University of Buffalo Publications in Philosophy.
Popper, Karl. 1968. *Conjectures and Refutations*. New York: Harper and Row.
Postel, Jacques (ed.), with collab. of David Allen. 1994. *La psychiatrie (Textes essentiels)*. Paris: Larousse.
Poster, Mark. 1975. *Existential Marxism in Postwar France: From Sartre to Althusser*. Princeton, NJ: Princeton University Press.
———. 1978. *Critical Theory of the Family*. New York: Seabury.
Rabow, Jerome. 1983. "Psychoanalysis and Sociology." *Annual Review of Sociology* 9: 555–78.
———. 1987. "The Field of Psychoanalytic Sociology." Pp. 3–30 in *Advances in Psychoanalytic Sociology*, edited by Jerome Rabow, Gerald Platt, and Marion Goldman. Malabar, FL: Krieger.
Reich, Charles. 1991. "The Individual Sector." *Yale Law Journal* 100:1409–48.
Reich, Wilhelm. 1972. *Sex-Pol: Essays 1929–1934*, edited by Lee Baxandall. New York: Vintage.
Reiche, Reimut. 1970. *Sexuality and Class Struggle.*, translated by Susan Bennett. London: NLB.
Rieff, Philip. 1966. *The Triumph of the Therapeutic*. New York: Harper and Row.
Rogers, Mary F. 1981. "Ideology, Perspective, and Praxis." *Human Studies* 4: 145–61.
Rose, Nikolas S. 1990. *Governing the Soul: The Shaping of the Private Self*. New York: Routledge.
Sallnow, Michael J. 1989. "Cooperation and Contradiction: The Dialectics of Everyday Practice." *Dialectical Anthropology* 14: 241–57.
Samuels, Andrew. 1993. *The Political Psyche*. New York: Routledge.
Schneider, Michael. 1975. *Neurosis and Civilization: A Marx/Freud Synthesis.*, translated by Michael Roloff. New York: Seabury.
Semiotext(e). 1977. Special issue on *Anti-Oedipus*. 2:3, 5–189.
Séve, Lucien. 1972. "The Structural Method and the Dialectical Method." *International Journal of Sociology* 2: 2/3 (Fall):195–240; "Reply to Maurice Godelier." Ibid.: 281–314.
———. 1974. "The Class Struggle and Marxist Reversion of the Hegelian Dialectic." *Dialectics and Humanism* (Poland) 4, 61–66.
———. 1975. *Marxism and the Theory of Human Personality*, translated by D. Pavett. London: Lawrence & Wishart.
———. 1978. *Man in Marxist Theory and the Psychology of Personality*, translated John McGreal. Sussex: Harvester Press.
Spiegelberg, Herbert. 1972. *Phenomenology in Psychology and Psychiatry: A Historical Introduction*. Evanston, IL: Northwestern University Press.
Stillman, Edmund. 1969. "Herbert Marcuse." *Horizon* 11:3 (Summer): 26–31.
Swingewood, Alan. 1977. Review of Gabel's *False Consciousness*. *American Journal of Sociology* 83: 222–24.
Thomas, Louis Vincent, Bernard Rousset, and Trinh Van Thao (eds). 1977. *La mort aujourd'hui* [actes du colloque organise par le C.U.R.S.A., octobre 1975]. Paris: Editions Anthropos.

Timpanaro, Sebastiano. 1975. *On Materialism*, translated by Lawrence Garner. London: NLB.
Tristram, R.J. 1976. "Extended Review" of Gabel's *False Consciousness*. *Sociological Review* 24:4 (November): 928–32.
Turkle, Sherry. 1978. *Psychoanalytic Politics: Freud's French Revolution*. New York: Basic Books.
Voloshinov, V.N. 1976. *Freudianism: A Marxist Critique*, translated by I. Titunik; edited by N. Bruss. New York: Academic Press.
Wallerstein, Robert and Neil Smelser. 1969. "Psychoanalysis and Sociology: Articulations and Applications." *International Journal of Psychoanalysis* 50: 693–710.
Warren, Mark. 1989. "Liberal Constitutionalism as Ideology: Marx and Habermas." *Political Theory* 17:4 (November): 511–34.
_____. 1990. "Ideology and the Self." *Theory and Society* 19: 599–634.
Warren, Scott. 1985. "Joseph Gabel." Pp. 156–57 in *Biographical Dictionary of Neo-Marxism*, edited by Robert A. Gorman. Westport, CT: Greenwood Press.
Watzlawick, Paul. 1978. *The Language of Change: Elements of Therapeutic Communication*. New York: Basic Books.
Weinstein, Fred and Gerald Platt. 1969. *The Wish to Be Free: Society, Psyche, and Value Change*. Berkeley: University of California Press.
_____. 1973. *Psychoanalytic Sociology: An Essay on the Interpretation of Historical Data and the Phenomena of Collective Behavior*. Baltimore, MD: Johns Hopkins University Press.
Wolfenstein, E. Victor. 1993. *Psychoanalytic-Marxism: Groundwork*. London: Free Association Books/New York: Guilford Press.
Yannis, Gabriel. 1983. *Freud and Society*. London: Routledge and Kegan Paul.

1

Utopian Consciousness and False Consciousness

The concept of false consciousness occupies a unique place in Marxist theory, although it is still rarely used by Marxists and, unlike the theory of alienation, is just beginning to infiltrate non-Marxist intellectual life. This concept has only recently become accepted in the university, having been previously rejected by both orthodox Marxists and "bourgeois" intellectuals. Following Lukács, Lucien Goldmann was very interested in the problem of false consciousness, though it did not become the central theme in his work.[1] Despite his shaky interpretation of the issue, he did have the merit of posing an important problem. Goldmann essentially saw the phenomenon of false consciousness as a collection of errors—or inadequate theories—conditioned by a given sociological situation. From this perspective, the theory of false consciousness should be situated in the trajectory of the sociology of knowledge and of epistemology.

For me, on the contrary, false consciousness appears indeed to be a form of inadequacy, but one that goes beyond the notion of error. False consciousness is a type of *insane (délirant)*—more precisely—*schizophrenic*—"inadequacy." Consequently, it should be studied as an extension of the theory of alienation and of

---

Edited and slightly condensed from a lecture given at the colloquium on "Utopian Discourse" (Cerisy-la-Salle, summer 1975). Translated from the French by Lynn Layton and Russell Berman.

psychopathology and should only indirectly concern epistemology and the sociology of knowledge. The following simple example illustrates the difference between ordinary and pathological error. Imagine two neighbors, a foreign military attaché and a peaceful business man. Their telephone lines are connected to the same cable which is not functioning properly. They hear interference and both come to the same conclusion: their lines are tapped. Materially, they are making the *same* mistake, and yet, in another sense, *it is not the same*. For the possibility of tapped lines is mostly probable and possible in the mode of "being-in-the-world" of the military attaché. Thus, his error is the result of an inadequate choice between two legitimate possibilities. By contrast, the identical error of his neighbor is symptomatic of a profound disturbance in the coordinates of his existence (in the sense of a deterioration of the dialectical quality of the insertion of the Self into the World) and could be a preliminary manifestation of a paranoid sequence. It is in this latter sense that I have previously tried to speak of the schizophrenic character ("morbid rationality") of false consciousness. It is this "existential" interpretation—as opposed to Goldmann's cognitive-Manichean version—that I will attempt to apply to the problem of utopian consciousness.[2]

Is utopian consciousness false consciousness? Mannheim thought so and his formulation was unequivocal: "The common and ultimately crucial characteristic of ideological and utopian thinking is that one experiences with both the possibility of false consciousness."[3] But Mannheim makes such an assertion without any proof, and within the context of a general theory of utopia that is often rejected. For Mannheim, as for Ernst Bloch, utopia is a positive historical phenomenon, a factor of social change with liberating potential. Elsewhere, Mannheim unenthusiastically predicts a decline of the utopian element in our civilization.[4] Yet if the eventual disappearance of the utopian element from our political space would leave such a vacuum, how could Mannheim speak about a *false* utopian consciousness? Here we are confronted with one of the major inconsistencies in Mannheim's work which forces us to rethink our concepts, especially that of utopia.

The concept of utopia has been characterized by its ambiguity; both its negative and positive role have been subject to debate. However, such a terminology conveys disturbing Manichean overtones. In one of my earlier studies, I suggested a distinction between two types of psychopathological impairments: the *surrealist*, characterized by an overly dialectical, and therefore insufficiently reified perception of reality, and the *subrealist* presenting a diametrically opposed structure.[5] This distinction has interesting sociological applications for the study of utopian consciousness. The surrealist concept of utopia sees it essentially as a factor of sociohistorical change, as a revolutionary instrument that "shatters" being (*"fait éclater l'etre"*). On the contrary, the subrealist concept points to unrealizable projects without historical validity elaborated by marginal people. Instead of displaying a "historical-generative" (*"historiogéne"*) quality, the subrealist version offers a pretext for escaping from history.

As an example of the ambiguity of the concept of "utopia," the traditional designation by Thomas More could prove useful. He is generally considered to be the first and model utopian, whereas Marx is considered to be a "futurologist."[6] However, when one recalls that More anticipated social imperialism or colonialism, the utilization of fifth columns, and slave labor, while Engels had "envisioned" the withering away of the state, one can wonder which one is the utopian and which one is the futurologist. With good reason, true utopians have often been reproached for failing to recognize the coherence of historical situations, that is, for ignoring the historical validity of the dialectical principle of totality. Yet More's sense of this coherence is astonishing. He understood perfectly that the socialist organization of society has for its permanent and necessary corollary, the existence of a strong state—a fact which an Engels could never comprehend. Strange as it may seem, the creator of the word "utopia" must be excluded from the circle of traditional utopians even though he undoubtedly considered himself to be one. In fact, More unknowingly discovered one of the great historical laws of the founding of collectivist systems. This process has nothing to do with either the "withering away" of the state or the leap from the "reign of necessity" to the reign of "freedom" as expounded by the "utopians," Marx and Engels.

64   Ideologies and the Corruption of Thought

The category of false consciousness does not belong to the surrealist conception of utopia represented by the writings of Bloch and Mannheim. In this context, a precise example can be provided by the question of a Zionist "utopia."[7] According to Bloch and Mannheim, Zionism is entirely utopian: an instrument which shatters Jewish "being"—the long reification and extra-historicization of the exile *(galuth)*. Hence, if Zionism seems to be a typical utopia,[8] can one still speak of a Zionist false consciousness? Personally, I do not think so. The Zionist idea may have crystallized a political error and it may have brought forth injustice, but it is very difficult to describe it as a form of false consciousness. False consciousness is a corollary of alienation and reification. Racism is an "alienating ideology" not because it perceives ethnic differences, but because, by biologizing these differences, it reifies them, and then legitimates this reification with terms drawn from the natural sciences. In contrast, Zionism constitutes a sociohistorical functionalization or relativization of such differences. It is by no means certain that the "Zionist man" occupies on the human scale, a higher position than the pre-Zionist Jew. His advances in "civic" virtues and dignity may be compensated and overcompensated by a regression of intellectual insight and of universalistic inclinations.

I understand fully the nostalgia for the Jew of yesterday as a representative of this *"sens de la souffrance"* (Scheler) and at the same time, as a bearer of universal messages; in this sense we may say—and Nietzsche would not disagree—that no Jew was more Jewish than Christ. It follows that from another perspective, it nevertheless seems true that the prodigious human mutation instigated, in such a short time, by Zionism constitutes an ultimate refutation of racism. Zionism is a disalienating ideology that has killed the stereotype of the masochistic, cowardly Jew. But it is impossible to kill a stereotype without shattering all other stereotypes such as the "lazy Negro" or "inefficient Arab" and all sterotypical thinking in general. Therefore, Zionism offers a "principle of hope' not only for the Jews, but for all oppressed or "undervalued" minorities in the world. Perhaps, the time will come when an objective historian will explain the relation between the contemporary Arab renaissance and this

Zionist model; there is certainly a phenomenon of "identification with the aggressor," in Anna Freud's terminology. Indeed, in turning back on this model, black Africa makes a dangerous concession to racism. Hence, the Zionist example proves that Bloch's surrealist utopia is not necessarily a corollary of alienation or of false consciousness.

Following Laplantine's formulation, I understand the "subrealist" conception of utopia as the "mathematical, logical and rigorous construction of a perfect city subject to the imperatives of an *absolute plan* which tolerates neither deviations nor questionings: it becomes a *synonym for totalitarianism*. The ethno-psychiatric diagnosis which can be applied to utopia is that of a devitalizing nationalism, a morbid inclination for stereotypes and abstraction, and political schizophrenia."[9] This judgment is severe, but not in the least unwarranted, for it is only the assimilation of utopia to totalitarianism that gives rise to reservations. Unequivocally, the term "political schizophrenia" poses the problem of utopian false consciousness.[10] My principal reference on this question will be Ruyer's classic work *Utopie et les Utopies* which delineates the most important features of this utopian consciousness, namely: (a) fixism; or the fact that "Utopia is essentially anti-historical," or according to Döblin, it is "a human plan to interrupt history, to jump out of history and reach a stable perfection;"[11] (b) the feeling of omnipotence,[12] frequent in the type of schizophrenic psychosis defined by Roheim as a "magic psychosis"; (c) the intellectualism of utopian constructions whereby individuals seem to completely lack an unconscious, as well as human warmth (which recalls Minkowski's characterization of "morbid rationalism" or Binswanger's analysis of the temporality of love); (d) its comic aspect which is essentially the consequence of dissociation;[13] and finally (e) its antidialectical character. This last point is a key one, for in the universe of utopian construction, quantity is never transformed into quality: "Utopia . . . is at the antipode . . . of a dialectical conception of things."[14]

As a consequence, the dialectical category of totality is alien to the utopian mentality that mechanically juxtaposes incompatible assertions linked by the common denominator of their positive valuation. An unexpected analogy can be drawn between the structure of the utopian universe and political demagoguery which also blithely juxtaposes incoherent themes and issues, but generally with a rather negative valuation. According to Aron, "one chooses, in history, between sets (*ensembles*). The worst form of utopian thought leads to the failure to recognize the interdependence between some goods and evils or the incompatibility between some equally precious goods."[15] Here is one of the reasons why Marx should not be classified among the utopians; his historical vision is in fact *very totalizing*. He "chooses between sets," knowing perfectly well that in politics, at least, every rose has thorns.[16]

The schizophrenic structure of utopian consciousness is particularly clear in the genre called anti-utopia or dystopia.[17] In reality, nothing unites utopias and dystopias except the description of an imaginary society based on Reason. Otherwise, they are opposed in all aspects. And even if the term is recent, the genre of dystopian literature has a long history behind it. Perhaps Aristophanes' *Women* is the earliest significant example of a dystopia. Certain chapters of *Gulliver's Travels* are authentically dystopian, especially the journey to Laputa-Balnibarbi which presents a caricature of a society integrally founded on reason and also constitutes a coherent description—perhaps the first in literature—of the "morbid rationalist" variety of schizophrenia.

The master of the genre, however, is Orwell. His novel *1984* is certainly one of the key works of our epoch. Based upon an ingenious extrapolation of the lessons of the Moscow show trials, it provides a description of a totalitarian society which has successfully utilized scientific progress to establish a *total* control of private life. The dominant chracteristics of this world are: (a) a suppression of history by a constant re-evalution of the past based on the exigencies of the present; (b) a dissociation of thought ("doublethink") as a consequence of extreme subordination; (c) a repression of sexuality; (d) an antihumanism and a generalized depersonalization; and finally (e) the development of a new artificial language ("newspeak") designed to enforce intellectual uniformity.

Some claim to discern certain traits of the People's Republic of China in Orwell's satire, whereas, myself, I find a curious analogy with the development of one of the most important currents of contemporary Marxism: the Althusserian school. This analogy is centered on two important and corollary points: its antihistoricism, which is symptomatic of a hidden rejection of the dialectic,[18] and its antihumanism. Furthermore, it is an *ideology*, that is, the theoretical expression of a form of false consciousness.[19] The popularity of the Althusserian school is contemporary with the profound crisis in the European Left. We have entered a historical period in which egalitarian demands are increasing in the West—May 1968 was essentially a "leveling" movement—while a hierarchic orientation is appearing in these countries which officially claim to be Marxist. The consciousness of the Left is thus a dissociated or split consciousness. Perhaps, here we have a sociological explanation of the general direction of this Marxist school that, while introducing the fundamental structures of subrealist utopian discourse—a-dialecticism, antihistoricism, antihumanism—and faced with increasing evidence about the utopian character of egalitarian demands, still practices a sort of flight forwards. In short, the contradiction between an egalitarian ideal and a hierarchical reality reappears in the consciousness of the European Left, either as a structural assimilation into a reified utopian discourse (Althusser) or as an ideological-utopian (surrealist) affirmation, that is, with no relation to the concrete historical possibilities of the egalitarian ideal (the student movement).

At this point, a simplistic but unavoidable conclusion emerges which is the necessity of working with well-defined concepts. The human sciences would be able to advance much faster if some consensus existed on the main research concepts. It would be particularly desirable to find the appropriate vocabulary for the concept of utopia. The demonstration of this urgency is perhaps the principal result of our examination of the relations between utopian and false consciousness.[20] Mannheim recognized the existence of a possible relationship between the two and searched for a common denominator. Working with a barely differentiated conceptual apparatus, however, he sought a common denominator in the notion of the "transcendence of being." This approach leads to an impasse since the desire to "transcend being" is not in the least related to an alienating attitude.

I have tried to show that this common denominator exists, but that it must be found elsewhere and that this search must begin with a preliminary effort at conceptual clarification.

To conclude, I would like to advance a hypothesis concerning the anthropological function of utopian consciousness. Why does man create utopias? For Lapassade, utopia gives an "illusion of completion" (*achévement*), designed to compensate for the feelings of incompleteness which man owes to the particularities of his evolution.[21] This sense of incompleteness is a challenge to which history, dialectics, the universe of values, that is, culture, respond. Utopia, however, can be a pretext to avoid this challenge. This leads to a rather surprising conclusion: the anthropolgocial significance of utopianism in its "subrealist" form is not so distant from that of racism. The universe of racism and of subrealist utopia are two forms of ahistoricism and two variations of the illusion of completion.

Hence, an explicative hypothesis surfaces from these arguments that leads us into psychology. I can only briefly sketch it here. Man displays a sort of fascination for identity which greatly transcends the epistemological realm. It expresses itself in various phenomena such as sexual fetishism, morbid rationalism (and schizophrenia generally), a taste for the uniform (both in dress and thought), and what Bouthoul calls "heterophobia." One can even wonder if, in the last instance, the death instinct in psychoanalysis is not related to it. Clearly the "subrealist" utopia primarily emerges out of this inclination: "What is remarkable in all these constructions which ruthlessly exorcise the collective memory of the group is the deliberate will to reduce the exuberance, the richness and *diversity* of a village or city worthy of the name—i.e., infused with a mythical density only realized slowly, generation after generation—to the monolithic coherence of identity."[22] Once again, in the study of utopian consciousness, we find the analogy with clinical schizophrenia, but at the same time, we reach the limits of the competence of the sociologist who must here make way for the psychoanalyst.

Utopian Consciousness and False Consciousness 69

Notes

1. Lucien Goldmann, "Conscience réelle et conscience possible: conscience adéquate et fausse conscience" (1959), now collected in *Marxisme et sciences humaines* (Paris, 1970), 121–29.
2. Thus I am attempting to apply a personal conception of false consciousness to the problem of utopia. In contrast to Goldmann, my central category is *dedialectization* rather than *inadequacy*; see my *False Consciousness*, trans. Margaret A. Thompson (Oxford, 1975).
3. See Mannheim, *Ideologie und Utopie*, 3rd ed. (Frankfurt, 1965), p.53.
4. Mannheim, *Ideology and Utopia*, trans. L. Wirth and E. Shils (New York, 1936), 262–63.
5. In the *Actas Luso-Expanolas de Neurologia y Psyquiatria* [Madrid] (November, 1946). These concepts are, of course, understood as ideal types; actual utopians and utopias present mixed features.
6. While futurology is a new discipline whose status still remains imprecise, from now on it is possible and necessary to distinguish it from utopianism. In René Dumont's *L'Utopie ou la Mort*, surrealist utopian and futurological tendencies are combined. Orwell's *1984* combines, on the other hand, antiutopian and futurological characteristics. In fact, the antiutopian genre may be viewed as a forerunner of futurology.
7. See the chapter on "Zionist Utopia" in Ernst Bloch, *Freiheit und Ordnung: Abriss der Sozial-Utopien* (New York: Aurora Verlag, 1946), pp. 160–74.
8. To support this interpretation I would like to cite three facts: (1) according to Bloch, utopia is a "principle of hope" and, in fact, the Zionist anthem is entitled "Hope" (*Hatikvah*); (2) the temporality of the surrealist variant of utopia—reminiscent of Bergsonian "duration"—is a living temporality, dialectical as well as value-creating rather than, as in the case of subrealist utopia, corrupt, spatialized, noneventful. One of Theodor Herzl's works is thus entitled *Altneuland* (the"old-new country") which clearly reflect the dialectical structure of historical temporality within the unity of opposites; (3) finally, recall the subtitle of Herzl's work: "If you will it, it is not a fable."
9. *Les trois voix de l'imaginaire* (Paris, 1974), 255–56.
10. Paris, 1951. My observations of political schizophrenia were published as early as 1952, and now appear as "Réveries utopiques chez un schizophréne," in *Ideologies*(Paris, 1974), 313–24.
11. Ibid, p. 70.
12. Ibid.
13. Ibid., p. 107.
14. Ibid., p. 98.
15. *L'Age des empires et l'avenir de la France* (Paris, 1946), 15.
16. In *politics*, because one can try to create it in botany. Hence one might ask if a certain "botany of roses without thorns" (Lysenko) is related to a utopian dimension in Russian Marxism.
17. This dichotomy is to be distinguished from that of Laplantine who identifies"utopia" and "totalitarianism" and then uses the term "counter-utopia" ("*contre-utopia*") to refer to projects founded on liberty, such as that of L'Abbaye de Thélème.
18. After L. Althusser's defense at Amiens, one of the members of the jury (M.

D'Hondt) observed that the German term *Verschiedenheit* (difference) had been translated as "opposition." This is more than M. D'Hondt understood, since a *dialectical* notion, the role of which was so important in the thought of H. Lefebvre, was rendered as a *Manichean* and *reified* expression.
19. In *L'Homme et la Société*, 35–36 (1975), 57ff.
20. During the colloquy, the terms "dionysian" and "apollonian" were suggested. The former would refer to the "surrealist," the latter to the "subrealist." The concept "energetic" has also been discussed. It is essential to underscore the ambiguity of the concept of utopia.
21. See G. Lapassade, *L'Entrée dans la vie* (Paris, 1962).
22. Laplantine, *Les trois voix*, p. 187.

2

Political Delusion of a Paranoid Patient

The present chapter revolves around a psychiatric case that is perhaps more significant for a critical theorist of ideology than for a psychopathologist. In some essays of the present volume as well as in previous work,[1] I have highlighted the schizophrenic character of the fundamental logical features of ideological distortion as analyzed by Karl Mannheim in *Ideology and Utopia*. L.M., who was my patient during my internship in the French State Hospital of Saint Etienne de Rouvray (a suburb of Rouen), presented a spontaneous confirmation of this interpretation by elaborating a delusional totalitarian utopia. His case also presents a genuine textbook case of "morbid rationalism" (Minkowski).

Unfortunately in this case, the past history of the patient was unavailable. As a "social reformer," L.M. willingly explained the principles underlying his "political delusion," but was silent about his own personal past. Let us add that he was reluctant about the use of psychological tests and injections. For all these reasons, the present study cannot claim to be a genuine clinical observation in the classical ("historicist") sense of this term (*Krankheitsgeschichte* according to German medical terminology); but is exclusively a descriptive analysis of individual delusions. Nevertheless, in spite of its static character, this study is not without interest for a sociologist since this political delusion involves both current and recent political themes.

Translation by author and friends, David Allen and James McCrate.

L.M. is a man in his forties with a proud and visionary face. The main source of his rudimentary learning is an old edition of the *Larousse Dictionary*. In spite of his protests, he seems well adjusted to his confinement in a mental hospital, since this confinement is integrated into his delusions as being the outcome of a plot by his political opponents. He promulgated several "laws" for an imaginary state which were gathered in a strange notebook, a "Journal of Parliamentary Decrees." Among his papers, I have also found several copies of a curious "Catholic Diary" (*Journal des Catholiques*) entirely written by him. In order to complete this description, let us add that this "pope" bears a ligature around his penis and wears a "papal badge" with nine stars on his jacket sleeve.

His political delusion revolves around a limited number of simple but coherent ideas. While being certainly autistic, L.M. does not exhibit any symptoms of schizophrenic dissociation. The symptomatology of his mental illness calls to mind Minkowski's theories rather than those of Bleuler. The two principal elements of his delusion are (a) the belief that he is a pope (the first of five popes) and (b) the construction of a theocratic and geometric utopia that results in an imaginary totalitarian society that exhibits some commonalities with the left-wing totalitarianism at its zenith when this clinical observation was made (1949).

L.M. considers himself first and foremost to be a Catholic, but his "Catholicism" is very distinct from any teachings of the Church, becoming merely a term referring to the totality of his delusional ideas. For L.M., the criterion for a genuine Catholic is the unconditional acceptance of his delusional utopia, and it is for this reason, that Pius XII (pope at this time) was considered to be a "heretic pope." For L.M., the term "heretics" includes Protestants, anarchists, "krauts,"[2] that is, all persons who do not share his prescriptions for ensuring mankind happiness. Hence, it appears that L.M. practices "unwarranted extrapolation" (Whitehead), one of the outstanding logical features of ideological distortion.[3]

This case of delusional utopianism is not unique. In a doctoral thesis defended in 1965 at the medical Faculty of Nancy (France), Dr. Jean-Marie Delassus analyzed an almost identical case.⁴ Moreover, in his classical work *L'Utopie et les Utopies*, the philosopher Raymond Ruyer highlighted the antidialectical structure of utopian consciousness.⁵ Since "morbid rationalism" is characterized by its antidialectical tendency,⁶ it is by no means surprising to meet morbid utopians in State hospitals.

Here is a transcript of my conversation with "His Holiness" the Pope L.M:

L.M.: There are five Popes. I am the leading one. These are the Catholic rules. Now, in order to be Pope, one must respect the Catholic constitution and whoever does not respect it cannot be Pope.

J.G.: Who is the second Pope?

L.M.: I do not know him. I know their names, I don't know their names. They are sixteen years younger than me. It goes from sixteen to sixteen years. There is one who is fifty-five years old, another who is seventy-one, another who is eighty-seven, and so on. In case of death there is another one who is sixteen. It follows. If the one who is eighty-seven years old does not die, that makes six popes. This holds for all levels of the hierarchy. There are five archbishops per archdioceses.

The five popes are the five leaders of France. They are its governors. There are five cardinals at the head of five continents which amounts to a total of twenty-five cardinals. In each subbishopric there are five archpriests as the heads of boroughs. Each borough contains four townships and each township is headed by five priests.

In order to be elected Pope, it is necessary to be a 100 percent Catholic. If one is 25 percent or even 50 percent catholic, this is not sufficient for obtaining this title. But I myself, have not always been a 100 percent Catholic.

I have elaborated this constitution in order to facilitate the management of the State. Every district contains thirty-six municipalities which are ruled by thirty-six deacons. Every municipality contains sixteen rectangles of which 130 are destined for farming and the other thirty for zoological parks and for sport.

My principal purpose is to impose respect for my Catholic legal system. I chose Rome as my residence, and, I asked to be sent there but this project was thwarted by my anarchist opponents. They are responsible for my presence here (in the State Hospital) and are willing to kill us with their rifles and guns.

J.G.: It seems to me that anarchists are against militarism.

L.M.: Not at all. They are warmongers. My father died at fifty-six, as a martyr to the heretics and the anarchists. You are simply either a Catholic or a heretic. For me, one is always one or the other.⁷

The present departments are an expression of anarchist confusion. It is impossible to find one's way in them for they are each unique.

The Catholic method consists in censoring lies in order to reach the truth.

74   Ideologies and the Corruption of Thought

J.G.: Are you for censorship?

L.M.: Yes, but in my view the censor's target is the lie and not the truth.

J.G.: What is your opinion concerning Pope Pius XII?

L.M.: It is necessary that he becomes 100 percent catholic.

J.G.: I suppose that he is.

L.M.: No. He will be a 100 percent Catholic when he has ratified my Catholic constitution. If he does not then he is an accomplice of the heretics. Are you divorced?

J.G.: No, I am a bachelor.

L.M.: In my view, a man who has never impregnated a woman is a divorcee. I am not divorced since I once made a woman pregnant. Impregnating someone is necessary in order to increase the population in France. One cannot be pope without being married.

J.G.: Is your father still alive?

L.M.: No he was killed by "krauts" and heretics. A "kraut," a heretic and an anarchist are all the same.

J.G.: I would like to know one additional thing: why must there always be a difference of sixteen years in the ages of the popes?

L.M.: This is based on the issue of fertilization which must take place every sixteen years.

J.G.: ???

L.M.: This is in order to better organize society. I considered that it was easier than spreading it over each year. This way, I am able to calculate the population of France, taking as a basis the present population which is two billion and three hundred and seventy five million.

J.G.: But France does not have so many inhabitants.

L.M.: But Frances does while Gaul has only 40 million. France is the five continents.

J.G.: Well, then there should be a French governor in the U.S.A.

L.M.: The U.S.A. is a French country governed by archbishops and by bishops.

J.G.: The archbishop of New York is Msgr. Spelmann and he is not French.

L.M.: I do not know the name of all these bishops.

J.G.: And the Swedish? They are Protestants.

L.M.: Protestants are those who make war. It is possible to govern without war, for in war, one can only destroy. We do not need a war; it is the heretics who make war.

In order that France[8] be populated correctly, it will need more than ten billion inhabitants, to be exact: twelve billion inhabitants. Not all of France is "cultivated" (in the agricultural sense of this term), for it also contains desert areas and their agricultural clearing would provide refuge to a great number of inhabitants. It is not the war which "conserves France" because warmongers which are factors of destruction. It is not bombing which transforms deserts into fertile plains but work.

J.G.: And the soldiers? What are your intentions towards them?

L.M.: We have to make them wise (*On les assagira*) until they become Catholics.

J.G.: It seems to me that there are many outstanding Catholic soldiers.
L.M.: It is not illicit to be a soldier when one belongs to Catholicism. Peace is civilization, war is barbarism. Barbarism is tantamount to heresy, and civilization to Catholicism.

This conversation sheds light on L.M.'s "Catholic doctrine." His central idea is the reorganization of the social hierarchy. Everything is supposed to be ecclesiastical in this imaginary society; nonecclesiastical "dignities" are suppressed and their "titulars" are directed towards the "wise makers" (*assagissoires*)[9] or specific reeducative institutions.

Here is another typical written recommendation from our "Pope:"

> Information drawn form an illustrated magazine.
> Population of France in 1949:
> 2 billion, 374 million, and 456,000 inhabitants.
> 75 percent heretics, 74 million, 456,000, inhabitants.
> 50 percent heretics, 62 million, 500,000 inhabitants.
> 25 percent heretics, 37 million, 500,000 inhabitants.
> 100 percent catholics, 2 billion, 200000000 inhabitants.
> Approximative statistics established by Mr. L.M. Pope of first rank.
> The "wise-making" of these heretics requires thirty-six "wise-makers" (*assagissoires*) in each township along with a criminal court (that is to say a church)
> Law promulgated in 1949 and improved the March 5, 1950 by Mr. L.M. Pope of first rank. So be it.

A "papal decree" of March 10, 1950, abolishes all civilian and military ranks and defines the degree of "wise making" (*assagissement*) imposed on their respective titulars. A field marshal should spend twelve years in an "*assagissoir*," while it is sufficient for a sergeant to commit four years, and for a private soldier to give two years. Our "lawmaker" did apparently not take into account the fact that in the case of these latter, military activities are a legal obligation.

The persons most severely penalized by L.M. for their uselessness in the collectivity are beyond doubt the military personal. L.M. is a pacifist "or better an anti-militarist." His doctrine is stamped with an abstract humanitarianism as it appears in a decree targeted against "infernalities which have to be discarded" (*Infernalités a supprimer*).

76 Ideologies and the Corruption of Thought

This is the list of the "Decree discarding infernalities. Thursday May 11, 1950":

> Cannons, fusil, baionnette, sabre, épée, poignard, revolver, pistolet, grenàde, obus, torpitle, balle, tank, torpilloir, bombardoir, bombe, matraquoir, électro-choquoir, piqûoir, guillotinoir, potence, citadelle, caserne, cloître, abbaye, hôpital, arsenal, préfecture, mairie, sur terre, sur air, sur eau, dans tere, dans pierre et dans l'eau". L.M. 1er, 1er chef suprême du R. F. et de la justice.[10]
> "Friday May 12, 1950. Decree by Mr. L.M., man of highest rank and head of State of the French Republic and of the Justice."

"Wise-making" (*assaigissement*) begins at the age of eight years. Shower baths take place on the fifth, twelfth, eighteenth, twenty-fourth and thirtieth of every month between fifteen and sixteen hours. Shaving takes place on the same dates; and, haircuts on the twenty-fourth of every month.

As of the territorial organizations, it is first necessary to call to mind that for L.M. France = the five continents. French is supposed to be spoken everywhere; so, the other languages are for him provincial dialects (*patois*). The French territory is for L.M. the Gaul. Mr. Vincent Auriol (head of state of the French Republic at this time) is seen by L.M. as an "autonomist."

> L.M.: The President of the Republic is the Pope. M. Auriol is an autonomist since he confuses Gaul and France, notwithstanding the fact that France spreads over the five continents.
> J.G.: For you France is the universe. And England?
> L.M.: It is a French province. Europe is a continent of France.
> J.G.: And French is spoken everywhere?
> L.M.: There are persons who are jabbering *patois*; this fact is devoid of interest for me. There are communal schools in which they have to learn linguistics.

Continents are numbered; America is for L.M. the continent number 1. France is seen by L.M. as the whole universe (the Five Continents) and also as the country number 1. I perceive here a kind of indecision in his delusional system, or, better, a contamination of the delusion by reality according to the term coined by the German psychiatrist Jacob Wyrsch.

The world is divided into areas (see illustration p. 82) and the areas in bishoprics. These rectangular bishoprics are all equal the respective dimensions of their coastlines being of 100 kilometers. L.M. dislikes the *"comitats"* stigmatized by him as resulting from a "revolutionary" or "anarchist" confusion. He blames their "illogical" form as well as their unequal dimensions. As for the communes, they are also organized according to geometric principles. They are all equal and their organization is based on the principle of a rational exploitation of areas where food can be grown.

Importance of Sexuality in L.M.'s Utopia

Sexuality is very important in L.M's utopia. We have seen above that a Pope has to be married. He even added, that this dignitary should also have made a woman pregnant. Nobody can be appointed Cardinal (he writes sometimes "carnidal"), unless he is interested in love. Having applied for appointment to the rank of "Cardinal of Europe," L.M. submitted to me a questionnaire concerning the recognition of his papal authority along with others concerning private life. My answers to these questions resulted in my rejection for the rank for the following reasons:

"Sotteville-lés-Rouiens
le Mercredi 20 Sétembre 1950
Syndicat civil, de la Sécurité sociale, territoriale, et océanique, protégrant, les corps des deux sexes, et tout ce qui est indispensable à l'économie des nationalistes.
Décret loi, du Samedi 29 Juillet 1950.
Le chef suprême.
.... lucien, grade 1er Pape. Elu par le pourcentage catholique du monde entier.
Cher monsier Gabel
J'ai l'honneur.
A la question: T'intéresses tu à l'amour? tu a répondu,non. Vu le décret loy, du Lundi 9 Janvier 1950, concernant les moeurs, tant que tu ne t'interesseras pà à l'amour il es pà possible que je te conféře le grade deCardinal.
Signature
...... lucien, grade 1er Pape
l'incorruptible[11]

78   Ideologies and the Corruption of Thought

The moral legislation of this strange utopia is reminiscent of the laws of Aldous Huxley's *Brave New World*. Childbearing women who nevertheless are not pregnant "obtain the favor of being directed towards a wise-maker."[12]

The Wise-Makers *(Assagissoirs)*

Coercive institutions are the natural corollary of such an ambitious social reformism. Let us consider the characteristics of these "wise-making institutions." L.M. precisely calculated their number, and suggested that every township should possess several of them. At the time of this clinical observation (1949), some historical records were still vivid in our memory; it seemed justified to ask the question of a possible kinship between the "wise-makers" of our patient and a world famous institution which is far from being a honor to our epoch. To this question, L.M. gave a clear answer: no cruelties in the wise-makers, for this is contrary to my Catholic law. Nevertheless and inspite of some other differences, this aspect of his delusion may be called "concentration camp reveries." Persons considered useless to society, such as, among others, soldiers (of all ranks as we have seen above) and all nonconformists, sexual nonconformist included—unified under the extrapolating term of "heretics"—are all directed towards these "wise-makers." Economic planning is one of the foundations of L.M.'s morbid utopia. These plans proliferate in a great number of notebooks and in a large part of his correspondence. However, this planning is autistic and a sign of maladjustment; L.M.'s calculations are exclusively based on his pathological imagination and devoid of any relation to reality. One may imagine L.M. as a member of the "Academy of Planning" in the schizophrenic kingdom of Balnibarbi[13] as described by Jonathan Swift in his famous novel.

The monotony of his themes, along with an extraordinary profusion of schizophrenic neologisms, renders the reading of these documents laborious. The size of these "documents" as well as their monotony also makes their insertion into a scientific publication very difficult. The principal themes revolve around plans for alimentary reserves (forecasted for three decades), plans for sowing crops and uniformization of human activities. In L.M.s political delusion, there is a paradoxical coexistence of an egalitarian nostalgia along with a very clear sense of social hierarchy.[14]

At the time when we ceased our contacts, L.M. devoted his energy to an important and difficult task: the revision and refinement of the French *Larousse Dictionary* with regard to what he called "linguistical barbarism." For instance, the French verb *massacrer* means to slaughter; and an *humeur massacrante* means rotten or foul temper. For L.M., this is an example of "linguistical barbarism;" a "temper" cannot be "slaughtering." For L.M., the term *obscurantisme* exclusively refers to any opposition to (his) Catholic ideology, which is another curious and significant instance of the trend towards egocentrization of meaning. This egocentrization of (political) concepts is also a typical feature of ideological distortion,[15] which leads us to believe that we have here a genuine textbook case of "morbid rationalism" (in the sense of E. Minkowski's theories). However, our patient applies this schizophrenic logic to highly topical social and political themes which gives a particular character to his delusion.

Interpretation of the Case

The interpretation of a psychiatric case can never be completely objective since a cross-questioning involves, in psychopathology as well as elsewhere, the interaction of two minds. The present interpretation is thus one working hypothesis among others, for this case contains objective documents which may allow a reader opposed with the suggested (Marxist) interpretation to proceed to another one in conformity with his/her own ideological preferences. My interpretation consists in a psychiatric application of the concept of reification which plays a central role for the "Hungaro-Marxist" school[16] (expressed first and foremost in the works of Georg Lukács).

According to Lukács, reification is characterized (a) by a specific form of rationalization "based on what is and can be calculated" and which involves "the progressive elimination of the qualitative human and individual attributes of the worker";[17] (b) a "fragmentation of the object of production" which necessarily entails "the fragmentation of its subject";[18] (c) the spatialization of temporality in the universe of reification:

time sheds its qualitative, variable flowing nature; it freezes into an exactly delimitated, quantifiable continuum filled with quantifiable 'things' (the reified, mechanically objectified 'performance' of the worker, wholly separated from his total human personality): in short, it becomes space.[19]

This quotations clearly shows an analogy between Lukács's notion of reification and Minkowski's "morbid rationalism" as exemplified by L.M. In another article (1991), I have already called Minkowski "the Lukács of morbid consciousness" and Lukács "the Minkowski of Class Consciousness."[20] These analogies can be explained by the common influence of Bergson on these two outstanding thinkers.

On the basis of these considerations, the introduction of the concept of "reification syndrome" into psychiatric nosology appears well-founded and even to some extent useful. It is an extrapolation of morbid rationalism since it involves symptoms that are absent from the classical symptomatology of this variant of schizophrenia identified by Minkowski. Between the schizophrenic dissociation (Bleuler) and the spatialization of temporality (Minkowski), there exists, of course, an empirical but not a logical relation. However, they are both present and logically linked to each other in Lukács's analysis of reification. In psychopathology, the concept of false consciousness allows a precise delimitation of schizophrenia as a nosological entity.[21]

In L.M's symptomatology, the principal features of reification are clearly present: (a) first and foremost, a typically totalitarian, that is, depersonalizing form of economic planning along with a homogenization of all human activities—including sexuality; (b) a tendency towards abstract (and antihistoricist) equality: illustrated by the conception of geometrical artificial bishoprics in opposition to the historically established departments; (c) and last, but not least, strong "concentrational" phantasms (the *assagissoirs*) whose uncommon presence in the symptomatology of a genuine schizophrenic deserves[22] to be highlighted.

One may wonder about the reasons for identifying the historical phenomenon of concentration camps, which sullied our civilization some decades ago, as a symptom of social reification. The answer lies in these facts: first, this phenomenon expresses the pretension of a totalitarian society to homogenize the behavior of its subjects.[23] Penal institutions are destined for delinquents while concentration camps are directed at non-conformists ("heretics" according to the favorite expression of L.M.).

Secondly, one should also remember that the institution of the concentration camp—much more than the penal institutions— involves an axiological devalorization of its victims. A condemned person's execution still involves some solemnity (the presence of a priest and of a lawyer) as an indication of the fact that society recognizes the axiological importance of the legal death of a stigmatized criminal. Whereas, the death of victims of concentration camps is not only bereft of any solemnity, but also an object of atrocious mechanization, foreseen by Kafka in his inspired story *In the Penal Colony*. Furthermore, the remains of these victims were frequently used for unspeakable functional purposes, which can be seen as a symptom of a reified (racist) perception of a discriminated ethnic minority.[24] Hence, the factors of reification, of impersonalization and of devalorization inherent in the concentration camp phenomenon appear to be a typical aspect of the "schizophrenic hue of our civilization," according to Henry Ey's formulation. Seen in this light, the presence of "concentrationary phantasms" in the symptomatology of a genuine schizophrenic seems highly significant.

This interpretation of L.M.'s case does not pretend to be either exhaustive or definitive; it is merely one perspective and a working hypothesis. It seeks to propose the possibility of a sociological application of the concept of morbid rationalism, as well an application of psychoanalytic theories to sociological phenomena. The present observation exhibits one curious particularity. In this case, the application was advanced by a psychotic and not by a sociologist.

A similar observation was made by the psychoanalyst Zulliger:[25] A young child witnesses a discussion between his parents; afterwards, he sees a rooster fornicating with a hen. He kills the rooster and eats it with his brothers. According to Bastide, "we have here all the elements of totemism;"[26] we are therefore in the presence of an individual experience of a sociological phenomenon. The same statement holds true for L.M's case, which appears in this light as an individual experience of false consciousness by a psychotic.[27]

FIGURE 1
Thw World Divided into Zones

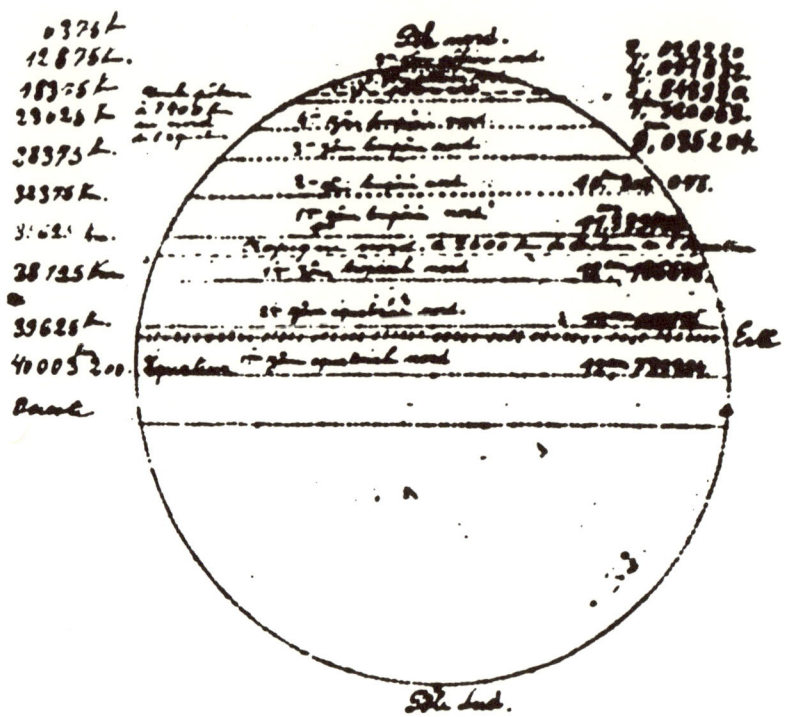

FIGURE 2
"Wise-Making Centers" (Concentration Camps)

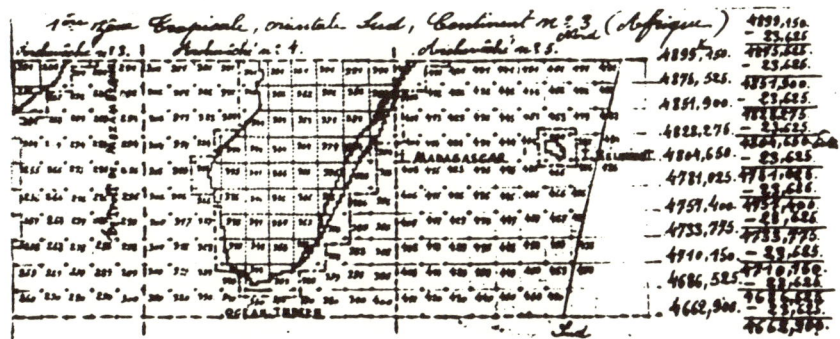

Une zone divisée en "évêchés"

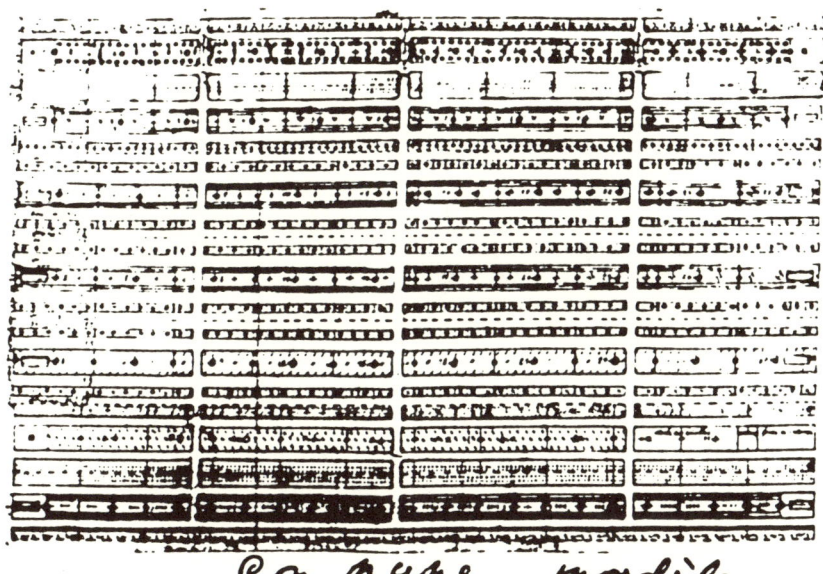

Commune modèle.

FIGURE 3
Human Being as Seen by a Psychotic

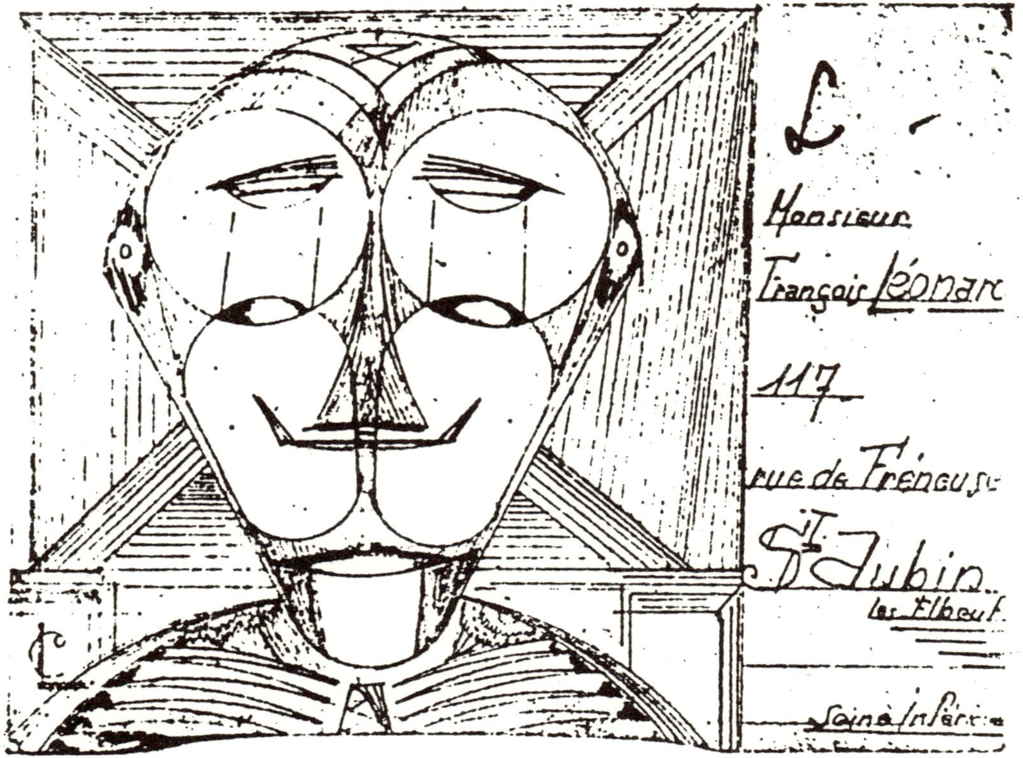

FIGURE 4
"The Arms of France"

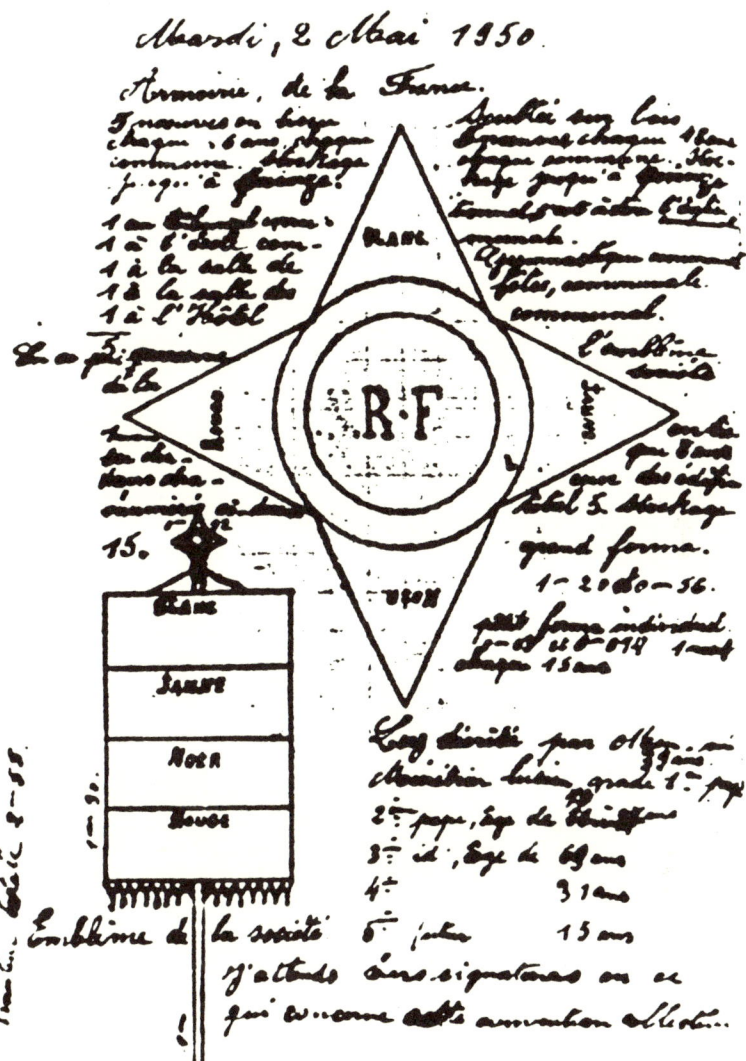

Notes

1. See Gabel, *False Consciousness* (Oxford: Blackwell Publishers, 1975). See also "Stalinism as Ideology" and "Eugéne Minkowski and the Problem of Alienation" in the present volume.
2. The term *boche* (kraut) is a nickname targeting the Germans in the past. It is no longer used today.
3. See chapter 8 of the present volume. For the Stalinist "ideology" (in the Marxist critical sense of this concept), all opponents were identifiable members of the same conspiracy (e.g., Trotsky considered as Hitler's accomplice). The same unwarranted, extrapolated corollary to false identification or the "perverse equation" (a term coined by the French author Alain Dieckhoff) characterizes the use of the concept of racism in some left-wing press. The same phenomenon was detected in the logic in schizophrenia by Silvano Arieti and by the present author.
4. J.M. Delassus, *Contribution à l'étude des délires schizophréniques: L'oeuvre et l'utopie de G.* (Contribution to the study of schizophrenic delusion; the work and the utopia of "G."). The political delusion of this patient is virtually identical to that of L.M. Minkowski is, of course, quoted by Delassus.
5. This statement is clearly formulated by Raymond Ruyer: "L'utopie . . . est aux antipodes par son académisme d'une conception dialectique des choses"; Ruyer, *L'Utopie et les utopies* (Paris: P.U.F., 1950), p. 98. (The academicism of utopian consciousness ascribed it to the antipodes of a dialectical conception).
6. "Morbid rationalism" was interpreted by the present author in *False Consciousness* (Oxford: Basil Blackwell, 1975) as a pathological form of dedialectization, that is, as reification of consciousness. This Marxist interpretation (*Umstülpung*) of this theory was ratified by Minkowski in his last important work *Traité de Psychopathologie* (Paris: P.U.F. 1966), p. 595.
7. This Manichean vision of human reality (a typical feature of ideological distortion) was detected in schizophrenia by Minkowski, who characterized the psyche of such psychotics as a "polar region of intellectual antitheses"; Minkowski, "Contribution à l'étude de la pensée et de l'attitude autistes (Le rationalisme morbide)," *L'Encephale* (Paris) April, 1923, p. 16.
8. Let us remember that for L.M., France is the totality of the five continents.
9. The French term *"assagissoir"* (wise-maker) is a schizophrenic neologism difficult to translate. The German translator of this article used the term *Bravmacherei* (Gabel, *Formen der Entfremdung* [Frankfurt: Fischer Verlag, 1964], pp. 42–43). This term designates in my view the Gulag of this imaginary totalitarian State.
10. Since this list of "infernalities" is teeming with schizophrenic neologisms, it is almost untranslatable. It contains weapons (guns, rifles, bombs, etc.), instruments of the death penalty (guillotine, gallows), social institutions such as police headquarters, town councils and also instruments of psychiatric treatments, like electroconvulsive therapy. This list is also a textbook example of "unwarranted identification" (perverse equation) which characterizes schizophrenic logic (Korzybski, Arieti, Gabel) and that of ideological distortion (Fogarasi).
11. "You declared that you are not interested in love. According to my papal

decree promulgated, January 9, 1950, a person who is not interested in love cannot be appointed cardinal."
12. "Graciées à l'assagissoir," according to the fanciful term employed by L.M.
13. See the chapter on Jonathan Swift in the present volume.
14. Let us remember that this apparently paradoxical coexistence of an egalitarian ideology along with an acceptance of social hierarchy was a specific trend of Stalinism as ideology.
15. For concrete examples of this egocentrization of political concepts, refer to pp. 129–144 of the present volume.
16. Term coined by the present author in an article about Karl Korsch in the review *Lettres Nouvelles* (Paris), July/August/September, 1965, p. 179.
17. Lukàcs, *History and Class Consciousness* (translated by Rodney Livingstone) (London: Merlin Press, 1971), p. 88.
18. Ibid., p. 89.
19. Ibid., p. 90.
20. Joseph Gabel, "L'oeuvre d'Eugéne Minkowski et la philosophie de la culture," *L'Evolution Psychiatrique* (Paris, 1991), pp. 429–34 and pp. 165–174 of the present volume.
21. For details of this nosological delimitation, see Gabel, *False Consciousness* (Oxford: Blackwell, 1975) and David Frank Allen, "Fausse Conscience" in Jacques Postel (ed.), *Dictionnaire de la Psychiatrie* (Paris: Ed. Larousse, 1993), p. 231.
22. This case is rare but not unique; see the doctoral thesis of Jean Marie Delassus quoted above.
23. The German term, *Gleichschaltung*, frequently employed by the Hitlerian press, is difficult to translate into French or English.
24. As pointed out by Adorno et al., *The Authoritarian Personality* (New York: Harper, 1950).
25. Quoted by Roger Bastide in *Sociologie et Psychonalyse* (Paris: P.U.F., 1950).
26. Zullinger, "The Totemic Meal of a Child of 5 Years," *Imago* XIII, 1927, quoted by Roger Bastide, *Sociologie et Psychoanalyse*, p. 37.
27. These developments are completed by the interesting drawings of L.C., another inmate of the same state hospital, author of a delusional physiological theory of exaggeratedly mechanistic (i.e., reified) character. Unlike L.M., this patient is not well disposed to explain his "theories," which makes it difficult to publish that case. Nevertheless, his drawings are significant as an expression of a reified perception of human beings.

3

Axiology and Dialectics

The hypothesis advanced in this paper is that the axiological experience (i.e, the perception of reality as a value) is equivalent to its dialectical (i.e., historicist and totalizing) perception—the postulate of axio-dialectical equivalence. Today, the concept of dialectics, which is central to political debate, has become highly ideologized. Just as Raymond Aron spoke of "Marxisms" in the plural, the same can be said about dialectics. Therefore, it becomes necessary to specify precisely which form of dialectics one adheres to.

The dialectics underlying the present research is the one used by Georg Lukács in his classic *History and Class Consciousness*[1] and by Lucien Goldmann, Henri Lefebvre and Maurice Merleau-Ponty. The two pillars of this conception of dialectics are the historicity of reality and the category of concrete totality, the latter being synonymous with "Gestalt" as it is used in psychology. Each of these assumptions has been subject to criticism by the supporters of sectarian Marxism. As far as the historicist dimension of dialectics is concerned, this criticism is directed against the Althusserian school in France,[2] which pretends to constitute (or "reconstitute") a form of Marxism freed from the "historicist burden," which is seen to be a legacy of pre-Marxist (idealist) philosophical influences.

It is strange that certain Marxist criticisms of the Gestalt school impugn the absence of a historico-genetic dimension in the works of the main representatives of that school. According to Roger Garaudy (a well-known French theorist of Marxism who later converted to Islam): "what Pavlov reproaches in Gestalt theory is not that it insists on the character of unity of perception but its idealistic conception of this unity whereby its antecedents and origins remain unknown."[3] In the same passage, while Garaudy uses a suggestive quotation from Hegel to question the Gestaltists' attempt to revamp a century-old idea, he does not realize that this questioning of the originality of Gestalt theory is implicitly a recognition of its dialectic value. Garaudy's criticism, like that of Jean Piaget's,[4] may then be directed against the personal views of some Gestaltists guilty of not recognizing the importance of the genetic dimension of the problem. But it cannot call into question the validity of the dialectical category of totality as conceived by Lukács and Goldmann.

Goldmann defined Marxism as a "genetic structuralism," though the synonymous expression, "historicism of totality," is perhaps preferable for it avoids all confusion with another school's terminology.[5] What is essential is to highlight clearly the intimate links between the two dimensions of dialectics: historicity and totality. Without a historical dimension, totality appears to be suspended in a vacuum and— as Garaudy explained—is unable to ward off any idealistic temptation: "Dialectics is a logic of movement, and in this world full of antagonistic forces, movement is a corollary of universal interdependence. Garaudy suggested that "if everything holds together, then everything moves."[6] Let us add that the dialectical law of transformation of quantity into quality may be perfectly deduced from the validity of the category of totality, as it is clearly brought to light in a text by Engels.[7]

Bergsonism and Dialectics

Lukács' concept of dialectics is similar to the one formulated by Bergson. Before the First World War, a considerable part of the progressive intelligentsia in Budapest perceived Bergson's philosophy as a dialectical philosophy of disalienation.[8] In fact, however, from its very beginnings, Bergson's philosophy—especially in his essay on the meaning of the comic (*Le Rire*, 1900)— embodied a form of thinking that Marxists would later designate by the term "reification." Such explanations are necessary since the work of a great psychopathologist of Bergsonian persuasion (E. Minkowski) is one of the principal references in this present study. Now it appears that each of these two components of Lukács dialectics belongs to the domain of axiology as exemplified on the one hand by Wilhelm Ostwald's treatment of the historicist component and by Wolfgang Köhler's treatment of its totalizing aspect.

Historicity and Value: Ostwald's View

Ostwald's axiology was published in 1913.[9] At that time, the theory of entropy was in vogue and inspired several philosophical positions. According to the physicist Eddington, there is "an arrow in time," an irreversible temporality in the double meaning of this term (*Sinn* and *Richtung*). In a continuum without an arrow (as in space), a destruction of values (such as for example the burning of books under the Nazis) would not be serious since one could go back in time to cancel out its effects. The irreversibility of historical time attests to the seriousness of the axiological fact that one cannot reverse history and return to the starting point. Ostwald's axiology posits the autonomous and axiogenous quality of historical time.[10] History creates its own values and is not a mere realization of extrahistorical values, such as the notion of divine origin in the religious philosophies of history (Bossuet), or that of biological origin in racist philosophies. This "axiological autonomy of historicity" is an important dimension of historicism. By crowning Charlemagne emperor, Pope Leo III created a historical value which, however, takes on a different meaning with each historical era; thus, it is, to use the terminology of Eugéne Dupréel, simultaneously consistent and precarious.[11]

Axiologies of Totality: Köhler and Lukács

Wolfgang Köhler's axiology is a gestaltist theory of value and consequently a dialectical one. According to the French philosopher Raymond Ruyer, "the recent attempt by Köhler, though deeper and less ambitious than Ostwald's theory, is essentially no different."[12] Not only is this theory "not essentially different" from Ostwald's, but, in fact, constitutes its very complement. Ostwald highlights the axiogenous character of historicity, while Köhler shows its dialectical totality (*Ganzheitsprinzip*). These two approaches converge towards the same conclusion: the "axiogenous" nature of dialectics in the sense of the Lukács school.

A very significant confirmation of this axiodialectical correlativity is demonstrated by racism. The racist perception of a discriminated ethnic group is a devalorizing one; this point needs no commentary. But a racist perception is also a reified (i.e., antihistoricist and dedialectizing) form of perception as established by Theodor Adorno's experimental investigation in *The Authoritarian Personality*.

The starting point of Köhler's philosophical enterprise was the study of "physical totalities" (*physische Gestalten*);[13] his procedure calls to mind that of Engels in his *Naturdialektik*.[14] These physical forms (totalities) spontaneously tend towards an equilibrating order. A glimpse of axiological behavior is to be noted here just as one can discern an anorganic outline of the memorization function in classical cases of hysteresis. To prevent any disagreement among authors over the establishment of the domain of axiology, Köhler introduces the concept of "requiredness."[15] A melodic structure requires the presence of certain notes to avoid the pitfalls of cacophony. For Gestaltist axiology, "dynamic form and requiredness of value with exactly the same properties are one and the same thing."[16] Thus, we find the dialectical concept of "axiogenic totality" in the writings of two non-Marxist authors. For his part, Lukács did not await the relatively recent rise of Gestalt theories to confirm in 1911 (before he even became a Marxist) that "form is the highest judge of life. The structuring capacity includes a directing force, an ethical factor; the simple fact of being structured thus implies a value-judgement."[17]

The Dialectical Axiology of Eugéne Dupréel

It is in this spirit that my own dialectical rereading of Dupréel's axiology seems justifiable. Depréel's axiology conforms to an implicit philosophical criticism of reification, though this Marxist term is not part of his fundamental vocabulary.

Dupréel maintains that superior values are the result of the contradictory (dialectical) unity of two apparently irreconcilable dimensions: consistency and precariousness. A uniquely consistent (i.e., "reified") value would therefore be a false value. The history of ideologies presents remarkable examples of reified values of pure consistency, such as the idea of Grace according to Calvinist theology or that of racial "value" in racist theories. It has been postulated that one can find a certain historical continuity between these two last forms of a "reified" axiology.[18] Whereas exclusively "precarious" values (a satisfying meal, a passing adventure) are not necessarily false values, they are doubtless inferior ones.

> To put forward a value as being unique is to set it up as being other than a value, *as being a thing*, not being consistent since it varies according to the determinations that are given to it, or being precarious since it would have to be held to exist in all events. Once more, such is indeed the error of the classics, the inventors of the Sovereign Good, of a model order both unique and universal, and also that of all fanaticism, no matter how lofty be their inspirations; in the name of a unique form of value is only calumny and disdain for the value which it is advised to sacrifice. *We wish that renunciation might mean giving up nothing, all that is good and desirable being on the side where we must go.*[19]

This important text of Dupréel highlights the dialectical structure of the world of values while including both a totally explicit criticism of reification and a philosophical indictment of totalitarian mentality. In the light of Dupréel's axiology, pluralist democracy appears in fact to be the axiogenous political regime par excellence. By underlining the importance of virtue for democracy, the thinkers of the Enlightenment were posing essentially these same claims.

This dialectical axiology is connected with certain aspects of Christian theology, as well as with the Freudian theories of drives. The presence of a death drive in our psychological constitution does not mean that one seeks to die, but rather, expresses the fact that life is considered to be a value, in Dupréel's meaning of the term—a dialectical synthesis of consistency and precariousness. An illustration of this idea can be found in Jonathan Swift's *Gulliver's Travels*. One day, the hero of this novel lands in a strange country (Luggnagg) among whose inhabitants are the immortal "Struldbrugs." Dr. Gulliver learns with satisfaction the unexpected demise of his traditional enemy, Death, but soon feels despondent for, against all reasonable odds, the "beneficiaries" of this value, now devoid of precariousness, feel deeply sad. As in the case of Saint Theresa of Avila, they are dying to die (" . . . *yo muero porqué no muero*"). In this outstanding passage, Swift comes across as a genuine precursor of Dupréel and also, to a certain extent, of Freud.

In Christian theology, the dual nature of Christ: both divine, and thus consistent, and human—that is, precarious—posits the same underlying idea. Gods of Greek mythology were especially precarious; Chronos was deposed along with his collaborators in the same manner in which an ordinary prime minister of the French Third Republic would be dismissed. However, whereas Chronos = Time, Jahweh, the Jewish divinity, is sometimes designated by the pseudonym "Hamakom," that is, place or pure space. Hence, among all the great monotheistic religions, Christianity stands alone on an underlying dialectical axiology (another common denominator between Marxism and Christianity).

Reified Logic and Axiological Regression in Schizophrenia

Described as early as 1929 as "a great experiment of Nature" by the Austrian psychiatrist J. Berze, schizophrenia is an important mental illness today. Eugéne Minkowski, a non-Marxist but doubtless, an outstanding dialectical thinker in the line of Bergson, pointed to a genuine reification of logic in schizophrenia: "morbid rationalism."[20] While the well-known American psychiatrist Silvano Arieti, showed the abnormal preponderance of identification in schizophrenic logic, others have insisted on the atrophy of praxis (Binswanger) and of the perception of totalities (Lauretta Bender) as characteristic of that illness. This atrophy of the dialectical quality of mental functions runs parallel to an axiological degradation. The affective coldness of schizophrenics is a clinically documented fact. The isolation of these patients—their "autism"—is probably a symptom of axiological deficiency. Their immobility, known as "catatonic syndrome," might be interpreted as the outcome of an existence in an axiologically homogenous space—the space of Buridan's donkey—where no privileged stimulus drives action. Although this interpretation does not prove or disprove biological or medical explanations, for example catatonic syndrome as a result of an infectious or toxic effect (Baruk), it is situated on a different level. As medical considerations do not concern me here, the only important conclusion drawn from our observations is that these patients suffer simultaneously from a dialectical degradation and axiological regression.

Perversions

Some time ago, Erwin Strauss pointed out the obvious role of phenomena of devalorization in sexual perversions. The expression "reification of sexuality" was coined by my late friend Igor A. Caruso who detected reification not only in fetishism where it is quite obvious, but in a more discreet fashion in several other sexual perversions.[21] Can we speak about a process of "dedialectization" of sexual relations? Without much detail, it seems sufficient to refer to the old but brilliant article by von Gebsattel, who interpreted fetishism in terms of a detotalization—in other words dedialectization—of sexual alterity.[22] Though important, the psychoanalytical dimension of the problem does not need to be included at this juncture. What is essential is to find once more the concordance between a process of dedialectization and axiological degradation.

Axiological Reification and Predialectical Logic in Children

In a nonpolitical context, Jean Piaget's work *Le jugement moral chez l'enfant* (1927), contains an implicit criticism of quantitative morals (ethics of pure utility) such as the ethical principle of "reasons of state." Until a certain age, when asked about the moral value of generous but harmful acts, and about the value of self-centered acts responsible for minimal damage, the child systematically exhibits a preference in favor of the latter. In children, an equally reified, predialectical logic corresponds to this "reified morality."[23] In his polemic against Gestalt,[24] Piaget showed that the totalizing structure of perception, highlighted by the Gestalt theorists, is not an innate constant of psychological life, but is the fruit of maturity. According to Peter L. Berger and Thomas Luckmann, "It would be a mistake to look at reification as a perversion of an originally non-reified apprehension of the social world, a sort of cognitive fall from grace. On the contrary, the available ethnological and psychological evidence seems to indicate the opposite, namely, that the original apprehension of the social world is highly reified both phylogenetically and ontogenically."[25] Man is not born a dialectician, but becomes one.

Dialectics and Axiology in Stalinism

The relations between Stalinism and dialectics have always been paradoxical. Although, theoretically, Stalinism always claimed a kinship with dialectical materialism, the logic underlying its concrete intellectual manifestations (journalism among many others) was radically opposed to dialectics.[26] Even before Lenin's death, Karl Korsch diagnosed the effects of this paradoxical evolution, which reached its apogee under the sway of Zhdanov during the Stalin era. This process of dedialectization took place at two levels: (a) through a logic of amalgamization (false identification) in the political discourse of this epoch, and (b) through a constant censorship justified as a reaction to the "idealism" of such genuinely dialectical theories as psychoanalysis, relativity, or Gestalt psychology. In the mental world of Stalinism, the axiological corollary of logical dedialectization was the forgotten phenomenon of objective morality (*morale objective*) which started to receive attention around 1950. Important thinkers such as Simone de Beauvoir or Maurice Merleau-Ponty showed interest in this phenomenon without noting its evident analogies with the data analyzed by Jean Piaget in his *Jugement moral chez l'enfant*. All this is relegated today to the history of ideologies; the rejection of dialectics by official Marxism has become less noticeable and no one any longer speaks of "objective morality." Nevertheless, their past coincidence, as well as the simultaneity of their regression, still remain significant.

Historicity and Axiology in Nazi Ideology

The ideology of the Nazi movement was obviously antihistoricist according to Adorno's analysis of the antihistoricist character of racism and Lukács' discussion in *The Destruction of the Reason* (*Zerstorung der Vernunft*). Such antihistoricism is a serious argument against the supporters of an imaginary "antihistoricist Marxism" articulated, for instance, by the Althusserian school. Although the term "history" frequently appears in Nazi political discourse, in fact, this ideology negates the postulate of the axiological autonomy of historicity since the "values" defended by the Third Reich, were of extrahistorical (biological) origin. For racism, history is *ancilla biologiae*. In Nazi ideology, this antihistoricism is echoed by a curious political axiology characterized by the dissociation of the two normally inseparable dimensions of consistency and precariousness. According to the powerful expression forged by René Alleau "the monstrous nature of Hitlerism derives from the total heterogeneity of the logic of deification and the logic of reification, applied simultaneously to the human condition, which had never been so fanatically exalted nor so inordinately vilified throughout the course of history."[27]

Without attaining the level of "total consistency" given to the notion of "grace" in Calvinist theology, the racial "value" remains, nonetheless, a highly reified value dominated as such by the dimension of consistency. Seen in this light, racism appears as a confirmation of Dupréel's axiology, precisely as an antitotalitarian indictment.

Some American theorists of the problem of alienation (under the probable influence of Melvin E. Seeman) regard "normlessness" as the essence of alienation. This conception is slightly dangerous when applied to Nazism, for it would not consider itself to be an "alienating" ideology. The "proper world" (*Eigenwelt*) of Nazism was in fact far from being "normless" since it was saturated with a privileged racial "value" surrounded by severe legal sanctions. If the theory of alienation entails even a partial ideological justification of Nazism, then such a theory should be discarded, as some sectarian Marxists would advise.

The axiodialectical approach presents a way out of this impasse. The mental universe of Marxism was not alienating because it was devoid of values, but precisely because it was saturated with a reified pseudo-value which disturbed the dialectical balance of "consistency-precariousness" in the political domain.

We have already mentioned that Piaget revealed a significant parallelism between the axiological and dialectical maturation of the individual. It is at the end of dialectical maturation that the individual accedes to the rank of a "valorizing animal" capable of transcending axiological immediacy (the axiology of elementary values). Such an evolution naturally includes the possibility of a phenomenon of regression on an individual or collective scale, a regression whose study comes under the heading of the general problematics of alienation. The "fall into ideology" (in other words, the rise of false consciousness) is tributary to an axiodialectical regression of this type which renders analogies between ideological logic and schizophrenic logic understandable. As Emmanuel Todd writes: "The relationship in structure between certain psychoses and between the old category of schizophrenia (paranoiac variant) and ideological fixation is truly astonishing."[28]

Notes

1. George Lukács, *History and Class Consciousness*, translated by Rodney Livingstone (London: Merlin Press, 1983 and 1990). This outstanding work of the Hungarian Marxist philosopher is in fact an ideological indictment of Stalinism that was consequently rejected by "official" Marxism.
2. The Althusser school (an "imaginary Marxism" according to Raymond Aron) advocated the absurd idea that Marxism has nothing in common with historicism. This antihistoricist, imaginary "Marxism" is a negative print of Lukács and Mannheim's historicist conceptions. As a form of antihistoricism, Althusserianism is situated in the ideological trajectory of Stalinism. For details see Gabel, *Ideologies II* ("Althusserisme et Stalinisme") (Paris: Anthropos, 1978).
3. Roger Garaudy, *La théorie matérialiste de la connaissance* (Paris, 1964), p. 164.
4. For details of this question, see chapter 3 of the present volume.
5. With that of the Althusser school.
6. Garaudy, "Contradiction et totalité dans la logique de Hegel"; *Revue Philosophique* (January-March 1964), p. 69. Mannheim for his part underlined the importance of the dialectical category of "totality" for historicism. See Mannheim's "Historismus" in *Soziologische Texte (Wissenssoziologie)* (Berlin: Luchterhand Verlag, 1964), p. 249 and *passim*. See also Eva Gàbor,

"Mannheim et la Dialectique" in Gabel, Rousset, and Trinh Van Thao (eds.), *Actualité de la Dialectique* (Paris: Anthropos, 1980).
7. "To finish, we invoke yet another witness in favor of the conversion of quantity into quality: Napoléon. This is how he describes the poorly mounted but well-disciplined cavalry in their battle against the Mameluks, without doubt the best horsemen of the time, but without any discipline. Two Mameluks were far superior to three Frenchmen, but 100 Mameluks were the equivalent of 100 Frenchmen. Normally 300 Frenchmen would be superior to 300 Mameluks and finally 1000 Frenchmen would win the day over 1500 Mameluks. . . . A cavalry detachment of a determined minimum size was necessary so that the strength of discipline could grow and triumph over greater numbers of well-mounted but irregular horsemen" (F. Engels, *Anti-Dühring* [Paris: Editions Sociales, 1963], p. 162.) This example clearly shows that the dialectic law of transformation between quantity and quality is linked with the category of totality as envisaged by Lukács in *History and Class Consciousness*.
8. The influence of Bergson on *History and Class Consciousness* is beyond doubt. As for the dialectical dimension of Bergsonism, see Werner Stark, *The Sociology of Knowledge: An Essay in Aid of a Deeper Understanding of the History of Ideas* (Glencoe, IL: The Free Press, 1958), p. 315. In his essay on Bergson (Paris: P.U.F., 1959), the French philosopher, Vladimir Jankélevitch, underscores the role of the category of totality in Bergson (pp. 5–27). Lukács' *The Destruction of Reason* contains very critical judgments of Bergson. But Lukács' letters from 1912–17 (Budapest: Ed. Magvetö, 1980), in which Bergson is often quoted, on the contrary, contain no unfavorable criticism. This correspondence attests also the interest in progressive Hungarian circles at the time to Bergsonian thought.
9. W. Ostwald, *Die Philosophie der Werte* (Leipzig: A. Kröner Verlag, 1913), p. 112 and especially pp. 123–24. See Raymond Ruyer, *Philosophie de la Valeur* (Paris: Armand Colin, 1952), p. 141; and Alfred Stern, *Le philosophie des valeurs: Regards sur ses tendances actuelles en Allemagne* (Paris: Hermann, 1934), p. 9.
10. The assertion of the axiogenous quality of irreversible historic temporality does not mean that time is the repository of values; such a banality would be just as true for space. It means in the Ostwald theory that temporalization and axiogenesis are consubstantial; time is axiogenous by its very nature, which is not true for space. Two well-known social facts attest to this: the prescription and naturalization of aliens. The phenomenon of prescription implies that time makes a delinquent innocent in spite of the fact he has escaped the action of justice. If space were axiogenous, then would be spatial prescription, but this is not the case. Spatial distancing from the place of the crime may give immunity but has never made anyone innocent. As for the naturalization of aliens, it is accorded—in France and also in the USA—after a long stay in the host country even if the stay has no particular merit. Likewise, in international law, time creates rights. Thus, it is axiogenous.
11. E. Dupréel, *Esquisse d'une philosophie des valeurs* (Paris: P.U.F., 1939).
12. R. Ruyer, *Philosophie de la Valeur.*, p. 141.
13. Wolfgang Köhler, *Die physische Gestalten in Ruhe und im stationären Zustand* (1920).

14. Raymond Ruyer classifies Köhler's theory among the "naturalist" axiologies (Ruyer, *loc. cit.*). Its dialectical nature appears more obvious.
15. Wolfgang Köhler, *The Place of Value in a World of Facts* (New York: Liveright, 1938), p. 63 sq.
16. Ruyer, *Philosophie de la Valeur*, p. 145.
17. "Dir Form ist die höchste Richterin des Lebens. Eine richtende Kraft, ein Ethisches ist das Gestaltenkönnen, und ein Werturteil ist in jedem Gestaltetsein enthalten"; Lukács, *Die Seele und die Formen* (Berlin, 1911), p. 370.
18. "Calvin's theory of predestination has one implication which should be explicitly mentioned here, since it has found its most vigorous revival in Nazi ideology: the principle of the basic inequality of men. For Calvin there are two kinds of people - those who are saved and those who are destined to eternal damnation. Since this fate is determined before they are born and without their being able to change it by anything they do or do not do in their lives, the equality of mankind is denied in principle. Men are created unequal." Erich Fromm, *Escape from Freedom* (New York: Rinehart and Company, Inc., 1941), p. 89.
19. Dupréel, *Esquisse*, p. 101. Passage italicized by the present author.
20. Since this summary is so short, may I direct the reader's attention to the chapter about this "dialectical" interpretation of schizophrenia ("The Dialectical Drama of Alienation") in my *False Consciousness* (New York: Harper Torchbooks, 1978), pp. 218–32.
21. Igor A. Caruso, "Notes sur la réification de la sexualité," *Psyché* (Paris, 1952), reproduced in extended form in *Psychanalyse pour la personne* (Paris: Ed. du Seuil, 1962).
22. Von Gebsattel, "Über Fetischismus," *Der Nervenarzt*, 1929.
23. Piaget does not use the term *reification*, but the phenomenon described certainly merits this qualification; the primacy of quantity in relation to quality is central in Lukács description of a reified universe.
24. Jean Piaget, *La psychologie de l'Intelligence* (Paris: A. Colin, 1947), p. 74.
25. Peter Berger and Thomas Luckmann, *The Social Construction of Reality* (New York: Doubleday Anchor Books, 1967), p. 90.
26. For this particular question—the dedialectization of Marxism under Stalinism—the work of Karl Korsch (*Marxismus und Philosophie*, Leipzig, 1923) is a classic of its kind. Cf. also Assen Ignatow, *Entdialektisierung des historischen Materialismus* (1981). According to Leo Kofler (*Stalinismus und Burokratie*, Berlin: Luchterhand, 1970, pp. 86–87), the three most characteristic forms of falsification of Marxism by Stalinist bureaucracy are (a) the disappearance of dialectics, (b) the nondialectical conception of the relationship infrastructure and superstructure, and (c) the disappearance of Marxist humanism.
27. René Alleau, *Hitler et les sociétés secrétes. Enquéte sur les sources occultes du nazisme* (Paris: Grasset, 1969), p. 215. The cult of reified "racial value" under the Third Reich was perhaps a reaction to the extreme precariousness of (economic) values under Weimar.
28. Emmanuel Todd, *Le fou et le prolétaire* (Paris, 1939), p. 32.

4

Durkheimianism and Political Alienation: Durkheim and Marx

A few years before the First World War, a young ethnologist of the Durkheim school, Robert Hertz, described an unusual ritual.[1] In some Borneo tribes, important persons are entitled to double funerals, the length of the interval between the two ceremonies being proportional to their social status. Ethnologists, and some sociologists too, now regard the Durkheim school as obsolete. Yet perhaps it has undergone only its first funeral; the second and final one may be long in following, or may even be postponed indefinitely. Durkheimianism's importance in the ethnological field has declined, since its basis (totemism) has been undercut by recent field research. But an important part of its findings, concerning so-called "primitive" societies and mentalities, are still applicable to a much-discussed contemporary phenomenon: totalitarian ideology and its various aspects, one of which is racism. I believe that the question of Durkheim's currency can be linked here with the problem of alienation.

Lévy-Bruhl is usually regarded as belonging to the Durkheim school. In fact, he was by no means a "disciple" of Durkheim, and his work was even subjected to criticism by orthodox Durheimians. However, there is an important parallel between the two authors, if not an actual convergence of views. Whether Lévy-Bruhl should be regarded as a dissident member of the

---

Earlier version delivered at the World Congress of Sociology (Uppsala, Sweden, 1974). Edited by Alan Sica.

Durkheim school, or as one of the two heads of the French school of sociology in the nineteenth century, is a historical problem that does not concern us here. But there is little doubt that his work was affected by the scientific discredit attached to the Durkheim school: its Eurocentrist terminology (*pensée prélogique, mentalité primitif*) undoubtedly contributed to this discredit. However, as a typical representative of the leftist French intelligentsia, Lévy-Bruhl was neither a colonialist nor a racist. As Leon Poliakov observes,[2] he could have escaped many criticisms simply by using the term *prescientific* instead of *prelogical*.

Primitive Mentality and Racist Consciousness

Rediscovering Lévy-Bruhl

It is significant that the author who most contributed to the renewal of interest in Lévy-Bruhl is not an ethnologist, but a well-known historian whose scientific work is chiefly centered on the problem of racism. The theory of "diabolic causality" (*causalité diabolique*) proposed by Poliakov substantiates the validity of Lévy-Bruhl's categories as instruments for a critical analysis of racism as ideology.[3] Insofar as we consider racist consciousness as a peculiar form of "false consciousness," these categories appear instrumental in unmasking this specific form of ideological distortion. A first point of convergence between Marxism and Durkheimianism can be noted here.

Albert Einstein—quoted by Poliakov[4]—thought the principle of causality was linked in its origins to the belief in the action of demons; primitive causality seems to operate in a similar manner. A man who dies from organic disease, from a snake's bite, or from a tiger's attack is viewed as having been "doomed" by a sorcerer. The tiger or snake is merely an arbitrary instrument of the sorcerer's action (Lévy-Bruhl). It appears that this form of archaic causality may persist in more rationalistic contexts and surface during intensive collective emotion. For example, Jews were often blamed for the medieval plague, despite the fact that they paid themselves a heavy tribute to it because of poor sanitation in the ghettos. A more recent example is evoked by Poliakov: around 1910, the well-known French anti-Semitic columnist, Leon Daudet, blamed Jewish real estate brokers for having caused floods owing to commercial deforestation.[5] The diabolical causal agent seems endowed with both absolute ill will and unlimited, super-social power; it appears to act in a sociological vacuum. Diabolic causality correlates with the "society-blindness" characteristic of ideological thinking in general. Jews have also been blamed for having triggered the Second World War, notwithstanding the fact that they were, prior to 1939, a minority of little influence even in democratic countries, notoriously unable to resolve the problem of their own refugees. In the same spirit, King Faysal of Saudi Arabia accused medieval Jewry of being responsible for the Crusades! Many other typical examples are to be found in the work of Poliakov.

Durkheimianism is also instrumental in unmasking racism through a different approach. This doctrine is above all a *sociologism*: a doctrine that claims the autonomy of social reality in relation to psychologism (Tarde) as well as in relation to biologism (Spencer). Racism is an antihistoricism since it postulates an extratemporal, reified permanence of ethnic features; it is an antisociologism since it proceeds from organicist sociology through the mediation of social Darwinism (Gumplowicz, Ratzenhofer, etc.). The two basic categories of racism are: (a) a reified and nonhistorical perception of ethnic minorities, and (b) a biological vision of society which jeopardizes the autonomy of the social sphere. With its strong emphasis on the autonomy of social reality, Durkheimianism is invested with a potentially disalienating tendency. The same holds true for the historicist variant of Marxism (Lukács, Mannheim, and, to some extent, Lefebvre and Goldmann), whose perception of social reality involves a historicist criticism of social reification as well as racism. Thus, one of the most serious reproaches that may be formulated against the antihistoricist interpretation of Marxism (Althusser) is that it invalidates Marxist criticism regarding this important question.

Ethnologists now agree in viewing the concept of "primitive mentality" as a scientific artifact of armchair theory, with little or no pertinence for genuine field work. This is an internal discussion for ethnologists in which the present author has no competence. From a purely philosophical point of view, it seems unlikely that a theory able to offer a valuable contribution in unmasking multiple forms of alienation could be completely devoid of pertinence in its own field of origin. It might be possible to preserve Lévy-Bruhl's contribution to ethnology by discarding its Europocentrist terminology—a purely parasitic phenomenon which answers no logical requirement. One might also consider this concept as an *ideologique*,[6] as a fruitful attempt to introduce into the field of the sociology of ideologies another important concept proposed by the second giant of contemporary French ethnology, Lévi-Strauss. The precise definition of the boundaries between *"mentalité primitive"* (Lévy-Bruhl) and *"pensée sauvage"* (Lévi-Strauss), as well as their respective contribution to the problem of ideology and alienation, could offer a fascinating field of research for sociologists of the coming generation.

The Division of Labor in Society,[7] is an anticipated criticism of totalitarian (false) consciousness. In this work Durkheim opposes *mechanical solidarity* (the mere juxtaposition of interchangeable elements) and *organic solidarity*, implying that each individual plays the role of an autonomous "entity" which, in principle, is not interchangeable within the overall functioning of society. Societies incorporating organic solidarity show, I think, a *dialectical totality* in Lukács' meaning. Where mechanical solidarity prevails, society shows characteristics of reification and, paradoxically, a relatively weak cohesion, notwithstanding its ideological homogeneity. Its legal system is dominated by repressive laws at the expense of restitutive laws. This was, as is well known, one of the leitmotives in French anthropology at the beginning of the present century. In so-called "primitive societies" the individual being is absorbed by the ocean of collectivity, and restitutive law simply loses all meaning because—in the face of the tyrannical power of the collective mind—a mere transgression of rules, a mere nonconformist action, entails a *penal* sanction. For Durkheim, the transition from mechanical to organic solidarity, following an increase of "social density," is the fundamental mechanism of social change.

Today's economists read Durkheim's work with some amusement. Moreover, his credibility has suffered from attacks directed towards its ethnological basis, that is, totemism. Today this Europocentrist, stereotypical theory of the "primitive"—as being depersonalizing, prelogical, and without historicity—is no longer accepted. But recent history, with the emergence of totalitarian states, has conferred an unexpected relevance to the postulates of the Durkheim school. The implicit criticism of the totalitarian mind in *De la division du travail social* appears particularly relevant today. Durkheim criticizes the existence in monosegmental societies of a homogeneity of thought, a preponderance of collective consciousness and, as a corollary, of mechanical solidarity and repressive law. But he considered this type of society as a thing of the past. Like most French intellectuals of the Belle Epoque, he believed that historical evolution tends irreversibly towards more and more individualism. He might have been afraid of the potential excesses of this tendency. The idea of a regression to archaic depersonalizing structures was never considered by him as a concrete historical possibility.

The historical perspective is no longer the same. Five years after Durkheim's death, there arose an historical phenomenon whose future impact could not be adequately appreciated at the time. Italian fascism was nothing but the first, timid start of a political adventure, the ultimate consequences of which were experienced only some years ago in Kampuchea and somewhat earlier in the Chinese Cultural Revolution. In spite of an ebb of this tendency in the Far East, we are now obliged to consider the possibility of a general decline of individualism together with its consequences, such as intellectual conformism, the reappearance of charismatic prestige in politics, and so on. In *Oriental Despotism*, Wittfogel, an ex-Marxist, anticipated the possibility of a regression to an "Asian" situation. Such an evolution again confirms Durkheim's views: totalitarian law in the twentieth century is, in fact, more repressive than the liberal law of the nineteenth century.

Decay of the Concept of Responsibility

Rediscovering Paul Fauconnet

Paul Fauconnet was one of the last personal disciples of Durkheim. His name and work are now nearly forgotten. With men such as Lagneau, Ravaisson, and others, he belonged to the respectable category of university people who prefer verbal to written transmission of knowledge, and who, for this reason, are frequently victims of undeserved oblivion. In fact, the only noteworthy book of Fauconnet is his doctoral thesis on the historical evolution of the concept of responsibility,[8] an outstanding contribution to the global achievement of Durkheimianism.

According to Harry Elmer Barnes, Fauconnet "starting with Durkheim's conception of crime as an act which offends strong states of the collective conscience, and of punishment as the need for a restoration of emotional equilibrium, tries to show that the function of 'responsibility' is simply to provide a focus for the application of punishment. In former times, children, the insane and even physical objects have been held responsible and have been punished, and only by a gradual process of social evolution has there emerged a modern conception of responsibility as limited to the free and rational agent."[9]

Durkheim foresaw an uninterrupted progression of the social division of work, from mechanical to organic solidarity. Fauconnet believed in a parallel process: a shifting of the notion of responsibility from collective to personalized forms (the "spiritualization of responsibility"). Recent political evolution—the generalization of hostage taking, the growing impact of racist theories—belies this optimism as it also belies forecasts, whether optimistic or not, concerning the division of labor and the future of individualism.

Durkheimianism and Marxism

These comments lead to the controversial issue of the relationship between Marxism and Durkheimianism. Orthodox Marxists are generally inclined to consider "bourgeois" Durkheimianism and "proletarian" Marxism as theoretically antagonistic. Lucien Henry's book, *Les origines de la religion*,[10] is chiefly representative of this position in French sociological writing. An opposite approach has been brilliantly advocated by Armand Cuvillier.[11] Durkheim's introduction to his book *De la division du travail social*, where recourse to corporations is considered as a remedy to the threatening social chaos and "anomie," has certainly contributed to the image of Durkheim as a reactionary social philosopher.

We saw above that Durkheimianism, in the broad sense of the word (including the works of L. Lévy-Bruhl) is quite useful in unmasking different forms of modern political alienation. This fact offers a valuable common denominator with the Marxism of the young Marx as well as with some variants of this doctrine, such as Lukácsism.

Reification *(Verdinglichung)* is without doubt the central concept of Lukácsism. The word reification is, of course, absent from Durkheim's terminology, but the idea clearly appears in his work at three levels: (1) at the methodological level as a working hypothesis; (2) as an element of a critical analysis of religious alienation; (3) in the division of social labor.

There is little to be added to the first point. In his methodology *(The Rules of Sociological Method)*, Durkheim emphasized the necessity of treating social data as if they were things. But this was, for him, just a working hypothesis which did not interfere with historical evolution. In Lukács' *Geschichte und Klassenbewusstsein*, the reification of social life is a transitory illusion—an element of bourgeois "false consciousness"—which is supposed to disappear gradually with the achievement of a socialist society.

Alienation and Reification in Archaic Religions

In his book *Les formes elémentaires de la vie religieuse*,[12] Durkheim (to put it simply) states that a member of an archaic tribe feels that his membership in a community increases his own efficiency and value; the community as a concrete dialectical totality (to use the Lukácsian concept) is more than the sum of its parts. This increased efficiency and value is explained by the archaic man as a sacred principle ("mana"). According to Durkheim, man worships through religion his *own sociability as being projected into nature*. The analogy with the mechanism of reification of Lukács is quite evident.

This theory to has been subjected to criticism by specialists. The methodological extrapolation of the results of the study of archaic religion, to the phenomenon of religion as such, has been correctly criticized. Whatever the pertinence of these objections, the Durkheimian interpretation still offers a valuable approach to "religious alienation" (with reification as its corollary). Considered from this standpoint, archaic religions appear to be an excellent example of *false consciousness*, exclusive of any suspicions of deliberate mystification at the service of social or economic exploitation. I wonder whether, in this case, Durkheim is not *plus royaliste que le roi*, that is, more Marxist than Marx himself, the theory of the "peoples' opium" being reminiscent of the pre-Marxist ideologies of the Enlightenment period.

Let us conclude this point by recalling that the Durkheimian definitions of religion postulate a dichotomy of the sacred and the profane, with no reference to a necessary presence of personified deities, is applicable to modern "secular religions" (Monnerot) such as Stalinism.

Finally, reification appears very clearly in Durkheim's description of mechanical solidarity as opposed to an organic one:

> The social molecules which can be coherent in this way can act together only in the measure that they have no actions of their own, as the molecules of inorganic bodies. That is why we propose to call this type of solidarity mechanical. The term does not signify that it is produced by mechanical and artificial means. We call it that only by analogy to the cohesion which unites the element of an inanimate body, as opposed to that which makes a unity out of the elements of a living body. What justifies this term is that the link which thus unites the individual to society is wholly analogous to that which attaches a thing to a person. The individual conscience, considered in this light, is a simple dependent upon the collective type, and follows all of its movements, as the possessed object follows those of its owner. In societies where this type of solidarity is highly developed, the individual does not appear (as we shall see later). Individuality is something which the society possesses. Thus, in these social types, personal rights are not yet distinguished from real rights.[13]

The meaning of this passage is clear. Societies with mechanical solidarity are reified societies; those with organic solidarity represent concrete dialectical totalities. The opposition between dialectics (and, more specifically, the dialectics of concrete totality) and reification, which is the main framework of Lukács' early philosophy, appears with the utmost clarity in the Durkheimian approach of archaic sociology. Are we entitled to see a *Marxiste malgré lui* in Durkheim? Certainly not, but neither can we see a pure anti-Marxist: his approach to methodology contains more dialectical elements than, for example, that of Max Weber. The term "bourgeois Marxist," applied also to Mannheim, seems to suit him to a certain extent. The Marxist determination of consciousness (*Bewusstsein*) by social being (*Sein*), as postulated by historical materialism, is present under a different name in Durkheimianism.

In a well-known article published in *Année Sociologique*, Mauss and Beuchat[14] had tried to show that the seasonal variations of the social organization of Eskimo tribes bring about corresponding variations in superstructures such as religious practices, legal relationships, property status, or sexual behavior. The Hungarian sociologist Oscar Jàszi[15] sees in this research an "inductive vindication of historical materialism." The same holds true for the so-called "primitive mentality" of Lévy-Bruhl. Once we have discarded a Europocentrist terminology, a fundamental idea remains: a given form of social organization entails related forms of logic. Marxist sociology has really no reason to challenge this view. The disalienating tendency common to Marxism and Durkheimianism results by no means from a fortuitous coincidence; it is a consequence of a fundamental homology in their respective perception of social reality.

Conclusion

Durkheimianism was the ideological expression of the Golden Age of the French bourgeoisie. It was an epoch of triumphant liberalism and individualism, of faith in science and in the unlimited and uninterrupted progress of civilization. It was also an epoch of colonial expansion and firm belief in the dogma of the "white man's burden." Durkheim and his colleagues were never "colonialists" in the pejorative sense of the word. But they were men of their time, patriotic citizens of one of the most important colonialist states. They could not escape the influence of the "spirit of their epoch," hence their highly Eurocentrist terminology, one of the main causes of their future discredit.

They constructed the ideal-type of an archaic society in a Europocentrist spirit as an antithesis to their own. The superstructural analysis of the "primitive" society arises from a curious convergence of secondhand information and theoretical

110   Ideologies and the Corruption of Thought

elaboration. These theorists, even a man such as Mauss, never performed personal field work. This concept of "primitive society" has not resisted the effects of time, results of field work, and perhaps, the impact of decolonialization. But the new social phenomenon arose which the Durkheimians and their contemporaries could not predict: totalitarianism. And it appears that some results of the research work of French sociology which are no longer valid, and may never have been valid in ethnology, are now useful in the critical analysis of this wrenching adventure in human history.

Notes

1. Robert Hertz, "Contribution à une étude sur la représentation collective de la mort." *L'Année Sociologique* (1907), 48–137.
2. Léon Poliakov, "Causalité, démonologie et racisme: Retour à Lévy-Bruhl?" *L'Homme et la Société* (Jan-Dec. 1980), p. 217.
3. See pp. 185–190 of the present volume.
4. Poliakov, "Causalite."
5. Poliakov, *La Causalité diabolique: Essai sur l'origine des persécutions* (Paris: Calmann Levy, 1980).
6. Francois Bourricaud, *Le bricolage idéologique: Essai sur les intellectuels et les passions démocratiques* (Paris: P.U.F., 1980).
7. Emile Durkheim, *De la division du travail social* (Paris: P.U.F., 1960). English translation by George Simpson, *The Division of Labor in Society* (New York: The Free Press, 1933).
8. Paul Fauconnet, *La Responsabilité* (Paris: Alcan, 1920).
9. Harry Elmer Barnes (ed.), *An Introduction to the History of Sociology*, (Chicago: University of Chicago Press, 1961), p. 522–23.
10. Henry Lucien, *Les origines de la religion* (Paris: ESI, 1935).
11. A. Cuvillier, "Durkheim et Marx." *Cahiers Internationaux de Sociologie* (1948), 75–97.
12. Durkheim, *The Elementary Forms of the Religious Life*, translated by J.W. Swain (London, 1915).
13. Durkheim, *The Division of Labor in Society* (translation by G. Simpson), p. 130.
14. M. Mauss and H. Beuchat, "Essai sur les variations saisonniéres des societes eskimos: Etude de morphologie sociale," *L'Année Sociologique* (1906), 39–130.
15. Oscar Jàszi, An inductive vindication of historical materialism, *The Review: A Quarterly of Pluralist Socialism* (1963), 51–65. (The Hungarian original has been published in 1906, in the monthly *Huszadik Szàzad*. French translation in Gabel, Rousset, Trinh Van Thao: L'Aliénation aujourd'hui [Paris: Anthropos 1974], 349–63).

5

Jonathan Swift as Forerunner of the Theory of "Morbid Geometrism"

Jonathan Swift was perhaps the first author to describe the mental disease known today as "schizophrenia." The kingdom of Laputa-Balnibarbi, described in his famous novel *Gulliver's Travels*, appears today, in the light of Eugene Minkowski's psychopathological theories, as a kingdom governed by "morbid rationalists" and "morbid geometrists," that is, by schizophrenics.

Laputa is governed by mathematicians and geometers whose heads are "all reclined either to the right or the left; one of their eyes turned inward, and the other directly up to the zenith."[1] These "scholars" are so distracted that a servant is continually charged with waking them up during a conversation.

Their existence is dominated by a strange form of geometrism closely similar to that mentioned in Minkowski's works. An example of this geometrization of existence is illustrated by the specific character of their meals, since dishes are cut up in geometric forms: "a shoulder of mutton cut into an equilateral triangle, a piece of beef into a rhomboids, and a pudding into a cycloid."[2] "The servants cut our bread into cones, cylinders, parallelograms, and several other mathematical figures."[3] Similarly, tailors also use instruments such as quadrants, rules, and compasses. However, this strange form of professional rationality results in very ill-fitting clothes.[4] Seen in the light of Minkowski's theories, this excess of rationality appears as a result of maladjustment, characteristic of full schizophrenia. The same statement holds true with regard to their behavior towards the fair sex: "If they would ... praise the beauty of a woman or any other animal (*sic*), they describe it by rhombs, circles, parallelograms, ellipses, and other geometrical terms."[5] Hence, it is not astonishing that the wives dislike this geometrical form of courting and "choose their gallants"[6] among the aliens who are less skilled in geometry than their erudite husbands. In fact, these people are "clumsy, awkward and unhandy"[7] in all practical problems of existence, except mathematics, geometry and music." Their houses are badly built, the walls crooked, without a single right angle in any apartment. These defects derive from their contempt for practical geometry, which is despised as vulgar and mechanical, so that the refined instructions given to the workmen are always misunderstood which leads to perpetual mistakes."[8] Most often, they reason badly and are vehemently given to opposition, except when they are of the right opinion, which rarely happens. They are strangers to imagination, fancy, and invention and have no words in their language to express such ideas; the whole range of their thoughts and minds is enclosed within the two forementioned sciences."[9] Two centuries before Minkowski, the brilliant author of *Gulliver's Travels* clearly saw the correlation between a geometrization of thinking and maladjustment to practical life, becoming the first author to theorize the problem of schizophrenia.

The kingdom of Balnibarbi (a colony of Laputa) is obsessed with the idea of planning. It seems that Swift lucidly foresaw one of the typical features that will reappear, centuries later, in the ideology of Stalinist Russia. Several "Academies of Projectors" are built in Lagado, the capital of the kingdom, and several other similar academies follow in the principal towns. The main objective of these "projectors" is to increase productivity. They contrive "new rules and methods of agriculture and building, and new instruments and tools for all trades and manufactures, whereby, as they undertake, one man shall do the work of ten; a palace may be built in a week, of materials so durable as to last forever without repairing. All the fruits of the earth shall come to maturity at whatever season we think fit to choose and increase a hundred fold more than they do at present, with innumerable other happy proposals."[10] Another "scholar," mem-

Swift as Forerunner of the Theory of "Morbid Geometrism" 113

ber of this Academy, sought to "reduce human excrements to their original foods, by separating the several parts, removing the tincture which they receive, making the odor exhale, and scumming off the saliva."[11]

This obsession with planning is also symptomatic of schizophrenia; it is an aspect of morbid rationalism. In his classical analysis of this mental illness, Minkowski quotes a patient who considers planning as one of the most important elements of life: "I don't want anything to disturb my plan; I prefer to disturb my life. It is my taste of symmetry and regularity which attracts me to the plan. Life is devoid of regularity and of symmetry and it is for this reason that I forget reality."[12]

This pathological reasoning is reminiscent of the thinking of Balnibarbi's scientists. As a citizen of this imaginary country, Minkowski's psychotic patient could have been elected to the "Academy of Projectors." The same "obsession with planning" is one of the principal elements in the symptomatology of the "paranoid utopist," L.M. (chapter 2 of the present volume). The "scholar" who transforms excrements into foods negates the irreversibility of a physiological process and consequently a spatialization of time. Seen in this light, it is significant that coprophagy characterizes the symptomatology of some cases of mental illness.

Last but not least, the schizophrenic character of the state's ideology clearly appears in the linguistic reform. According to these "reformists," to some degree, "every word that we speak diminishes our lungs by corrosion, and consequently contributes to the shortening of our lives." Therefore, an expedient method was offered to suggest that, if words are merely names for *things*, it would be more convenient for all men to carry along the necessary *things* to express the particular business they are to discuss."[13] In addition, discourses could be abbreviated by "cutting polysyllables into one and leaving out verbs and participles, because in reality all things imaginable are but nouns."[14] Devoid of terms expressing action, spontaneity, and movement, this "anti-Bergsonian" language becomes as such the reified reflection of a reified universe.

Geometrism, practical maladjustment, reification of the "proper universe" (*Eigenwelt*), a morbid obsession with planning and coprophagy constitute the complete symptoms of schizophrenia. A last analogy could be added: a judicious hierarchization of different possibilities is a determining factor of vital adjustment. An "obsession with the possible" has been detected in some cases of schizoid psychology, as it was pointed out by Swift in the collective psychology in Laputa-Balnibarbi's inhabitants. "These people are under continual disquietudes, never enjoying a minute's peace of mind; and their disturbances proceed from causes which very little affect the rest of mortals. Their apprehensions arise from several changes they dread in the celestial bodies. For instance, that the earth, by the continual approaches of the sun towards it, must in course of time by degrees be encrusted with its own effluvia, and give no more light to the world."[15] They are "so perpetually apprehensive of these and the like impending dangers that they can neither sleep quietly in their beds, nor have any relish for the common pleasures or amusements of life."[16] This obsessional fear of the "possible" is the logical corollary of morbid geometrism, since geometry is a science in which reality coincides with the "possible."

A question arises: where is the origin of this brilliant psychopathological intuition of *Gulliver's* author? Is it the fruit of a morbid introspection? This seems to be the opinion of Mario M. Rossi and Joseph M. Hone who detected a form of "egotism" in Swift's psychology—an egotism which has nothing in common with egoism (selfishness). According to these authors "The egotist has no ambitions in life, while the egoist enslaves his human relations to his ambitions. Being isolated in the society, the "egotist" cannot follow the egoist's example; it is uneasy to act with plenty of drive when one is isolated.[17] The "egotism" defined in this way is closely akin to "autism" as defined in psychiatry. Seen in this light, Swift's critical description of Laputa-Balnibarbi's inhabitants may be interpreted as the product of a clearsighted, and to some extent, masochist autoanalysis; it is also an important element of Swift's political criticism. Along with his compatriot Francis Bacon (theorist of the "idols" as factors of distortion), Swift appears as a genuine forerunner of the Marxist theory of false consciousness.

Our present civilization is not bereft of some schizophrenic elements. "The world is victim of a collective schizophrenia,"[18] as expressed by Gilbert Robin. The structure of false consciousness wonderfully analyzed by Lukács in *History and Class Consciousness* is a schizophrenic one; it locates the human being in a reified universe in which quantity prevails over quality, space over time, and material achievements over moral intentions. It was a mistake to interpret the "geometrism" of the inhabitants of Laputa as an underhanded ironic gesture towards Isaac Newton and his colleagues of the "Royal Society." Swift's historicist intuition was far more profound. The passages quoted above have contemporary echoes so that today his message remains topical. And for the psychopathologist, Swift's work presents a literary confirmation of the sometimes controversial nosological reality of schizophrenia as pictured by Minkowski and others.

Notes

1. Jonathan Swift, *Gulliver's Travels* (Baltimore, MD: Penguin Books, 1967). p. 200.
2. Ibid., p. 202.
3. Ibid., p. 203.
4. Ibid., p. 204.
5. Ibid., p. 205.
6. Ibid., p. 207.
7. Ibid., p. 205.
8. Ibid., p. 205.
9. Ibid., p. 205–6.
10. Ibid., pp. 221–22.
11. Ibid., p. 224.
12. "Le plan c'est tout pour moi dans la vie . . . Je ne veux à aucun prix déranger mon plan, je dérange plutôt la vie que le plan. C'est le goût pour la symétrie, pour la régularité qui m'attire vers mon plan. La vie ne montre ni régularité ni symétrie et c'est pour ca que je fabrique la réalité. Minkowski réalité." Minkowski, *La Schizophrénie* (Paris: Payot 1927), p. 119.
13. Swift, *Gulliver's Travels.*, p. 230.
14. Ibid., p. 230.
15. Ibid., p. 206.
16. Ibid., p. 207.
17. Mario M. Rossi and Joseph M. Hone, *Swift, or the Egotist* (London, 1934), p. 27.
18. Gilbert Robin, *La Guerison des défauts et des vices d'enfants* (Paris, 1948), p. 17.

6

Althusser and Orwell

To compare Orwell and Althusser may, at first glance, appear surprising. The former is an outstanding novelist and a genuine political theorist, whose work in 1984, the year of the predicted realization of his political nightmare, was once more in the limelight. The latter was, before his last decade of life, an influential philosopher, who has led for decades an important but waning current of contemporary French Marxism. In my opinion, the common denominator that invites comparison between the two is the problem of historicism, which occupies a central position in both their works. Althusser sought to construct a paradoxically antihistoricist and antihumanist "Marxism,"[1] while Orwell is an outstanding literary representative of humanist historicism. His work belongs to the lineage of great English utopians that runs from Thomas More to Huxley, and includes Bacon, Swift, Butler, and Morris, among others.[2] It also belongs—and perhaps in a more significant way—to the line of the great historicists, such as Troeltsch, Dilthey, Lukács, and Mannheim. Of course, Orwell, a novelist rather than a philosopher, never explicitly claimed to be a historicist. Nonetheless, by attacking the antihistoricism of totalitarian regimes, that is, their notorious tendency to rewrite history according to the ideological requirements of the present political situation,[3] Orwell, wittingly appointed himself an advocate for the historicist school of thought.

Earlier version delivered at Orwell Seminar (Cerisy-la-Salle, 1984). Initial English translation edited by David Frank Allen and James McCrate.

In fact, historicism was in dire need of an advocate to combat the dominance of antihistoricism represented by the well-known polemical work of Karl Popper: *The Poverty of Historicism*.[4] In spite of its unquestionable scientific relevance, historicism seems at present to be in a sort of ideological quandary. Under the influence of Stalinism and Althusserism, Marxism turned its back on historicism despite its debt towards a school of thought that includes, amongst others, Hegel, while others such as Raymond Aron, whose thought is objectively close to historicism, no longer overtly proclaim their link to it. Nevertheless, Orwell's widening audience, and the recent renewal of interest in Karl Mannheim's work, raises the possibility of reviving this weary but not yet dead body. This is one of the aims of the present chapter.

We have far too many different and divergent definitions of the concept of historicism. A definition is not a theory for it cannot be refuted. However, it may prove more or less operational in solving problems though it may, in certain cases, lead to a dead end. Such is the case with Althusser whose interpretation pivots around Gramsci's definition of historicism. Gramsci's notion of "absolute historicism" captures an essential aspect of Marxist thought: the practical role of theory in real history.[5] According to this definition, any political doctrine that has exerted some historical impact could legitimately claim to be historicist. In the light of this definition, the concept of historicism is emptied of any concrete significance.

According to Alfred Stern, and several other authors, the essence of historicism resides in its questioning of "the external and supra-historical validity of scientific statements as well as of moral values."[6] This point of view also appears to lead to an impasse. If all theories are historically limited in their validity, why should historicism not suffer the same fate? This impasse is exemplified by Oswald Spengler who started by an audacious historicist relativization of all cultural values and ended paradoxically in a European—and even to some extent German—cultural provincialism. Nevertheless, this dead end is perhaps more apparent than real. Historicism seems justified in its demand that we appreciate alien institutions and moral norms in terms of their own specific axiological context, though it does not preclude us from comparing these contexts with ours and establishing a hierarchy. For instance, we ought to understand the practice of human sacrifices which was customary in the highly sophisticated pre-Columbian civilizations of South America, in terms of a specific axiology that does not place personal existence among its fundamental values. But this point of view does not jeopardize our right to prefer our old "Judeo-Christian" civilization which upholds individual existence and individual salvation as its highest values.

At this juncture, it would be appropriate to reintroduce Karl Popper's *Poverty of Historicism*. A Marxist of the Lukács school (a "Hungaro-Marxist" according to the terminology coined by the present author) may gain some valuable arguments in favor of a historicist interpretation of Marxism from this otherwise trenchant critique of both Marxism and historicism.

Popper underscores the importance of social change and that of a "holistic" (i.e., totalizing) perception of social reality as the two theoretical pillars of historicism:

> Most historicists believe that there is an even deeper reason why the methods of physical science cannot be applied to the social sciences. They argue that sociology, like all 'biological' sciences, i.e. all sciences that deal with living objects, should not proceed in an atomistic, but in what is now called a 'holistic' manner. For the objects of sociology, social groups, must never be regarded as mere aggregates of persons. The social group is *more* than the mere sum total of its members, and it is also *more* than the mere sum total of the merely personal relationships existing at any moment between any of its members. A group founded by A and B will be different in character from a group consisting of the same members but founded by B and C. This may illustrate what is meant by saying that a group has a *history* of its own, and that its structure depends to a great extent on its history.[7]

This methodological holism (i.e., totalism) combined with a theory of social change is, for the reader familiar with the ideas of Georg Lukács, reminiscent of dialectics. Popper's struggle against Marxism and dialectics is also a struggle against historicism. The kinship of these two currents, which is a blind spot of dogmatic Marxism torn between its theoretical tradition and its practical demands, is clearly revealed in this Popperian perspective. Antihistoricist Marxism is also antidialectical Marxism and as such, an anti-Marxist Marxism.[8] According to the young

Marx, ideology is either an erroneous conception of human history, or its complete abstraction.[9] This statement is in my view sufficient to classify Marx as a historicist and could have equally well been used by Orwell as an epigraph to *1984*.

The problem of the irreversibility of historical duration—a logical consequence of its structured character—is central to *1984*. The dichotomy "space versus time," that underlies our interpretation, may appear to be simplistic in the eyes of a professional philosopher. Yet, this commonsense view is legitimized by one essential criterion: one moves at will only in space, never in time. As Eddington stated, "There is an arrow in time." I can go to Paris, return to Cerisy and finally come back to Paris, merely limited by my modest material means of transportation. Yet all the treasures of the King of Arabia would not permit this potentate to recapture the minute that has just slipped away. It is on this basis that we are entitled to speak of a "spatialization of historical duration" in Orwell's novel.

A well-known Peruvian psychopathologist, Professor Honorio Delgado, pointed out that schizophrenia involved a *reificacion del tiempo* along with a *invalidacion del acaecido*.[10] This seems to describe exactly the structure of the ideologico-utopian temporality of *1984*. The ambiance of this novel has undoubtedly a schizophrenic character. The "double-think" that characterizes the psychology of its protagonists is reminiscent of schizophrenic dissociation as pointed out decades earlier by Bleuler. The same holds true for the *novlangue*, or neologisms constituting meaningful symptoms of this mental illness.

The spatialization of duration was the central leitmotif in the work of Minkowski.[11] Orwell's novel is a provocative literary illustration of the schizophrenic structure of political alienation. Winston Smith and his lady friend, Julia, try to escape this nightmarish world by practicing free love[12] and by joining a fake "resistance movement," which was in fact a trap and finally by a *recherche du temps perdu*.[13] This Proustian terminology is fully adequate to describe Winston's strategy in this novel. This attempt at personal disalienation leads the tragic couple to catastrophe. The temporality of *1984* is characterized by an arbitrary erasure of the past by the power structure, and by the absence of any opening towards the future. Hence, the homogeneous structure of time tends to align itself with that of space.[14] The reading of it only reaffirms Lukács's identification of spatialization and reification. Along with the novels of Kafka, *1984* is perhaps the most adequate literary depiction of a reified social universe. According to Gisela Pankow, a psychoanalyst whose work provides a synthesis of the psychoanalytic and phenomenological approach to the psychopathology of schizophrenia,[15] the therapeutic act consists essentially in a reconstruction of the concrete totality of a dissociated morbid personality along with a therapeutic temporalization of a "*Dasein* prisoner of spatiality." Ms. Pankow cures her patients by making them simultaneously aware of their personal historicity and of their sex; in Orwell's novel the couple Winston-Julia proceeds in exactly the same manner. But what seems feasible or easy in the consulting room of a psychoanalyst, becomes utopian for a couple crushed by the terrifying social pressures of a totalitarian state.

The Moscow purge trials of the thirties were obviously the main target of Orwell's *1984*. But this arbitrary restructuring of the historical past revealed by the young Marx a century before Orwell, was not the monopoloy of Stalinism. Here, we will present a few examples drawn, in the main, from recent political history.

McCarthyism in the USA

This current is now past, but it played an important role in American public life in the fifties. To a large extent, it was responsible for the undeserved and highly paradoxical unpopularity of the U.S. in postwar Europe after a victory over Nazism in which the United States played a major role.[16] Along with the doctrine of Barry Goldwater, McCarthyism constitutes a typical American form of antihistoricism,[17] and is as such a typically American manifestation of false consciousness. The work of the historicist Karl Mannheim contains an anticipated criticism of these "American Ideologies." It is rather astonishing that in the outstanding work of Guenther Lewy,[18] one of the rare works in American sociological writing dedicated to the problem of false consciousness, reference to these two currents is entirely absent.

In his book *Ordeal by Slander*, Owen Lattimore, one of the

victims of McCarthyism, touched upon the "time mastery" that underlay the political actions of the senator from Wisconsin.[19] This time mastery is closely akin to that depicted in *1984*. In Orwell's novel, three superstates, which are alternatively at war with each other, dominate the world: Oceania, Eurasia, and Eastasia. In a given moment, any modification that takes place in the network of oppositions and alliances is seen as retroactive, and all documents testifying to the contrary—such as collections of daily papers in public libraries—are destroyed by the Ministry of Truth: "Oceania is at war with Eastasia...Oceania has always been at war with Eastasia. Since the beginning of your life, since the beginning of the Party, since the beginning of history, the war has continued without a break, always the same war."[20] In fact, the declaration of war between Oceania and Eastasia took place only a few days before Winston's arrest. A month earlier, these two superstates were allies in the war against the third superstate, Eurasia. All printed documents testifying to this former situation were destroyed by the Ministry of Truth. An identical procedure is applied to political leaders who fall into disgrace, and all documents attesting to their revolutionary past are nullified.[21]

McCarthyism was, in some respects, a mirror image of Stalinism whose antihistoricism was shared by the late chairman of the Senate Investigation Subcommitte. The central categories of McCarthyism were (a) the negation of individual historicity,[22] and (b) the pretense at judging the acts of the Truman administration in 1945 according to criteria valid in 1952. In *The Fight for America* McCarthy blamed the Democrats, then in power, for releasing at the end of the war the surviving members of the pro-Soviet Sorge espionage network which worked very efficiently for the common victory during the Second World War.[23] In 1952, when McCarthy's book was published, the cold war was at its zenith, while in 1945 these two superstates were still allies. McCarthy projected the 1952 situation back to 1945. It seems that O'Brien of *1984* would have acted similarly.

The Retroactivity of Laws

For democratic legal sensitivity, the idea of retroactivity of laws is a shocking absurdity. For instance, the retroactive law, promulgated under the combined pressure of the German occupation authorities and its own extremist wing by the Vichy regime, was opposed in the cabinet by the minister of justice (Joseph Barthelemy) himself. The significance of this event was perfectly grasped by the German liaison officer to the Vichy government: "This text introduces a genuine revolution into the French judicial system. The retroactivity of the laws challenges the sacrosanct liberal principle *no poena sine lege*. On the other hand, the orders given by a government to a court constitute a break with the principle of separation of powers. Under the probable influence of her new Home Secretary, Pierre Pucheu, France is now in the process of drawing the outlines of a new state order."[24]

The Inca State and Historicity

In the Inca state—a genuine ideal-type of totalitarian socialism—the recollection of the historical past was considered to be a serious offense. According to the chronicler Fernando Montesinos, "The Inca government wanted to eradicate everything susceptible of evoking the history of subjugated peoples: traditions, legends, religion and all other expressions of spirituality. Education was dispensed in this country by the so called *amautas*, erudite persons who were commissioned to write history in two different versions: an objective one conserved in the form of *quipus* destined exclusively to the officials, and another version in hymns, told to the people at festivities. The name of any historical personality that ceased to be *persona grata* was erased from these commemorations."[25]

Thus, it appears that Orwell did not really invent anything, nor did Auguste Comte, who also proposed two histories. The Incas—just like their distant follower Big Brother—were perfectly aware of the fact that, in politics, the mastery of the past is a prerequisite to the mastery of the present. A structured and irreversible historical duration (*durée bergsonienne*), and a totalitarian or authoritarian mentality, are simply not compatible. The "Orwell phenomenon" is not at home and the "Orwell technique" is not really efficient except in a totalitarian or at least authoritarian political context. In an ambiance of pluralism and free discussion, their existence is precarious and their efficiency is limited.

After the liberation in France, there were some modest attempts to revise Marshall Petain's action in the First World War in the light of his behavior during the Second; this attempt found little resonance in the French public. For the totalitarian historical sensitivity, it is inconceivable that a man (Trotsky), officially branded as a traitor in the thirties, could have been the heroic creator of the Red Army two decades earlier. Its temporality appears in this light as a homogeneous, reified, and spatialized one. In contrast, a democratic and pluralist historical sensitivity accepts that the same personality could have been an outstanding war leader in 1916 and the collaborator with a victorious enemy some decades later. The temporality here is a dialectical one (unity of opposites). Space—or better, reified and spatialized historical time—is the milieu in which totalitarian (false) consciousness thrives. For a pluralist democracy, it is a deleterious atmosphere.

Here, in my opinion, lies the interest in this curious "negative convergence" of our two authors. Althusser advocated a nonhistoricist and nonhumanist Marxism and rejected the Luckácsian critique of reification, under the pretext of "idealism." Orwell presents a highly critical description of a reified and antihumanist social universe whose historicity is banned by the totalitarian state power. The question is not to examine the Marxist legitimacy of Althusser's point of view, but to elucidate its ideological function in recent political debate.

The question is linked to the problem of social equality. Since the Middle Ages, an "egalitarian nostalgia" runs like a burning thread throughout western ideological history. Millenarians, Anabaptists, levellers, and the doctrinaires of the revolutions of 1789 and 1848 all share this nostalgia, which is perhaps one of the specific features of Western consciousness. For several decades—since 1917 to be precise—this egalitarian nostalgia has been tempered by political experiences of a totalitarian character, and by non-Western inspirations. Totalitarian egalitarianism is not only nonexistent but also impossible, for this type of political regime always produces a privileged strata, and some comrades are "more equal than others" (Orwell's term in *Animal Farm*). Moreover, the non-Western tradition is not always favorable to the egalitarian idea.[26] By injecting egalitarian nostalgia into such different experiences, the Western intelligentsia set itself up for a rude awakening heralded by the Khrushchev report in 1956.

After the ideological collapse of Stalinism, egalitarian nostalgia turned towards "the new Mecca." Since the road to egalitarian paradise must pass through totalitarian purgatory, we were forced to tolerate the tyranny of our Chinese "Big Brother" in the hope that the birth of an egalitarian society would eventuate. During the Cultural Revolution, Maoism played the role of a "hope principle" (*Prinzip Hoffnung*)[27] for large sectors of the Western intelligentsia, so that a few lucid voices—such as Simon Leys'—were smothered with sarcasm. Althusser was certainly under the influence of this illusion, which is perhaps the secret of his undeserved success with the French intellectual public and one explanation for the particular structure of his "Marxism." In fact, he interjected into this theory the main features of the totalitarian discourse identical to those of utopia: antihistoricism, dedialectization[28] and dehumanization. All of this results in the "negative convergence" that Orwell pointed out above; a blind nostalgia met a lucid caricature.

Maoism reached its hour of truth only after the death of the "Great Helmsman" and after his widow's trial. Still, the widow's courage before her judges deserves some respect. Nevertheless the feminine personality that appeared in the light of this trial seems more reminiscent of an imperial concubine in prerevolutionary China than of a militant of an egalitarian ideology. She is much closer to Tz'u Hsi[29] than to Rosa Luxemburg as portrayed in a lucid essay by Simon Leys entitled "Broken Idols."[30] In fact, for a large segment of the Western intelligentsia and of the Third World, this trial meant the collapse of an entire system of values. Some psychoanalysts such as Leopold Szondi[31] explain psychotic breakdown by a devalorization of the patient's *Eigenwelt*; others, such as the late Daniel Lagache, speak of "manic mourning." I do not wish to mention here a tragic event known to everyone. Let me simply say that the catastrophe still present in our mind[32] was perhaps the "mourning" over a gen-

126   Ideologies and the Corruption of Thought

erous but unattainable egalitarian dream. There have always been—and there will always be in all societies—comrades "more equal than others." O'Brien is immortal, but so is Orwell.

Notes

1. The antihistoricist Marxism of Althusser is an "imaginary Marxism" according to Raymond Aron, an opponent of Marxism, yet an outstanding connoisseur of the theory.
2. In fact *1984* is rather a "counter-utopia" or "dystopia" since it is not the expression of nostalgia, but a warning.
3. I suggest designating this phenomenon as "ideological presentocentrism." It was one of the basic features of Stalinism (the real target of Orwell in *1984*) and of McCarthyism, too. As for Althusser, he underscored the privileged position of the present (*Lire le Capital* [Paris: Ed. Maspero, 1969], p. 168) while Lukács, whose conception of Marxism is a kind of reverse image of Althusser's, insisted on the "historicity of the present" (Lukács, *Histoire et Conscience de classe* [Paris: Ed. de Minuit, 1960], pp. 197–98).
4. Karl R. Popper, *The Poverty of Historicism* (London: Routledge and Kegan, 1972 [1957]).
5. Gramsci quoted by Althusser and E.Balibar in *Lire le Capital* (Paris: Maspero, 1971), p. 162.
6. Alfred Stern, "Quelques remarques sur l'historicisme," *Revue philosophique* (July-September, 1962).
7. Popper, *Poverty of Historicism*, p. 17.
8. "Imaginary Marxisms" is the subtitle of a work by Raymond Aron that targets Sartre, whose Marxism was perhaps less imaginary than Aron supposed, and who was foremost in formulating opposition to Althusser. See Raymond Aron, *D'une Sainte Famille à l'autre. Essai sur les Marxismes imaginaires* (Paris: Gallimard, 1969).
9. Pp. 129–143 of the present volume on "Political Ideologies". Marx was beyond doubt an historicist.
10. On Honorio Delgado, see pp. 120, 132 of the present volume. The "invalidacion de lo acaecido" (retroactive nullification of historical facticities) pointed out by the Peruvian psychiatrist is purely Orwellian.
11. E. Minkowski, *Contribution à l'étude de la pensée et de l'attitude autistes* (Le rationalisme morbide), L'Encéphale (Paris), April 1923; also *The Clinical Roots of the Schizophrenia Concept* (Cambridge: Cambridge University Press, 1987).
12. In fact the *vue de garconne* put into practice by Julia before her love affair with Winston, was first and foremost a protest against the intrusion of the totalitarian state into the private existence of its subjects.
13. "In search of lost time."
14. "This movement towards the homogeneous can be brought into a clearer perspective. The Now…(as in me, here, now) has a tendency to raise itself to a sort of absolutism and thus to reduce to nothingness all that it is not; it shows a disposition to include at most the nearest point of the before and of the immediate after. The present, whilst being opposed to the nonpresent, is situated at the very same level. That which is now exists and

present, is situated at the very same level. That which is now exists and then which is not now (i.e. before, after) exists not, as we stated above"; Minkowski, *Le Temps Vécu*, (Paris, 1933) pp. 33–34. Again, it is pure Orwell; one must nevertheless remember that Minkowski's brilliant book was first published before the Moscow trials and well before the first publication of *1984*. In his *Contribution to the Critique of Hegel's Philosophy* (Hallische Jahrbücher, 1839), Feuerbach, in a curious and adumbrative manner, poses "exclusive time" against "tolerant space."

15. Gisela Pankow, *Dynamische Strukturierung in der Psychose* (Berne: Huber Verlag 1956). According to Igor A. Caruso "reification of sexuality" is the common denominator of different forms of sexual perversions; Igor A. Caruso, *Notes sur la réification de la sexualité* (Paris: Psyché, Dec., 1952). The convergence of these points of view (vis-a-vis Pankow, Caruso, and Orwell) is significant, for if we hold with Caruso that sexual pathology is the clinical expression of a process of reification, then normal sexuality appears to function within the general realm of dereification and, consequently, of disalienation.
16. See the admirable passage on McCarthyism in Bertrand Russell, *Nightmares of Eminent Persons and Other Stories* (London, 1954).
17. Goldwater blamed American democracy for having "permitted our schools to become laboratories for social and economic change"; Barry M. Goldwater, *The Conscience of a Conservative* (New York: Macfadden, 1962), p. 86. In another of his works (*Why Not Victory?*, p. 78), he criticizes the foreign policy of the Democratic administration with arguments valid at the epoch of McKinley's presidency when the U.S. was invulnerable, but outmoded when faced with the USSR at the zenith of its military power. The common denominator of these two "American ideologies" is obviously their antihistoricism. Mannheim's work in his English (i.e., post-Weimar) period presents an anticipated criticism of these "American Ideologies" along with an attempt to smuggle, without employing this term, some dialectic and historicist elements into the American public spirit. For details see Gabel, *Mannheim and Hungarian Marxism* (New Brunswick, NJ: Transaction Publishers, 1991), p. 69.
18. Guenther Lewy, *False Consciousness: An Essay on Mystification* (New Brunswick: Transaction Books, 1982).
19. Owen Lattimore, *Ordeal by Slander* (Boston: Little Brown & Co., 1950), p. 208.
20. Orwell, *1984* (New York, 1961), p. 212. Discussion between O'Brien and Winston Smith, prisoners in the "Ministry of Love."
21. The allusion to Stalinism is clear. At the Paris World Fair of 1938, one could see in the Soviet Pavilion portraits of Lenin dated from 1917, while those of Trotsky, Kamenev, or Zinoviev had been deliberately suppressed. It is a well-known fact that in the communist press of this epoch the revolutionary past of these personalities had been systematically changed. In *1984*, Big Brother acted thus towards Goldstein (Trotsky).
22. "Before Russia was recognized by the United States in 1933, Dean Acheson was paid by the Soviet Union to act as Stalin's lawyer in this country"; McCarthy, *The Fight for America* (New York, 1952), p. 23. In 1933, there was no cold war between the U.S. and the Soviet Union. At the time McCarthy's book was published, Dean Acheson, as member of a government harshly opposed on the international scene to Soviet-Russia, was severely blamed

by the European communist and the fellow-traveller presses. Similarly to Stalinism, McCarthyism does not accept individual historicity.
23. This form of "time mastery" was also a typical feature of the communist press of this time. In the September 19, 1949 issue of the French communist daily *L'Humanité*, one could read "As early as 1943 Tito plotted with the Anglo-Saxons." In 1943, the U.S. and the Soviet Union were allies against the Third Reich. Tito was perfectly within his rights to "plot" with them.
24. Quoted by Hervé Villeré, *L'Affaire de la Section Spéciale* (Paris: Fayard, 1973), p. 200.
25. *Historama* (May 1977, n 307), p. 43; and Igor Chafarevitch, *Le phénomène socialiste* (Paris: Seuil, 1977), p. 161.
26. Here, I would refer to a well known work by Louis Dumont, *Homo hierarchicus* (Paris: Gallimard, 1966).
27. As used by Ernest Bloch.
28. The French philosopher Raymond Ruyer stressed the antidialectical character of utopian consciousness: "L'utopie...est aux antipodes par son académisme d'une conception dialectique des choses"; Ruyer, *L'Utopie et les utopies* (Paris: PUF, 1950), p. 98.
29. Tz'u Hsi, empress of China at the time of the Boxer revolt.
30. Simon Leys, *Images brisées* (Paris: R. Laffont, 1976).
31. Hungarian psychoanalyst, author of a well-known but severely contested projective test.
32. In 1980, Althusser killed his wife.

7

Political Ideologies

It is of paramount importance to define concepts in political sociology. In *Culture: A Critical Review of Concepts and Definitions*,[1] Kroeber and Kluckhohn listed more than a hundred different definitions of the term. And a comparable result would be obtained if we attempted a definition of ideology. At a certain moment, the convergence of various research efforts results in unanimously accepted concepts, especially in the exact sciences. However, political science is far from having attained this level of exactitude for it is widely accepted that important concepts such as socialism,[2] fascism, racism, left wing, right wing, and so on, do not have any consensually accepted definitions. The quest for a valid definition is the unavoidable prerequisite of any scientific approach to the problem of ideology. And, the best—and perhaps the only—way of reaching a certain degree of objectivity in this matter is to bring together a number of divergent definitions and construct an "ideal type" from them.

A Critical versus Neutral Concept of Ideology

It is important to note an ambiguity at the very heart of this problem of definition. Raymond Aron points out an "oscillation in the current use of the concept of ideology between a critical and neutral understanding. The former considers ideology to be a deliberate falsehood in the service of interests and passions,

---

Earlier version first published in *Encyclopedia Universalis* (Paris), vol. VIII. Translation initially edited by David Frank Allen and James McCrate.

and the latter considers that ideology shapes a certain vision of social reality according to the prescribed image of a desirable social future. Ultimately any philosophical discourse may be dubbed ideology; seen in this light the term loses its pejorative overtones and becomes a laudatory one."[3] The critical understanding of this concept in the early writings of Marx and Engels goes back to Napoleon, who branded his intellectual opponents as "ideologues," that is, theoreticians estranged from reality. Both the orthodox Marxism of the Stalinist era and some later Marxist theorists such as Althusser, frequently use this concept in its neutral meaning. This fact simultaneously points to a progressive distancing from the personal conceptions advanced by the "founding fathers" of Marxism and to its own ideologization.[4]

Ideology and Superstructure

We should emphasize another point: there is an important and persuasive distinction between "ideology" and "superstructure" that parallels the distinction offered by Werner Stark between the "social *origin*" and the "social *determination* of thinking."[5] The concept of social origin seems void of any ideological distortions and refers to a simple causal relationship between a given society and the intellectual and scientific achievements of its members. By contrast, the social *determination* of thinking pertains to the *affiliation* to a partial social structure (class, subculture, generation, or ethnic minority) often in conflict with other structures. Political egocentricity could in such a case harbor ideological distortion. According to this definition, superstructures are of social *origin*, while ideologies are *determined* by affiliation to subcultures.

The Typology of Karl Mannheim

The "bourgeois Marxist," Karl Mannheim used the concept of ideology almost exclusively in its critical sense. In his studies of ideology, three separate conceptions are introduced: (a) the "evaluative" versus the "non-evaluative"; (b) the "particular" versus the "total"; and (c) the "special" versus the "general." Earlier, I had[6] proposed a simplification of this interesting but

Political Ideologies 131

dense terminology; to wit, the division between a "polemical" (i.e., partial and particular) conception of ideology as opposed to a "structural" (total and general) one. The former attempts to legitimize the current egocentricity of committed political consciousness. In this light, ideology (in its critical sense) simply refers to the *opponent's* political perspective. On the other hand, the "structural" conception (total and general conception of ideology) postulates that *all* forms of committed political thinking are prone to ideologization, and that a genuine form of nonideologized consciousness does not reside within the working class committed to political action, but in the "rootless intelligentsia" *(freischwebende Intelligenz)*[7] protected, by its very rootlessness, from falling into the trap of sociocentric distortion (the *idola tribus* of Francis Bacon). In contrast to the "polemical" conception of ideology, the central category of the "structural" conception is not deliberate falsehood, but a sociocentric restructuring of a logical base of political consciousness to serve a specific and unilateral historical perspective. In extreme cases, this process may result in mental features reminiscent of schizophrenia. In order to clarify the psychopathological bases of the point of view advocated in the present work, I shall take a detour through the work of Minkowski.

Minkowski, an outstanding French psychopathologist of Polish origin (1895–1972), under Bergson's influence, defined and identified a specific form of schizophrenia which he termed "morbid geometrism and rationalism" (*rationalisme et geometrisme morbides*).[8] According to this interpretation, the universe of schizophrenia is characterized by an imbalance favoring the spatial dimension over the temporal one, and the rational over the instinctive one. Minkowski also underscored the existence of a curious Manichean feature in the psychism of these psychotics.[9]

Silvano Arieti detected a hypertrophy of the identification function[10] in the logic of these patients.[11] Based on Lukács's conceptions, I have tried to establish a synthesis of these different approaches by defining schizophrenic consciousness as a reified and consequently dedialecticized form of consciousness.[12] This attempt was in fact an *Umstülpun*[13] of Minkowski's theories, and was ratified by Minkowski in one of his last works.[14] Now, it seems that these features of schizophrenic consciousness are present in the structure of ideological distortion, that is, of political false consciousness. A Manichean perception of the political universe involves an "unwarranted identification," as its logical corollary.[15] The arbitrary reconstruction of historical facticities described by Orwell in his famous novel, was detected in schizophrenia by the Peruvian psychopathologist Honorio Delgado.[16] The very specific form of rationality that underlies Stalinism as ideology[17] was curiously akin to Minkowski's "morbid rationalism"[18] and to Aron's depiction of Stalinism as a "logical delusion."[19] Stalinism now belongs definitively to the past but, as a genuine ideal-type of ideological distortion, its critical analysis may shed light on some contemporary issues.[20]

Ideology and False Consciousness

The theory of false consciousness is likely the most important contribution of Marxism to political psychology, and perhaps the only element of this theory destined to survive the present demise of Marxist economic and political thought. Marxism gave political science not only the theory of false consciousness but also an outstanding historical example in Stalinism.

According to Mannheim, the concept of false consciousness offers a common denominator to both ideology and utopia: "The concepts of ideology and utopia have one common and essential point in the final analysis: they both postulate the possible existence of false consciousness."[21] In Mannheim's work, the problem of ideology is closely linked to that of false consciousness. Nevertheless, I cannot agree with the simplistic formulation of the French theorist P. Kahn who claims that Mannheim "identifies false consciousness with the total conception of ideology."[22] In a "polemical" (partial and particular) conception of ideology, the problem of the relationship between ideology and false consciousness is meaningless, since the opponent's ideology is branded as mere falsehood, while one's own perspective is supposed to be completely *seinsadäquat*, that is, free from all traces of ideological distortion. However, in the "structural" (i.e., total and general) conception of ideology, the relationship between ideology and false consciousness is analogous to those perceived by Pareto between "derivations" and "residues," for ideology is the theoretical crystallization of a form of false consciousness. According to this definition, a form of false consciousness constantly underlies ideology, but the opposite is not always the case; there are intense forms of false consciousness without any genuine ideological expression. Racism in the Third Reich was highly ideologized, while that of the southern states of the U.S.—although intense in the past—relied only on a moderate degree of ideologization. While, Adorno[23] claims to present a critical analysis of ethnocentrist *ideology*, in fact it is above all a very brilliant experimental study of racist *false consciousness*.

Definitions of Ideology and Construction of an "Ideal-type"

We shall consider several definitions of ideology in order to draw an "ideal-type" in the Weberian sense of this term. None of these definitions may be termed either "false" or "true,"—as each of them reflects a particular and significant aspect of the ideological phenomenon. A synthesis of these divergent definitions is a step towards objectivity.

Definitions

> Ideology is a process accomplished by the so-called thinker consciously no doubt, within a framework of false conscience. The real driving forces which set it off remain unknown for him, for, if the opposite were the case, there would be no ideological process at all. Moreover he imagines false or apparent driving forces. By virtue of its being an intellectual process, he deduces both content and form from pure thought, whether it be from his own thought or from that of his predecessors. He is exclusively dealing with intellectual matters: without closer study, he considers that such matters derive from thought and does not bother to find out whether they have some other more distant origins, independent of thought. This way of going about the problem is for him a matter of course for all human acts some to fulfillment through the intermediary of thought and thus appear to him in the last analysis as being founded on thought. (Letter from Engels to Mehring, July 14, 1893)[24]

> The History of Nature, what is called natural sciences, does not concern us at this point, but we will have to confront the history of men, since almost all of ideology may be reduced to either a mistaken conception of such a history or a complete abstraction of this history.(Marx and Engels)[25]

> An ideology is a system (with its logic and own rigor) of representations

(images, myths, ideas or concepts according to the particular cases) given an existence and a historical role within a given society. Without addressing the problem of the relationship between a science and its past (ideological), let it be said that ideology, as a system of representations, is different from science in that the practical-social function outstrips its theoretical function (or knowledge function). (L. Althusser)[26]

By ideologies, we understand those interpretations of situations which are not the outcome of concrete experiences but are a kind of distorted knowledge of them, and which serve to cover up the real situation and work upon the individual like a compulsion. (K. Mannheim)[27]

Ideology is a global system of interpretation of the historico-political world. (R. Aron)[28]

The function of an ideology is to give both individual and collective directives of actions. (M. Rodinson)[29]

Ideology is the intellectual expression determined historically of a system of (vested) interests. (Mennicke)[30]

Ideology is a thought charged with affectivity in which each of these elements corrupts the other. (J. Monnerot)[31]

An ideology is a complexity of ideas and representations which pass in the eyes of the subject for an interpretation of the world or of his own situation, which represent absolute truth, but in the form of an illusion through which he justifies himself, hides, or runs away from in some way or another, but always to his immediate advantage. To see that a thought is ideological means uncovering the mistake, showing evil, designating it an ideology, thus reproaching it with lying and being untruthful: there can be no more violent means of attacking it. (K. Jaspers)[32]

What characterizes, at least in principal, ideological deviance, is a misunderstanding of the practical setting up of categories which afterwards are treated on a higher level. The philosopher, the jurist, the theologian use concepts which seem obvious to them and to which they accord a quasi natural status; the formal problems which belong to them—a search for order, ultimate legitimization, coherence—and which seem to refer to hypercriticism, are posed from a naive acceptance of the terrain on which these problems flourish. The solutions are then taken to transcendental powers—God, Reason, or an Absolute idea—which are offered as the source of reality itself. Criticism of ideologies, stressing the discrepancy between Saying and Doing, bring back to man alone what had been taken from him by those extraordinary speculative expropriations that are Philosophy and Religion. (L. Sebag)[33]

To a great extent, the word *ideology* remains marked by the meaning which was given to it by the Marxists for whom the essence of ideology would be a wish to translate, as if it were question of expressing a disinterested thought, the vital interests of a social group or class. Thus ideology would proceed from a falsified conscience, the characteristic of ideology being to be unaware that this system of reflexion is the product of the material conditions in which it is placed. Expressing the relationships of property, ideology is linked to the division of society into social classes, with the dominating class making all the efforts to impose its own conception of the world on the whole of the community. From that moment onwards, the ideological procedure takes on the role of defensive factor or protector principle. As an element of social cover with a mystifying content, ideology plays the part of an instrument of combat between the groups. (J.Meynaud)[34]

The majority of ideologies of which we may think, whether major or minor ideologies, left-wing or right-wing ideologies, are characterized by the fact that they effectively lay claim to doctrines following scientific procedures. Both arguments demand a definition of ideologies as doctrines based on scientific theories, but on false or poorly interpreted theories, which are accorded a credibility that they do not deserve. Hence, the fundamental sociological problem to be posed is the knowledge of how much misinterpretations are possible, and why they are so wide-spread. (R. Boudon)[35]

Ideology and Dialectics

Jean Lacroix, one of the main representatives of Christian personalism in France, asserts, in the spirit of Lukácsism, that ideologization generally involves reification. "All ideology is reifying in so far as it seeks an enduring state of things, so consequently, it is anti-historicist."[36] This trend towards reification of the ideological discourse is particularly evident in racist ideology as demonstrated above by Adorno's inquiry.[37] In the quotation above, Maxime Rodinson highlighted the Manichean overtones of ideological discourse that idealizes the political in-group and "diabolizes" the opponent.[38] Meanwhile, a fruitful distinction between worldview *(Weltanschauung)* and ideology has been formulated by Lucien Goldmann: the former was characterized by its "totalizing" (i.e., dialectical) perception of social reality and the latter by its atomized (reified) perception.[39]

Now it appears that these three interpretations (that of Lacroix, Rodinson, and Goldmann) converge towards the same "fundamental disturbance,"[40] which is dedialectization. Here, I would like to especially refer to Lukács' work *History and Class Consciousness* which emphasizes the importance of the category of totality (wholeness) and of historicism as elements of a dialectical approach to sociopolitical realities. The universe of reification as described in the principal chapter of this book is ahistorical and a-dialectical. It is reminiscent of the atmosphere of Orwell's *1984*.[41]

On the basis of these considerations I suggest the following definition: Ideology is a system of ideas which express without reciprocity the more or less legitimate interests *(seinsverbunden)* of an economic, political, or ethnic entity. As an historicism, ideology also expresses resistance to social change and dissociation of concrete dialectical totalities.

This definition is essentially a *dialectical* one; seen in this light, ideologization is tantamount to dedialectization as already suggested above by Marx.[42] The young Marx could not, of course, foresee in 1844 that this statement inferred an anticipated criticism of what was to become a century later his own theory under Stalin and Zhdanov. Some other definitions quoted above (Engels, Sebag, Meynaud) emphasize the asociologism ("society-blindness") common to ideological discourse; Engels blames (German) ideologists for considering intellectual currents as autonomous facts independent from the social context and the class situation of the protagonists.[43]

So it seems that we are presented with two definitions both of Marxist origin: Ideology defined as "history-blindness" (Marx) or as "society-blindness" (Engels and Althusser). These two definitions are convergent inasmuch as they reflect two aspects of the same dialectical approach to social reality. Sociologism, in Durkheim's sense, is basically a dialectical doctrine, which is attested by the current use of the category of totality by authors such as Marcel Mauss and Durkheim himself.[44]

This dialectical and historicist definition of ideology offers a solution to a problem that seems to have become one of the main scientific preoccupations of Raymond Boudon: the paradoxical credibility of sometimes absurd statements in politics.[45] A historicist and dialectical understanding of social realities—"social awareness"[46]—is a difficult and sophisticated intellectual technique which is the fruit of a process of maturation. Man is neither born a dialectician nor a historicist, but *becomes one*.[47] Historical thinking about the present requires a certain degree of maturity and effort. Hence, ideology is attractive because of its antihistoricist and antidialectical character which offers an easy solution for the lazy mind *(Denkoekonomie)*. The success of such typically antihistoricist and nondialectical theories, such as Stalinism and racism, illustrates this.

In its original (genuine) form, Marxism is beyond doubt a historicism. Karl Popper speaks of the "deification of History" by Marx,[48] whereas the neo-Marxist vision of history (that of Stalinism) involves a genuine reification of historical duration. Some decades ago, the French intellectual public witnessed a paradoxical phenomenon: the rise of a deliberately antihistoricist and antihumanist Marxist school of thought which was consequently antidialectical.[49] Later, however, witnessed the dissipation of the influence of Althusserianism, adequately described as *"marxisme immaginaire,"*[50] despite the fact that it occupied a dominant position in French academia for a long period. This philosophical school involves a conception of ideology as a theoretical justification of the Stalinist "presentocentrism" and of ahistoricism exemplified by the Moscow trials in the thirties. Althusserianism introjected—in the psychoanalytic sense of this term—the critical aspect of *1984.*"[51]

Ideological (Diabolical) Causality

The term "ideological causality" is employed here for simplicity's sake; in fact, one should speak of "ideological distortion of the perception of social causality." The same problem is discussed by Leon Poliakov[52] who refers to the "diabolization of the opponent" (Maxime Rodinson) as one of the typical features of ideological behavior. Poliakov's book is an important contribution to the problem of political false consciousness. Investigations concerning the causes of historical events (generally in failures or defeats) occupy, indeed, a prominent place in the ideological approach to political problems. Sociology is foremost interested in "how" things happen, whereas ideology is more concerned with "why" they happen. This causal oversaturation is an important element and perhaps one of the causes of ideological distortion. The definition of magic by Marcel Mauss as a *gigantesque variation sur le thème de la causalité*"[53] also holds true for ideology. This causalist orientation of the ideological discourse expresses a trend that characterizes various aspects of political life, e.g., the search for scapegoats frequently followed by arbitrary penal sanctions, as exemplified by the Riom trial in Vichy France.

Thus, we see that the principal features of ideological causality are: (a) the detotalisation of historical situations; (b) its Manichean tendency; and (c) the inversion of cause and effect in the perception of causal relations.

Detotalization of Historical Situations

In reference to J.S Mill, MacIver highlights the fact that a genuine causal action goes from wholeness (totality) to wholeness and that the commonplace distinction between "cause" and condition is merely subjective:

> It is very common to single out any one of the antecedents under the denomination of Cause, calling the others merely Conditions. Thus, if a person eats a particular dish and dies in consequence, that is, would not have died if had not eaten of it, people would be apt to say that eating of that dish was the cause of his death.... But though we may think proper to give the name of cause to that one condition, the fulfillment of which completes the tale, and brings about the effect without further delay; this condition has really no closer relation to the effect than any of the other conditions has. All the conditions were equally indispensable to the production of the consequent; and this statement of the cause is incomplete, unless in some shape or other we introduce them all.[54]

Public opinion is inclined to perceive a genuine cause where an intervention or a penal sanction on the part of public authorities is to be envisaged; other factors are seen as mere conditions. This requirement of integral totalization is not realizable in our daily practice; we are obliged to employ detotalizing abstraction according to professional necessities and in consideration of the limits of our competence. Faced with a case of death by poisoning, a physician would be interested by the causal action of the poison on the victim's central nervous system; whereas the coroner would investigate the possibility of interpersonal conflicts. But in this case, detotalisation is based on rational considerations and does to involve ideological distortion.

Manichean Tendency

In case of ideological causality, detotalization is on the contrary reliant on generally irrational motivations. A well-known and provocative historical example is the explanation of Germany's defeat in the First World War by the "stab in the back" (*Dolchstoss*) theory. This defeat was obviously the result of the convergence of several economic, military, and political factors; right-wing propaganda in both postwar Germany and Nazism, singled out the actions of "inside foes" (left-wing pacifists and Jews) as the main, and even the sole, cause of this defeat. Nevertheless the extermination between 1933–1945 of the "inside foe" did not prevent a second defeat in 1945. This example shows clearly that ideological causality is corollary to a nondialectical (detotalizing and Manichean) approach to sociopolitical realities.

The Inversion of Cause and Effect:

The same holds true for the third typical trait of ideological causality: the temporal inversion of cause and effect. The propaganda of the Third Reich claimed that the anti-Germanism of some Jewish milieus after 1933 was a justification of Hitlerite anti-Semitism which had risen prior to that date. Zionism is often considered to be one of the causes of contemporary anti-Semitism; however, it is obviously a consequence rather than a cause. The communist press at the time of the Korean Civil War depicted the crossing in 1951 by General MacArthur of the 38th parallel as a proof of his imperialistic ambitions and consequently as a justification of the North Korean attack which took place a year earlier. It would be easy to multiply these examples; temporal inversion of cause and effect is a common feature of political debates. But since such inversion is inconceivable within the framework of normal (irreversible) duration, it appears as a clear symptom of reification (spatialization) of temporality. And since reification (according to Lukács) is tantamount to dedialecization, this confirms our "dialectical" interpretation of ideological distortion, and at the same time the hypothesis of the schizophrenic character of political alienation (of "false consciousness").

Notes

1. Kroeber, A.L and C. Kluckhohn, *Culture: A Critical Review of Concepts and Definitions* (New York: Vintage Books, 1952).
2. According to Alain Touraine "Socialism is nothing but a disparate group of those who use this term as a reference" ("Le Socialisme n'est plus rien d'autre que l'ensemble disparate de ceux qui se couvrent de son nom") Alain Touraine, *L'Après-Socialisme* (Paris: Ed. Grasset, 1980), p.1.
3. Raymond Aron, *Trois essais sur l'Age Industriel* (Paris: Ed. Plon 1966), p. 214.
4. "The valorization of the concept of ideology by Lenin who considered Marxism-Leninism as the ideology of the revolutionary class is to some extent in contradiction with the original conceptions of Marx." Henri Chambre, *Le Marxisme en Union Soviétique* (Paris: Ed. du Seuil, 1955), p. 49.
5. Werner Stark, *The Sociology of Knowledge: An Essay in Aid of a Deeper Understanding of the History of Ideas* (London: Routledge & Kegan Paul, 1958) p. 172.
6. J. Gabel, *Mannheim and Hungarian Marxism* (New Brunswick, NJ: Transaction Publishers, 1991), p. 44.
7. This theory of Karl Mannheim was often misunderstood. L. Goldmann and R. Aron interpreted it as an apologia of academic teaching staff. For details see Gabel, *Mannheim and Hungarian Marxism*, p. 59ff.
8. See Eugène Minkowski, *La Schizophrénie* (Paris: Payot 1927), and *Le Temps Vécu* (Paris: Collection de l'Evolution Psychiatrique, 1933), and J. Gabel, *L'oeuvre d'Eugène Minkowski et la philosophie de la culture, L'Evolution Psychiatrique* (Paris: 1991), p. 429–34.
9. According to Minkowski the schizophrenic consciousness is the "polar region of intellectual antithesis" (*La région polaire des antithèses intellectuelles*). Minkowski, *Contribution à l'étude de la pensée et de l'attitude autistes, L'Encéphale*, (April 1923), p. 16. The kinship of this morbid form of rationality with that underlying the ideological distortion of political discourse is obvious.
10. Any person who has a characteristic in common with an alleged persecutor, for example, having a beard or red hair or wearing a special dress, may become the persecutor, or a relative of the persecutor, or somehow associated with the persecutor. From all these examples it is easy to recognize that many patients at this stage indulge in what I have called an "orgy of identifications." A French psychiatrist, Gale (1948),independently discovered the same phenomenon in schizophrenia and called it a "hypertrophy of the sense of identification". See Silvano Arieti, *Interpretation of Schizophrenia* (New York: Basic Books, 1974), p. 232.
11. The same phenomenon was observed but only superficially exploited some decades earlier by Alfred Karzybski: "In heavy cases of dementia praecox we find the most highly developed "identification." Alfred Krzybski, *Science and Sanity* (The International Non-Aristotelian Library Publishing Company, 1980), p. 568.
12. Joseph Gabel, "Psychopatholgie de la pensée dialectique," *Esprit* 10 (Paris, 1951); and Gabel, *False Consciousness: An Essay on Reification* (New York: Harper Torchbooks, 1978), p. 139ff and *passim*.
13. The term was coined by Marx to designate the integration of Hegel's

idealistic dialectics into the framework of a materialistic philosophy.
14. "M. Gabel préfère, lui aussi, se limiter à un point de vue partiel: les rapports du phénomène réificationnel avec le fait pyschiatrique. Cette position nous est plus proche également." Eugene Minkowski, *Traité de Psychopathologie* (Paris: P.U.F 1966), p. 597.
15. This term was term coined by the talented Hungarian Marxist philosopher Béla Fogarasi. For details see Gabel, *Mannheim and Hungarian Marxism*, p. 20.
16. Honorio Delgado detected an invalidation of the facticities of the past ("invaledacion de lo acaecido" in the psychology of schizophrenics), see p. of present volume).
17. For more details see chapter 8 on Stalinism and also chapter 10.
18. See chapter on Stalinism of present volume.
19. Raymond Aron, "Ideologie communiste et religion," *La Revue de Paris*, May 1955.
20. This is in my view a justification of the insertion of this outmoded study into the present volume. The point of view advocated in this paper is akin to that underlying Orwell's *1984*. Orwell underscores the antihistoricism of the totalitarian mind while the article reprinted (pp. 145–158 of the present volume) points out its antidialectic features. For the Hungarian Marxist school (Lukács, Mannheim, and others) historicism and dialectics are two facets of the same philosophical approach.
21. Karl Mannheim, *Ideologie und Utopie* (1965), p. 53. This important passage of Mannheim's magnum opus has been for mysterious reasons discarded from the English (and also from the French) translation.
22. P. Kahn, *Ideologie et Sociologie de la Connaissance, Cahiers Internationaux de Sociologie*, vol. VII, 1950, p. 154.
23. Theodor Adorno, et al., *The Authoritarian Personality* (New York: Harper & Row, 1950).
24. Marx and Engels, *Etudes philosophiques* (Paris: Ed. ESI, 1951), p. 139.
25. Here is the German original of this statement of paramount importance which involves an anticipated criticism of the Stalinist vision of history and as such foreshadows *1984*. "Die Geschichte der Natur die sogenannte Naturwissenschaft geht uns hier nicht an; an die Geschichte der Menschen werden wir in dessen einzugchen haben da fast die ganze Ideologie sich etweder auf eine verdrehte Auffassung dieser Geschichte oder auf eine gänzliche Abstraktion von Ihr reduziert." (*Deutsche Ideologie-Frühschriften*, ed. by Siefried Landshut (Stuttgart: A. Kroner, 1953), p. 346.
26. L. Althusser: *Pour Marx* (Paris: Ed. Maspero, 1972), p. 238.
27. Karl Mannheim, *Diagnosis of Our Time: Wartime Essays of a Sociologist* (London: Kegan Paul, Trench, Trubner, and Co., Ltd., 1943/New York: Oxford University Press, 1944), p. 97.
28. Raymond Aron, *Trois essais sur l'âge industriel* (Paris, 1966), p. 215.
29. Maxime Rodinson, "Sociologie marxiste et ideologie marxiste," *Diogène* (64 Oct-Dec,. 1968).
30. See Mennicke's article, "Ideologie" in H. Schmidt, *Philosophisches Wörterbuch* (Stuttgart, 1943); second edition completely rewritten by W. Schingnitz and J. Schondorff.
31. Jules Monnerot, *Sociologie du Communisme* (Paris, 1949), p. 297.
32. Karl Jaspers, *Origines et Sens de l'Histoire* (Paris, 1949), p. 163–64.
33. L.Sebag, *Marxisme et structuralisme* (Paris: Payot, 1949), pp. 90–91.

34. J. Meynaud, "Destin des idéologies," in *Etudes de sciences politiques*, 4 (Lausanne-Paris, 1961), p. 9–10.
35. Raymond Boudon, *L'idéologie* (Paris: Fayard, 1986), p. 45.
36. Jean Lacrois, *Le personalisme comme anti-ideologie* (Paris: PUF, 1972), p. 21.
37. The ethnocentric "need for an outgroup" prevents that identification with humanity as a whole which is found in anti-ethnocentrism. (This lack in identification is related to the ethnocentrists' inability to approach individuals as individuals, and to their tendency to see and "prejudge" each individual only as a sample specimen of the reified group. Their experience of interpersonal relations involves, so to speak, the same stereotyping as their opinions regarding groups generally.) Adorno, *The Authoritarian Personality*, p. 148.
38. M. Rodinson, "Sociolgie Marxist."
39. Lucien Goldmann, *Sciences humaines et Philosophie* (Paris: P.U.F.,1952), p. 103ff.
40. The term "fundamental disturbance" (*Grundstörung*) belongs to the conceptual framework of phenomenological psychopathology (Binswanger, Minkowski, and others.) It does not refer to a pathogenic cause but to a general symptom from which thedifferent symptoms of a given mental illness can be deduced. In my *False Consciousness*, I have tried to show that reification of consciousness is the fundamental disturbance of schizophrenia and also of political alienation.
41. The antidialectical character of political manicheism such as it appears in totalitarian mentality seems to be an obvious fact which does not require any comment.
42. The main reference of this definition is the pioneering statement by the young Marx quoted above: ideology involves an arbitrary distortion or negation of historicity ("History-Blindness").
43. In his *History of the Peasant War in Germany*, Engels is ironical about the representatives of "German Ideology" who depict the French Revolution of 1789 as a somewhat animated discussion about the advantages of constitutional monarchy over an absolute one, and the social struggles at the end of the Middle Ages as passionate theological arguments devoid of any relationship to the class struggles (Engels, *La Guerre des Paysans en Allemagne* [French edition, 1974], p. 61.) For Engels ideological distortion is first and foremost tantamount to "society-blindness," while Marx, as a forerunner of Orwell, criticizes above all the "history-blindness" of the ideologues. But these two points of view are two facets of the same dialectical approach.
44. According to Durkheim, "society is not reducible to the properties of individual minds, but . . . it constitutes a reality sui generis which emerges out of the collocation and interaction of individual minds" (Harry Elmer Barnes, *An Introduction to the History of Sociology* [Chicago: The University of Chicago Press, 1961], p. 506). The Marxist author of *History and Class Consciousness* could have signed this statement, which is, in fact, a recognition of the importance of the dialectical category of wholeness (*Totalität*) for sociologism. Sociologism, no matter whether of Marxist or of Durkheimian origin, is tantamount to a dialectical perception of social reality, and consequently the society-blindness of ideology, as criticized by Engels, involves dedialectization. Raymond Boudon, the outstanding French representative of "methodological individualism" and as such an opponent to

sociologism, is consistent when he challenges the scientific pertinency of the category of totality; R. Boudon: *Les méthodes en Sociologie* (Paris: P.U.F., 1969), p. 29.
45. See Raymond Boudon, *L'idéologie ou l'origine des idées recues* (Paris: Fayard, 1986) and *L'art de se Persuader* (Paris: Fayard, 1990).
46. This is Mannheim's term. See J. Gabel: *Mannheim and Hungarian Marxism* (New Brunswick, NJ: Transaction Publishers, 1991), p. 73.
47. In his polemic against Gestalt theory, Jean Piaget underscores the fact that a totalizing (i.e., dialectic) perception of reality is not an innate capacity but the result of a process of maturation (Piaget, *La psychologie de l'Intelligence* [Paris: Armand Colin, 1947], pp. 47ff.
48. Karl Popper, "Prediction and Prophecy in the Social Sciences" in *Conjectures and Refutations* (New York: Basic Books, 1962), p. 346, quoted by Leon Poliakov, *La causalité diabolique* (Paris: Calmann Levy, 1980), p. 230.
49. See Henri Lefebvre, *Au dela du Structuralisme* (Paris: Anthropos, 1971), p. 336.
50. Raymond Aron, *D'une Sainte Famille à l'autre. Essais sur les Marxismes Imaginaires* (Paris, 1969).
51. "Althusser and Orwell", chapter 6 of the present volume.
52. Léon Poliakov, *La causalité diabolique*, vol. 1 (Paris: Calmann Levy, 1980).
53. Marcel Mauss, *Sociologie et Anthropolgie* (Paris: P.U.F., 1959), p. 56.
54. Robert M. MacIver, *Social Causation* (New York: Harper Torchbooks, 1964 [1942]), p. 41.

8

Stalinism as Ideology: An Ideal-Type of Ideological Distortion

> *"Fair is foul and foul is fair"*—Chorus of witches, *Macbeth*, Act I

The object of the present article is a critical analysis of ideological distortion as it appeared in Stalinism. One may wonder why such an outmoded political ideology would be of interest today. But if archaeology is a science whose usefulness has never been challenged, to some extent the same holds true for political archaeology. The construction of "ideal-types" (Max Weber) has generally been recognized as an important tool of research in the social sciences. As a coherent system of a nondialectical and antihistoricist vision of social reality, Stalinism offers political researchers a genuine "ideal-type" of ideological (sociocentric) distortion whose critical analysis may shed light on some crucial current issues.

Stalinism was probably the most extreme manifestation of false consciousness known to history. At that time, the discussion of political problems with partisans and the reading of party press gave one the impression of dealing with people with totally different minds. Angelo Rossi recalled a scientist "who waits ten years and conducts a great number of experiments before finishing a given atomic formula and who admits, as would the simplest of souls, that a man such as Trotsky could be on the payroll of the Nazi secret service and that the

Stalinist constitution is the most democratic in the world."[1] This statement is not a product of partisan imagination, for similar cases were familar during that period.

Andre Wurmser, a left-wing critic wrote the following astonishing statement: "What acts of aggression has a socialist State ever committed? And what expansionist war has Russia ever started? None."[2] Wurmser cannot be blamed for not having foreseen the Afghanistan war which started several decades later. Nevertheless by 1948, Soviet Russia had already started three wars against Poland, Finland, and the Baltic States. Whether these wars were justifiable or not on the basis of *raison d'etat* is irrelevant here. And, even if we admit that they may have been entirely legitimized by "historical necessities," disruptions of these nations' own histories still could not be justified.

The absurd idea of a formal alliance between Trotsky's supporters and the Third Reich marked the Moscow trials of the thirties. This allegation, without any material proof, was exclusively based on the defendants' confession. Nevertheless, a lingering doubt remained until 1945, after which it became totally untenable. The archives of the Third Reich have disclosed some of their secrets, and public trials took place where leading Nazi politicians were tried by an international court of justice with representatives of the victorious coalition, including those of Soviet Russia. It is inconceivable that the alleged Hitler-Trotsky conspiracy could have either remained secret during the court's sessions or left no traces in the archives of the Third Reich. Here, we are faced with conclusive evidence. The "Hitler-Trotsky conspiracy," targeted by the public prosecutor of the Moscow trials, can now be proven to have never existed. However, this fact did not deter the party press of that period from presenting this imaginary conspiracy as an unquestionable historical fact.

The logic that underpinned this mentality was impervious to factual experience (a sort of resistance to the obvious).[3] Hence, it is paradoxically opposed to dialectical logic, as brilliantly analyzed by party theorists such as the late Henri Lefebvre.[4] To study this particular form of logic, one should bear in mind the advice given by Levy-Bruhl to researchers in the field of the sociology of moral facts: dismiss norms and look only at facts.[5] Official textbooks of dialectical philosophy are of little interest

Stalinism as Ideology 147

for our present research; we shall attempt to investigate the real logical mechanisms of the process of ideologication as it appeared in public debates or in the party press of that time.

The False Identity Syllogism

The main logical feature of this mentality is the arbitrary identification (false identity) or "perverse equation," according to a more recent—and perhaps more appropriate—terminology coined by Alain Dieckhoff.[6] Paradoxically, this concept is of Marxist origin. Two philosophers of the Budapest school, Béla Fogarasi and Georg Nàdor, were the first to elaborate the idea that the abuse of identification may be a factor of dedialectization of political consciousness, and consequently an instrument of ideological distortion. Fogarasi explains this process:[7]

> The essential gambit used in anti-dialectical theories is false identification; the unjustified identification of contrary and different data. False identification plays an important part not only in economics but also in sociology and even in political practice.[8]
> An important form of false identification consists in identifying the work of a manual worker with that of a capitalist. In a brilliant analysis, Marx shows that when the capitalist works he does not do so as a capitalist. The "work" of exploitation is only work in appearance. The key to the paralogism is the following: identifying by basing on an apparent analogy the "work" of exploitation and the work of the exploited.[9]
> Each time that sophistry and demagogy raise their heads, false identification is to be found as one of the most important—sometimes decisive—"gambits" used to lead naive thought astray. The reason is that common sense tends to substitute easily unrefined identification with tiresome and finely differentiated mediations of dialectic thought. Nowadays one of the most blameworthy forms of the use of false identification consists in identifying fascism and communism, which has become the leitmotif of the ideology of world reaction.[10] Finally, if dialectics consists essentially of an adequate view, that is to say, as to the unity (identity) of opposites and their conflict, sophistry is essentially the subjective method of false identifications and false oppositions."[11]

Here a commentary seems hardly necessary. The analogy between the logical structure of false consciousness as depicted by the Marxist Fogarasi, and that of the logic of Stalinism is obvious. At first sight, Fogarasi's criticisms appear to target exclusively bourgeois ideologies. Nevertheless, it seems unlikely that a lucid thinker such as Fogarasi could be unaware that his depiction of unwarranted identification in right-wing ideologies implies an indirect criticism of one of the basic logical features of Stalinism. I am inclined to think that this was a deliberate ploy designed to convey a nonconformist message.[12]

Though arbitrary identification was one of the logical features of Stalinist ideology, it was by no means its monopoly. The examples quoted by Fogarasi are partly valid; the term "Judeo-bolshevism," pervasive in mainstream anti-Semitic literature, relies on an identical mental mechanism. The number of false identities in a given political discourse reflects the degree of its ideologization. The communist discourse under Stalin and Zhdanov was saturated with such false identities. After de-Stalinization, the number dropped to a large extent, but, one could nevertheless see in the party press an analogy between the 1956 Budapest freedom fighters and the Versailles smashing of the Paris Commune of 1870. Solzhenitsyn was falsely compared to Knut Hamsun, who was beyond doubt an outstanding novelist and a genuine quisling under the foreign occupation of his homeland.[13] More recently it is the anti-Israeli political discourse that probably harbors the most provocative instances of perverse equations, such as "Zionism = racism."[14]

Prior to de-Stalinization, the French communist press teemed with such "perverse equations," especially in the following argument: "Nazi foreign policy was anticommunist; America's post-war policy was also anticommunist; therefore the U.S. is a fascist power just as the Third Reich was."[15] The presence of U.S. armed forces in postwar Europe was frequently compared to the occupation of these countries by the *Wehrmacht* during the War. On November 18, 1948, French Communist Parliament members compared President Truman to Hitler. On May 7, 1948, the party daily *"l'Humanité"* issued an article by Pierre Courtade under the heading *"Hitler l'a déja dit,"* ("Hitler already said that"), containing numerous references to "Overseas Führers" and their European "Gauleiters." Commenting on a bill aiming at the exclusion of communist researchers from atomic commissions, V. Leduc goes as far as to coin the term "New Racism."[16] The common denominator in all these examples is their common identification of all political currents or personalities opposed to communism, even though they represent highly different political tendencies.

The Principle of Analogy in the Stalinist Code of Laws

A curious example of arbitrary identification is provided by the Stalinist code of laws. During the Stalinist era, the "principle of analogy" was the object of violent discussions in the USSR. An example of "judgment by analogy" is presented by Rudolph Schlesinger: the death sentence for counterfeiting a passport *by analogy* with the law against false coining.[17] There is, beyond doubt, a common element of counterfeit of a state document linking the two offenses, but their moral and intentional context cannot be compared. This principle of analogy also prevailed in the judicial system of the Third Reich. In his work on National Socialism, the pro-Nazi prelate Msgr. Alois Hudal, pointed out that "the law of June 26th, 1935, introduced the principle of judgement by analogy into the penal procedure in Germany."[18] Here, apparently, we are faced with a constant feature of totalitarian legal sensitivity rather than with a peculiarity of the Stalinist legal system.

A final example can be offered to show that this "ideo-logic" does not respect the barrier which is supposed to protect the field of science against the irruption of ideology. In the fifties, lobotomy was outlawed in USSR, while in America Freeman and Watts continued the large-scale testing of this technique. From a purely scientific standpoint, the Soviet legislation could marshall some valuable arguments in its favor; nevertheless, this procedure becomes a typical form of ideological distortion when a serious psychiatric monthly *La Raison*, the organ of Pavlovism in France, compared the American research with the criminal "medical" experiments in Hitler's concentration camps.[19]

Arbitrary identification includes "unwarranted extrapolation" (Whitehead) as its corollary in the formation of political concepts. In the party press of that period, the term "fascism" was not the conceptual counterpart of an observed sociopolitical structure but a mere caption, covering a wide range of political movements arbitrarily assumed to be identical because of a (frequently very tenuous) common element. It was also an egocentric concept inasmuch as this "tenuous common element" was generally the relationship with communism seen as the logical center of the political universe. This form of collective egocentrism (sociocentrism) ultimately resulted in mental structures akin to those described in child psychology by Jean Piaget.[20] Finally, every regime, regardless of its social structure or ideological make up, may be branded as "fascist."[21] In philosophical debates, the concept of "idealism" assumed the same ideological function and was often deployed as a pretext for dismissing dialectical theories such as the conceptions of Georg Lukács, Henri Bergson, and Gestalt theory.

This predominance of identification in ideological discourse is obviously incompatible with dialectics. Theodor Adorno defined dialectics as "the rigorous awareness of non-identity."[22] The arbitrary identification of disparate data involves, as its primary condition, the dissociation of concrete dialectic totalities formed by the data in question, as well as an occultation of their historical dimension. This approach is characterized by the fact that, in a given complex historical context, one trait is arbitrarily singled out as representative of the whole. Whenever two such traits can be found in two historically different situations, these situations are considered to be identical. In other words, in contrast with Gestalt theory (and Lukács's notion of dialectics), concrete totalities are dissociated and partial identities are raised to the status of global identities.

Totality and Identification

The dialectical concept of totality (wholeness) that pervades the criticism of "identifying expressions" (egocentric concepts) needs clarification. According to Lukács, totality (wholeness) is "the essential category of reality" (*Eigentliche Wirklichkeitskategorie*).[23] In opposition to this dialectical concept, stands the principle of identification whose role in mental processes was pointed out by the French epistemologist Emile Meyerson.[24] It represents the nondialectic (reified) pole of human intelligence, and is an indispensable instrument for fixing a dynamic reality behind the formation of concepts and in language. Moreover, Meyerson allows for an intuition of the diversity,[25] in addition to identification, as a necessary corrective. A rupture of equilibrium between these two components of normal thought processes may lead to ideological distortion at the social level and to mental disturbance at the individual level.

Several theorists (Alfred Korzybski, Silvano Arieti, and the present author[26]) have detected a morbid hypertrophy of the function of identification in schizophrenia. Eugene Minkowski also pointed out a Manichean mental structure in such patients.[27] Now, a Manichean perception of reality and unwarranted identification are two facets of a similar undialectical approach. The same "unwarranted extrapolation" which underlies, as we have seen above, the egocentric construction of political concepts, has also been detected in schizophrenia by Georges Devereux.[28] Hence, it appears that the hypothesis of the schizophrenic character of political alienation (of false consciousness) posited by the present author[29] may marshall some serious arguments in its favor.

Although Stalinism is a dead ideology, nevertheless, as a spontaneous ideal-type of ideological distortion, it remains very important for sociologists, as it sheds light on current issues. Let us take the problem of racism as an example. The role of reification as an outstanding element of the racist perception of ethnic alterity was clearly pointed out earlier in Adorno's inquiry.[30] Now, in the spirit of Lukácsism, reification is tantamount to dedialectization and antihistoricism.[31] This statement may have some practical implications regarding any social action against racism.

A democratic state has the right, and even the obligation, to combat dangerous ideologies by legal means, such as the banning of printed communications, but this is merely a symptomatic treatment which may involve undesirable "pernicious side effects."[32] Ideology is a social neurosis which may in some cases turn into social psychosis. Historicization and dedialectization of public opinion may act as a preventive therapy for these disturbances of the collective mind. This was one of the main leitmotifs of the second (English) period of the work of Mannheim, who wished to make the demystifying (dialectical and historicist) aspects of Marxism—considered by him at that time, and with good reason, as vulnerable—available to liberal democracy.[33] Meanwhile, Wittfogel,[34] criticized Mannheim as one of those bourgeois sociologists who pillage the ideological arsenal of the class enemy.[35] The main lesson to be drawn from a critical analysis of Stalinism as ideology is, in my view, a reappraisal of dialectics as an instrument of political demystification. Stalinism, as a typical manifestation of political falsehood, was compelled to turn its back on dialectics in spite of its Marxist origins. The same holds true for Althusser's school.[36]

Marxism will probably not outlive its present failure in the field of economics and politics; it would be regrettable that it should pull down, in its own fall, this precious weapon of demystification that is dialectics. The fate of Marxism is genuinely tragic.[37] It is true that the evolution of capitalism has continuously discredited many of Marx's predictions, but Marxism as a dialectic and historicist philosophy of demystification conserves its usefulness as an instrument of criticism for all forms of the totalitarian mind—left-wing totalitarianism included.[38]

Notes

1. A. Rossi, *Physiologie du parti communiste francais* (Paris: Self Publishers, 1948), p. 334.
2. Andre Wurmser, in the February 18, 1948 issue of the French Marxist weekly *L'Action*.
3. It would be easy to fill volumes with examples of this imperviousness to factual experience (a kind of resistance to the obvious) which characterized the communist mentality of that time. But the analysis of such authors as Raymond Aron, Arthur Koestler, and many others have rendered such an exercise unnecessary.
4. Among all French theorists of Marxism, the work of Henri Lefebvre (1901–1991), shows the most intensive dialectical tendency; see *Logique formelle, logique dialectique* (Paris: Anthropos, 1967), and "Le notion de totalitè dans les sciences sociales," *Cahiers Internationaux de Sociologie* (1955). It is not a fortuitous fact that he was also one of the first to be interested in the problem of false consciousness (*La conscience mystifiée*, Paris, 1936).
5. See Lucien Levy-Bruhl, *La morale et la science des moeurs* (Paris: Alcan, 1903).
6. Alain Dieckhoff, *Le sionisme comme racisme, genèse, expansion, itinéraires, résurgences d'une équation perverse* (Unpublished Ph.D Thesis, Paris X/Nanterre, 1983).
7. In a chapter of Fogarasi's work *Marxism and Logic* which includes Béla Fogarasi, *Marxizmus és Logika* (Budapest: Szikra Publisher, 1946), pp. 70–76, chap. XI "On false identification."
8. Fogarasi, *Marxism and Logic*, p. 71.
9. Marx, *Theorien der Mehrwert* (quoted by Fogarasi, *Marxism and Logic*, p. 72).
10. Fogarasi, *Marxism and Logic*, p. 74. This is, of course, the view of a party theorist: it is not certain that equation "fascism=communism" is really a perverse equation. For details, see James Burnham, *The Managerial Revolution* (New York: John Day, 1941).

11. Ibid., p. 75. Instead of "subjective" I should prefer the term "sociocentric" (collective egocentricity) which underscores the kinship of the logical features of ideological distortion with those of child psychology as established by Jean Piaget.
12. Béla Fogarasi (1891–1959) is along with Georg Lukàcs the most outstanding representative of the Hungarian Marxist school ("Hungaro-Marxism" according to the terminology coined by the present author), but much less well known abroad then his illustrious fellow countryman. As with Lukács, he was during his career a thinker torn between the obligations of political militancy and those of his message as philosopher. During the two communist experiences in his homeland (1919 and 1945), Fogarasi occupied important official positions involving the necessity of a conformist attitude in theoretical questions. Nevertheless, the collection of his essays published after his death in an epoch of relative intellectual freedom (Bela Fogarasi, *Parallele ind Divergenz/Ausgewählte Schriften* [Budapest: Archives Lukács, 1988]) contains highly nonconformist statements. Fogarasi was certainly aware of the fact that the chapter on "false identification" of his book was a subtle criticism of the logic that underlay Stalinism as ideology. Georg Nador, a Marxist philosopher in the wake of Fogarasi, published in 1952 in the official "Annals of Philosophy" (*Filozofiai Evkönyv*) a remarkable essay, "Contemporary sophistry: A contribution to the logical analysis of the fallacious thinking of the bourgeoisie in the imperialist era."

    This essay is one of the few examples of a critical analysis of ideological distortion (or false consciousness) in the official Marxist literature of that time. Nàdor emigrated from Hungary in the fifties. For more details see Gabel, *Mannheim and Hungarian Marxism*, (New Brunswick, NJ: Transaction Publishers, 1991), pp. 9, 12, 20, 22, 23. The later evolution of Fogarasi's career grants a certain credibility to this interpretation.
13. *Sovyetskaya Kultura* quoted by the Paris daily *Le Monde*, January 12–14, 1974.
14. For details see pp. 191–198 of the present volume.
15. For a typical example the work of the French fellow traveller, see Yves Farge, *La guerre d'Hitler continue* (Paris: La Bibliothèque Francaise, 1948).
16. Victor Leduc, "Le nouveau racisme," *L'Action* 1948 n° 182 (pp.24–30, March 1948).
17. See Rudolf Schlesinger, *Soviet Legal Theory* (London: Kegan Paul, Trench Trubner & C. Ltd., 1945), pp. 225 et sq. The main supporter of this principle was the famous public prosecutor in the Moscow trials in the thirties, Andrei Vishinski. But there is no absolute unanimity with regard to this question in the legal world of the USSR. Schlesinger points out that this principle was challenged by some Soviet jurists such as, among others, Tavgasov.
18. Msgr. Alois Hudal, *Die Grundlagen des National-Sozialismus* (Leipzig-Wien: Günther-Verlag, 1937), p. 167.
19. *La Raison: Cahiers de psychopathologie scientifique* (published in Paris circa 1953), 5, p. 7. On page 98 of the same issue, American society under Truman was termed "fascist"! This monthly had a good scientific reputation; the president of its editorial board was the famous psychologist Henri Wallon. Nevertheless its staunch left-wing political commitment often led it into scandalously absurd statements of which the example given is merely

154   Ideologies and the Corruption of Thought

a sample. The publication of this monthly ceased in 1954.
20. In his experimental research on child psychology Piaget pointed out a curious form of "objective morality" in the very young child. whose moral appreciation relies exclusively on the results and not on the moral intention (J. Piaget, *Le judgement moral chez l'enfant*; Paris: Alcan, 1926). This form of "objective (or better, "reified") morality was curiously akin to the axiological sensibility of Stalinism.
21. Yugoslavia was stigmatized as "fascist" after Tito's rupture with the Cominform; Israel, too, in periods of tension with the U.S.S.R.
22. Theodor Adorno, *Dialectique Négative* (Paris: Payot, 1978), p. 13.
23. Georg Lukács, *Geschichte und Klassenbewusstsein* (Berlin: Malik Verlag, 1923).
24. Emile Meyerson, *Identité et réalité* (Paris, 1908).
25. Emile Meyerson, *Du Cheminement de la Pensée*, (Paris: Alcan, 1931), Vol. 1, p. 93.
26. See Alfred Korzybski, *Science and Sanity* (Lakeville, CT: The International Non- Aristotelian Publishing Company, 1980 [first edition 1933]) p. 568; Silvano Arieti, *Interpretation of Schizophrenia* (New York: Basic Books, 1974), p. 232; and Gabel, *False Consciousness*, (New York: Harper Torchbooks, 1978), p. 224 and *passim*.
27. E. Minkowski, "Contribution à l'étude de la pensée et de l'attitude autiste" (Le rationalisme morbide) *L'Encéphale* (Paris), April, 1923. In this article, Minkowski evokes "the polar region of intellectual antithesis" ("région polaires des antithéses intellectuelles") as one of the typical features of schizophrenia. This is also an outstanding feature of ideological distortion.
28. Georges Devereux, *Essais d'ethnopsyciatrie générale*, (Paris: Gallimard, 1970), p. 236.
29. Gabel, *False Consciousness*.
30. "Antisemitism involves an inability to experience Jews as invidivuals. Rather each Jew is seen and reacted to as a sort of sample specimen of the stereotyped reified image of the group"; Theodor Adorno et al., *The Authoritarian Personality* (New York: Harper, 1951), p. 94. This statement holds true for all forms of racism, not exclusively for anti-Semitism.
31. This is one of the central leitmotifs of the chapter on reification in *History and Class Consciousness*.
32. The main *"effet pervers"* of the banning of publications of a racist character is to allow the authors of such works to appear as the defenders of freedom of expression. This phenomenon is commonplace in the French political scene today.
33. Mannheim's works was an anticipated criticism of the antihistoricism of McCarthyism (and of Goldwaterism too) which was at the same time a typical *"conduite d'échec"* in the field of politics. For details refer to Gabel, *Mannheim and Hungarian Marxism*, (New Brunswick, NJ: Transaction Publishers, 1991), p. 71–72 and *passim*.
34. Karl-August Wittfogel, *Oriental Despotism* (New Haven, CT: Yale University Press, 1957).
35. Wittfogel was the prospective author of a famous literary indictment of the totalitarian mind, but a staunch and even sectarian marxist at the outset of his career in Weimer Germany. See Karl-August Wittfogel, *Wissen und Gesellschaft. Neuere deutsche Litteratur zur Wissensoziologie* (*Unter dem Banner des Marxismus*, vol. 5, fasc. 1, p.83).
36. The late Louis Althusser, one of the most influential Marxist theorists in

postwar France, advocated an antihistoricist and antihumanist Marxism. This paradoxical point of view forced him to "evacuate dialectics" (according to Henri Lefebvre, *Au dela du structuralisme* [Paris: Anthropos 1971], p. 336).

37. Some decades ago, a French Marxist theorist, Michel Collinet, already issued a warning concerning this tragic fate in *La Tragédie du Marxisme* (Paris: Calmann Levy, 1947).

38. If by misfortune, Marx had been resuscitated in Stalin's Russia, he would certainly undergo the same tragic experiences as did Christ in Dostoevsky's tale of the Grand Inquisitor, in *The Brothers Karamazov*.

9

McCarthyism: An American Form of Political False Consciousness

McCarthyism represents a curious phenomenon in the ideological history of the United States. Although it belongs to a specific past, it is nevertheless a typically American form of political false consciousness. Its logical structure reveals some analogies with Stalinism, which is not very surprising when one compares the two ideologies theoretically.

McCarthyism thrust itself into the limelight after some notorious political trials that marked the final phase of Truman's presidency. The Alger Hiss case ended in 1950 with a prison sentence for one of Roosevelt's former aides at Yalta, charged with spying for the Soviets. Hiss contacted the communists at a time when this was neither prohibited, nor even considered to be in poor form. He may well have had some sympathy for the USSR which, at that time, was still an ally of the United States. Moreover, the charge of espionage depended, first and foremost, on the uncertain evidence provided by a disturbing personality, Whittaker Chambers. And the illustrious British jurist, Lord Jowitt, was quick to unveil the myth surrounding this evidence.[1]

The second of these trials involved Owen Lattimore, also a former Roosevelt aide, and an outstanding expert on Far Eastern affairs. He spent the greater part of his life in the Far East and had command of the Chinese and Mongol languages. As an advisor to Chiang Kai-Shek, he maintained cordial relations with the Generalissimo, whom he esteemed. However, this did not prevent him from diagnosing the immense corruption of the political structure in Kuomintang China. The abandonment of Nationalist China by the Truman administration, together with the former's collapse, remains one of the most mysterious chapters in postwar American history. Does this issue relate to the inevitable end of a regime condemned by its own corruption and dependent on the most massive American aid, or on the contrary, was it the price paid for carelessness, or even for the deliberate treason, of the Democrats in power? The answers to these questions will remain unknown until access is given to secret files. However, McCarthy did not hesitate to implicate Lattimore, who was influential in the State Department, as the "top Russian espionage agent in United States." As a result, Lattimore had to appear before the Un-American Activities Committee. He summed up his defense in his book *Ordeal by Slander*,[2] which remains a valuable source for the study of McCarthyism. This book is clearly written by a Roosevelt Democrat and not by an apologist of crypto-communism. While Lattimore might well have been mistaken in his opinions and advice, his anticommunism seems evident only insofar as liberalism and communism are considered to be antagonistic ideologies. Unlike Hiss, Lattimore did not suffer further prosecution but he remained suspect.

The "Dexter-White Affair" would have been the third of these "great scandals" were it not for the dramatic death of the main protagonist. Harry Dexter-White, a friend of Hiss and a close collaborator of Henry Morgenthau, Jr., seems to have been the real author of the "Morgenthau Plan," which aimed to reduce Germany to an exclusively agrarian economy. Elizabeth Bentley accused Dexter-White of having acted under direct orders from political circles in the USSR, for which Whittaker Chambers accused White of being a sympathizer and active member of a spy network. In his defense, White read an eloquent declaration of faith in American democracy to the Committee and died of exhaustion some days later (in 1948).

It was in the aftermath of these trials that a segment of the American public—which history will doubtless not confirm—became convinced that the Democrats were more or less conscious agents of Russian foreign policy. From then on, the foundations of McCarthyism were sufficiently institutionalized so that any personality from the American right could have assumed its leadership. McCarthy's own work, *The Fight for America*, provides an account—albeit somewhat incomplete—of these various trials.³ This book is written in the form of a catechism with questions and answers. It contains a summary of the Lattimore affair, glimpses of the activities of Dean Acheson and General George C. Marshall, as well as a plea *pro domo*. For McCarthy, Acheson was, to all intents and purposes, a communist sympathizer, and men like Truman or Marshall were "objectively" so. His critical judgment of the Marshall plan will not fail to interest the French, who still remember the communist criticisms of this very plan.

In contrast to other right-wing ideologies of this period, McCarthyism appeared to be a nonracist ideology. The Senator's two principal assistants were of Jewish origin and, moreover, his refusal to position himself on the Afro-American question was remarkably skilled. However, such an attitude may well have corresponded to electoral preoccupations, and it should be noted that while McCarthy was not overtly anti-Semitic, a majority of anti-Semites during that period, in the U.S. as well as in foreign countries, supported his ideas.⁴ This social fact is perhaps more significant than the senator's own personal opinions. It is possible, though, by no means, certain, that once in power, McCarthy would have followed the example of Mussolini and moved officially towards anti-Semitism.

In spite of the nonracist stance of McCarthy's official ideology, there is a common denominator with Hiterlism: an antiscientific (paranoid) interpretation of history. A sense of political frustration lies at the base of both McCarthyism and Hitlerism, in the common feeling of being "stabbed in the back" (*Dolchstoss*). For McCarthyism, the "stab in the back" came from the Democrats' "treason" in the Far East. This could be an instance of a form of antihistoricism common to all forms of totalitarian ideologies (e.g., *1984*), and a typical manifestation of a *conception policiére de l'Histoire* (a police-state attitude towards history), using to the term coined by Manes Sperber.⁵ Since the "collective ego" is deemed superior to all others, any failure can only be explained by some conspiracy. Here again, a distinct analogy between McCarthyism and Hitlerism seems appropriate.[6]

McCarthyism and Stalinism

At first glance, such a comparison would seem absurd: one cannot fruitfully compare a movement of the extreme right to one on the extreme left. However, scientific analysis should not be paralyzed by notions of "left-wing" and "right-wing," as they have lost any real meaning.[7] The analogy between McCarthyism and Stalinism results from the fact that they are both authoritarian ideologies, whether right or left being immaterial.

False Identification

Stalinist political (false) consciousness was characterized by the existence of curious "perverse equations," which are invariably unscientific, for example, "social fascism" or "Hitlero-Trotskyism." These are examples of the "false identities" central to Stalinist logic.[8] The existence of false identities presupposes a schematic (Manichean) conception of the political universe, analogous to the religious distinction between sacred and secular. Such a conception is essentially antidialectical and clashes with a doctrine which officially claims to be dialectical.

McCarthyism can be compared to Stalinist logic by virtue of the fact that it had its own system of "perverse equations." It is only in the ideological light of this leaning that Democratic statesmen, such as, among others, Dean Acheson, could be seen as genuine communist sympathizers.

Rejection of All Evolutionism (Antihistoricism)

Another common denominator between these two "ideologies" (in the Marxist-critical sense of this concept) lies in their antihistoricist attitudes. According to the brilliant and prophetic observations of the young Marx, the negation or arbitrary transformation of historical events ("Orwellization of the past," in my own terms) is one of the main features of ideological distortion. In Stalinist ideology, this rejection of historicity took two principal forms. On the one hand, Stalinist political consciousness refused to accept the evolution of society from an egalitarian society under Lenin into an authoritarian and hierarchical state under Stalin. This consciousness was thus "fixed" in the Russia of the beginning of the revolutionary period. This was the ideological mechanism by which one of the most conservative countries of that period could remain, for a long time, the point of crystallization and the universal symbol of the revolt against inequality and authority. Furthermore, this ideology refused to recognize the schism that had developed during this degradation of Marxism, as a dialectical doctrine of demystification, into Stalinism, as a reified ideology of political mystification.

This ideological refusal to change can be perceived at the level of individual evolution, too. In the light of Stalinist ideology, Trotsky was never the Lazare Carnot of the Russian October revolution. In the French communist daily *L'Humanité* (September 19, 1949), one could read that as early as 1943, "Tito conspired with the British and the Americans." This critique illustrates typical McCarthyist reasoning: in 1943 British and Americans were allied with Russia, consequently Tito was perfectly justified in his right to "conspire" with them. This is a significant example of "presentification of historical duration," that is, an arbitrary projection of present categories into the past. This involves a spatialization of time analogous to what may be observed in schizophrenia.[9]

The McCarthyist conception of history similarly contains a sui generis structuring of historical time. Owen Lattimore, a lucid observer (and principal victim) of McCarthyism clearly pointed out this tendency in the charge that his opponent was a "master of timing."[10] Put another way, this "mastering of the organization of time" is a geometrization of temporal experience. McCarthy's works include several examples of this "time mastery." Here are two typical examples.

In *The Fight for America* (p. 23), we read that "Before Russia was recognized by the United States in 1933, Dean Acheson was paid by the Soviet Union to act as Stalin's lawyer in this country." In 1933, when that happened, the relations between the

USSR and the U.S. were far from hostile. Moreover, it is absurd to blame a statesman in his sixties for his behavior as a young man. In their youths, Mussolini, Pilsudsky, and Koestler were all leftist militants. McCarthy was obviously antagonistic to the idea of personal historicity.

In the same work,[11] McCarthy accused the State Department of having ordered, in 1945, the liberation of Klausen, a member of the famous Sorge network in Japan, who had received a life sentence from the Japanese judicial system. However, in 1945, the USSR was a military ally of the United States which means that the Americans could not, in all decency, sanction an act of espionage perpetrated in wartime by an ally against an enemy. *The Fight for America* contains several other examples of such "time mastery." It appears that McCarthyism adopted the same temporality deployed by Stalinist ideology.

The two principal features, thus, of "ideological distortion are (a) false identification (perverse equation), and (b) antihistoricism. Both can be detected in the worldview of McCarthyism that appears, in this light, to be both a genuine mirror-image of Stalinism and another textbook case of false consciousness. Political false consciousness can be frequently identified as "failure-oriented behavior" (*Conduite d'échec*). The most significant illustration of this fact is presented by the racism of German Third Reich. The expulsion of outstanding scholars of Jewish origin from the scientific life of the country was highly instrumental in their own military defeat. To some extent, the same holds true for McCarthyism in the United States; as political false consciousness, it was a maladjusted form of anticommunism, broadly responsible both for the paradoxical lack of popularity of the United States in postwar Western Europe, and for the strange popularity of Stalinism in some intellectual circles of these same countries during that period.

Notes

1. W.A.J. Jowitt, *The Strange Case of Alger Hiss* (London: Hodder & Stoughton, 1953); see also Lucien Martin (J. Gabel), "L'Affaire Hiss", *Esprit* (Paris), May 1984.
2. Owen Lattimore, *Ordeal by Slander* (Boston: Little Brown & Co., 1950).
3. McCarthy, *The Fight for America* (New York: Devin-Adair Co., 1952).

McCarthyism: Political False Consciousness

4. In France the right-wing (anti-Semitic) reviews such as *Rivarol, Ecrits de Paris, Défense de l'Europe* (run by Maurice Bardéche) were all favorable to the senator's ideas.
5. Manes Sperber, "La conception policiére de l'Histoire," *Preuves* (Paris), February 1954.
6. The concept of *Dolchstoss* (stab in the back) by Jewish and leftist opponents, portrayed as the unique cause of the German defeat in 1918, was one of the central themes of Nazism.
7. This text was published in 1954. History has confirmed this point of view.
8. For other examples of "false identities," refer to chapter—of the present volume and to Gabel, *Mannheim and Hungarian Marxism* (New Brunswick, NJ: Transaction Publishers, 1991), pp. 21, 23, cf. the interesting point of view of the Hungarian Marxist philosopher, Bela Fogarasi.
9. In the "morbid geometrism" of E. Minkowski. See also the phenomenon of "invalidation of happened facts of (*invalidacion de lo acaecido*) pointed out in schizophrenia by Honorio Delgado. For details refer to chapter 7 of the present volume.
10. Owen Lattimore, *Ordeal*, p. 208.
11. McCarthy, *The Fight for America*, p.58.

10

Eugene Minkowski and the Problem of Alienation

Some decades ago, Professor Henri Baruk together with Eugene Minkowski—the most outstanding French psychiatrist of Jewish origin—elaborated a "test *Tsedek*" to evaluate the moral conscience of a person. From an exclusively scientific point of view, the idea behind this test is not above criticism. Nevertheless, its authors deserve credit for having drawn the public's attention to this interesting and in fact, little known (beyond traditionalist Jewish milieus) moral concept from the Old Testament. According to Robert Sommer, the *Tsedek* represents "a kind of mixture of justice and charity," whereas Professor Baruk sees it as "a cornerstone of Hebrew monotheism."[1] I do not share the latter's opinion on this last point. Philosophers such as Plotinus and Epictetus were, without knowing this particular term, genuine *Tsadikim*,[2] and Emperor Antoninus Pius was probably the unique historical example of a *Tsadik* on a throne. The concept of *Tsedek* cannot be considered as the monopoly of any particular religion; it belongs to the moral inheritance of humanity as a whole.

I did not have the opportunity to discuss the problems of this test with my late *maître à penser*, Minkowski, though I would not be surprised to learn that he had doubts and was even critical towards the research of his famous colleague. His Bergsonian philosophical sensibility was almost entirely incompatible with the idea of quantifiable moral data. However, he did much more than simply contribute to the theoretical elaboration and practical application of this test; he was a living example of a *tsadik*. He was a genuine sage in both the Biblical and Greek senses of that term—modest, courteous, and obliging, by the unanimous opinion of all who enjoyed his company. Today, in the race for honors, modesty is an unforgivable weakness, and it was his modesty that was to a large extent responsible for the paradoxical fact that in spite of his worldwide reputation, Minkowski occupied a modest place in the French academic hierarchy. He was never appointed to a professorship.

Are we entitled to speak of Minkowski's "failure?" The question could perhaps be raised. Some years before his death, in a lecture delivered in Paris at the College Philosophique, Minkowski himself evoked his "failed career." In considering this statement, we should however take into account his modesty and the depressed state of an unconsolable widower.[3] At the seminar "Psychiatry and Existence" (Cerisy la Salle, September 1989), Professor Arthur Tatossian opened the session with a lecture entitled, "Eugéne Minkowski, or the Missed Opportunity."[4] Minkowski was, doubtless, a well-known and respected personality, but this respect was directed more to the nobleness of his character than to his outstanding scientific and philosophical achievements. His funeral in 1972 was a solemn event, but the funeral orations delivered on this occasion paid more homage to the heroic First World War volunteer than to the brilliant thinker. One last and significant fact : Minkowski's name is not even mentioned in the first edition of the monumental *Dictionnaire des Philosophes*, which magnanimously allots entire pages to unknown young philosophers.[5] He is frequently quoted in scientific publications but, as perceptively observed by Professor Tatossian, these quotations are generally not the source of independent research work. Furthermore, according to Tatossian, Minkowski was "a thinker without disciples and without a master"; this sentiment would probably not have displeased Minkowski.

It is a fact that he had more admirers than genuine disciples. For example, in France, while the disciples of Jacques Lacan and Henri Ey are legion, the late Dr. Paul Citrome[6] and myself are perhaps the only psychopathologists who claim allegiance to Minkowski's school. I myself have also worked as a sociologist under the influence of Georg Lukács. This fact is by no means paradoxical, for there is a curious and significant convergence between the philosophical approach of Minkowski and that of Lukács. In my view, Minkowski is the Lukács of morbid consciousness and Lukács is the Minkowski of class consciousness. This formulation may appear shocking or even blasphemous to some, but we must keep in mind that there were two Lukácses: on the one hand, a man of the party driven by the demands of militancy to regrettable intellectual compromises, and on the other hand, an outstanding dialectical and de-alienating thinker, ostracized as such by ideological currents with good reasons to dislike the "logic of freedom" entailed by dialectics. Hungary, the first communist society to get rid of the Stalinist ideological tyranny, was consistently logical with itself in rehabilitating this second Lukács, who became the key reference for a whole generation of nonconformist intellectuals. The idea of a kinship between a great theorist of alienation (Minkowski) and an outstanding theorist of de-alienation (Lukács) is by no means paradoxical. Both Minkowski and Lukács have benefited from Bergson's seminal work in dialectics. This influence was overtly claimed by Minkowski, but was obscured for political reasons by Lukács and his followers.[7]

Bergson and Octave Hamelin are doubtless the outstanding dialectical thinkers of French origin. Bergson's remarkable essay *Le Rire* presents, without employing Marxist terminology, a severe indictment of social reification in Lukács's sense. The universe of reification described by Lukács in the principal chapter of *History and Class Consciousness*, is characterized by the spatialization of duration.[8] The same holds true both for the inner world (*Eigenwelt*) of morbid rationalism characterized by Minkowski as the polar region of intellectual "antitheses,"[9] and for the "Manichean" political consciousness (false consciousness). We have here the elements of a future synthesis in which the concept of morbid rationalism may extend beyond the boundary of psychopathology and claim its place in political science and in the philosophy of culture.

It may be wondered whether or not Minkowski was aware of these potential extrapolations of his psychopathological theory. I beleive that he was. In a conversation that took place between us around 1950, he stated that features of morbid rationalism were present in different aspects of contemporary political discourse. I suppose that he was alluding to Stalinism, then at the zenith of its influence, whose prestige, enhanced by the victory of Soviet Russia over the Third Reich, exerted a genuine fascination over some of the most brilliant intellectuals of the time.[10] Now it seems unquestionable that the logic underlying Stalinist ideology was a very close kin to the "morbid rationalism" pointed out in psychopathology by Minkowski. In his article "Communism and Religion,"[11] Raymond Aron characterized this form of ideo-logic (communism) as a "logical delusion" (*délire logique*) and, according to Emmanuel Todd, "the analogies between the structure of ideological fixation and that of the schizophrenic universe are astounding."[12] Let us conclude by pointing to the fact that the French daily press of recent decades teems with articles evoking "political schizophrenia."[13] This mental illness has become a key concept of cultural philosophy and, it seems clear that Minkowski's work was the point of departure, perhaps even the trigger, for such a development. Had it remained at the Bleulerian stage, the concept of "dementia praecox" would probably have never known such a triumph.

Minkowski seldom used the term "dialectics" and never in its Hegelian or Marxist sense. Nevertheless, along with Bergson, he was a brilliant dialectician. Since Hegel, we have been aware of the fact that, in the field of logic, the problem of dialectics is linked to that of "identity." According to Adorno, "dialectics is a rigorous consciousness of non-identity."[14] This formulation has several consequences, some of which concern the problem of morbid consciousness. A reified and dedialectized form of thinking implies, as a consequence, a form of logic in which the identificatory function, pointed out in epistemology by Emile Meyerson, prevails.[15] Silvano Arieti calls attention to a genuine "orgy of identifications" in the psychology of these cases. The same holds true for ideological distortion,[16] a fact which confirms the schizophrenic character of political alienation, or false consciousness. While this idea of morbid hypertrophy of identificatory functions in schizophrenia is central in Arieti's work, one may still ask whether Minkowski was not the first author to underscore its importance.[17] Here, a footbridge seems to link the morbid rationalism of Minkowski, interpreted as a pathological form of reified and dedialectized logic, with a psychoanalytic theory in which the concept of identification occupies a significant place. This fact is relevant since Minkowski, along with Henri Baruk, was somewhat reserved in his enthusiasm for Freud's theories. But the behavior of public ideas sometimes reminds us of children who, in the choice of their friendship or love relations, are not concerned with the preferences of their parents. It is not certain that the marriage of phenomenological psychopathology with psychoanalysis would be blessed by the former's father (Minkowski).[18] The conceptions of Arieti are similar to those of Minkowski but are bereft of any hostility towards Freudian theories. Hence, they are a link between these two conceptions, which is also true for the theories of Gisela Pankow.[19] Let us conclude by quoting my late friend, Igor A. Caruso, (who, along with Leopold Szondi, was the most consistently dialectical among the best representatives of psychoanalysis), who defined psychoanalysis as "a dialectical reaction against reification in psychology."[20]

Last but not least, the theory of Minkowski involves a criticism of utopian consciousness. This point is perhaps the most remarkable illustration of the "extra-psychiatric" pertinance of his theories, since the "utopian phenomenon" is one of the important features of our everyday life. Some decades ago, Herbert Marcuse (as well as Karl Mannheim) predicted the "end of utopias." This forecast proved sound, for recently we have witnessed a genuine historical earthquake—"utopias" are collapsing one after the other.

In his remarkable work *L'Utopie et les Utopies*, the French philosopher Raymond Ruyer presented a meticulous analysis of utopian consciousness.[21] His analysis shows that many features that characterize the *Eigenwelt* of Minkowski's morbid rationalism are present in the framework of utopian consciousness. Like ideological consciousness, utopian consciousness is reified, adialectical and ahistoric: it is a consciousness of *avenir chose* in the words of Simone de Beauvoir.[22] It is thus not surprising to meet sometimes psychotic "utopians" in mental hospitals. One typical case was presented by Dr. Jean-Marie Delassus,[23] whose work contains several references to Minkowski's theories.[24] This curious case is by no means an exception. The rationalities of both utopian consciousness and ideological consciousness appear to be, in the light of such clinical observations, forms of morbid rationalism and geometrism.[25]

I shall conclude this memorial to neglected thinkers by recalling the forgotten work of a French sociologist of Polish origin, Victor Zoltowski (1900–1970), who interpreted history as a cycle of periods of spatialization and temporalization.[26] The "spatializing periods" described by Zoltowski can be read, in the light of Minkowski's theory, as periods of morbid geometrism. These are characterized by an exacerbation of social and international antagonism, periods of political alienation in the sense of the "Hungaro-Marxists" Mannheim and Paul Szende.[27] According to Binswanger, temporality is a "bearer of love," whereas spatiality is often a locus of aggression, as shown in the often spatialized overtones of totalitarian discourse.

Did Minkowski represent "a missed opportunity?" Professor Tatossian's statement stands the test only if we exclusively consider his personal career, but not if we regard the rich openings created by his work. While Minkowski had few disciples during his life, it is possible that he will have more in the coming decades. Like George Orwell, whose philosophy is close to his,[28] Minkowski belongs to the category of authors who receive more tribute after their death than during their lifetime. In the future, Minkowski will probably be recognized, not only as an outstanding psychopathologist, but also as a key contributor to cultural philosophy.

Notes

1. Henri Baruk, *Civilization Hebraique et Sciences de l'Homme* (Paris, 1965), with a preface by Robert Sommer. See p. 9 (Sommer) and p.146 (Baruk).
2. In Hebrew *Tsedek* = Justice, *Tsadik* = the Just; *Tsadikim* = the plural of *Tsadik*.
3. Minkowski's wife, who died in 1950, was a well-known specialist of the Rorschach test.
4. Arthur Tatossian, "Eugéne Minkowski ou l'occasion manquée in Pierre Fedida et Jacques Schotte." *Psychiatrie et existence* (Paris: Jérome Millon Publisher, 1991), p. 11–22.
5. *Dictionnaire des Philosophes*, published in 1984 (Paris P.U.F.) under the direction of Denis Huisman. Our statement holds true for the first and second edition of this monumental work; the third edition in preparation at

the present moment contains an excellent article on Minkowski by David Frank Allen.
6. The late Paul Citrome deported during the Second World War and author of interesting articles on suicide in concentration camps, was a personal friend of Minkowski; they were co-authors of several publications.
7. The question of the "dialecticity" of Bergsonism is a complicated philosophical as well as a sociological problem. Stalinists criticized Bergson as an idealist and as a "destroyer of reason." In his well known work *Die Zerstörung der Vernunft* (Berlin, 1955), published in the Stalinist period of his career, Lukács is severely critical of Bergson; he even invoked the critical views of the charlatan Lysenko against Bergson.
Nevertheless, the early writings of Lukács prior to 1919 and republished in 1977 (Lukács, *Ifjukori müvek*, Budapest: Magvetö Publishers) contain views on Bergson bereft of any hostility. *Tempora mutantur*. The left-wing Hungarian intelligentsia of this time perceived Bergsonism as a philosophy of desalienation because of its unquestionably dialectical character, and also because of its French origin. For these progressive (and frequently masonic) milieus, the Republic of Combes and of Waldeck-Rousseau was an example of "realized utopia," as was Soviet Russia in the eyes of the "sympathizers" in our French postwar period.
8. "Therefore, we should not say that one man's hour is worth another man's hour, but rather that one man during an hour is worth just as much as another man during an hour. Time is everything, man is nothing; he is at the most the incarnation of time. Quality no longer matters. Quantity alone decides everything: hour for hour, day for day…Thus time sheds its qualitative, variable, flowing nature; it freezes into an exactly delimited, quantifiable continuum filled with quantifiable 'things' (the reified, mechanically objectified 'performance' of the worker, wholly separated from his total human personality): in short, it becomes space." Lukács, *History and Class Consciousness*, translated by Rodney Livingstone (London: Merlin Press, 1971), pp. 89–90.
Bergson's influence on Lukács is obvious. I cannot enter into the details of this question; but let us remember only the well known fact that Lukács was first and foremost a philosopher of dialectical totality; as for Bergson, the importance of this dialectical category in his conceptions was underscored by an outstanding connoisseur of his system, Vladimir Jankelevitch, *Henri Bergson* (Paris: P.U.F., 1959), chapter 1.
9. See Minkowski, "Contribution à l'étude de la pensée et de l'attitude autistes", *L'Encéphale* (Paris, April 1923), p. 16. Seen in the light of this interpretation, the "morbid rationalism" of Minkowski appears not as a symptom of "excessive rationality" (which would place it among the "destroyers of reason" in Lukács' terms), but as a symptom of the reification and dedialectization of rationality.
10. In his important work *Les Aventures de la Dialectique* (Paris, 1955), the outstanding French philosopher Maurice Merleau-Ponty characterized Soviet Marxism as a "marxism of antithesis": "Now the psychical universe (*Eigenwelt*) of schizophrenia according to Minkowski is the "polar region of intellectual antithesis." I perceive here a confirmation of the schizophrenic feature of political alienation as proposed in my *False Consciousness*, (Oxford: Basil Blackwell Publisher, 1975).
11. In *La Revue de Paris* (May 1955).

12. E. Todd, *Le fou et le prolétaire* (Paris: Laffont, 1979), p. 32.
13. Here are some typical examples: Louis Pauwels, "La schizophrénie nationale" *Le Figaro* (March 8, 1978); Emmanuel Leroy Ladurie, "Totalitarisme et schizophrénie," *Le Figaro* (February 20, 1979). In an article published in the Paris daily *Le Monde* (February 14, 1957), Maurice Duverger speaks of "political schizophrenia." These examples testify to the active presence of Minkowski's ideas in the current political debate.
14. Theodor W. Adorno, *Dialectique négative* (Paris: Payot, 1978), p. 13.
15. Emile Meyerson, *Identité et réalité* (Paris, 1908).
16. See Silvano Arieti, *Interpretation of Schizophrenia* (New York: Basic Books, 1974), p. 232 and *passim*. Representatives of the Hungarian Marxist School, such as Bela Fogarasi, Paul Szende and Georg Nador, underscored the importance of "unwarranted identification" ("perverse equation" according to the term coined by Alan Dieckhoff) as a factor of ideological distortion. For details see Gabel, *Mannheim and Hungarian Marxism*, (New Brunswick, NJ: Transaction Publishers, 1992), part I, chapter 2.
17. See Minkowski's article of 1923, p. 9. According to the Polish-American philosopher Alfred Korzybski "Psychiatry, and common experience, teach us, that in heavy cases of dementia praecox we find the most highly developed identification"; A. Korzbyski, *Science and Sanity* (The International Non-Aristotelian Publishing Company, 1980), p. 568. The first edition of this astonishing work dates back to 1933. It is regrettable that Minkowski's article which had already referred to the same phenomenon in 1923, is absent from Korzbyski's bibliography.
18. My late friend Nicolas Abraham (1919–1975), French psychoanalyst of Hungarian origin, supported the idea of such a synthesis in a lecture delivered at the symposium, "Genesis and Structure," which took place in 1959 in Cerisy la Salle (France). See. N. Abraham, "Réflections phénoménologiques sur les implications structurelles et génétiques de la psychanalyse" in *Entretiens sur les notions de genése et structure* (The Hague: Mouton & Cie Publishers,1959).
19. The psychotherapy advocated in these cases by Mrs. Gisela Pankow (*Dynamische Strukturierung in der Psychose* [Bern and Stuttgart: Huber Verlag, 1957] entails the reconstruction of the "concrete totality" of the psychotic's personality along with the therapeutic temporalization of existence—imprisoned by pure spatiality. This theory is a link between Freud's and Minkowski's theories; for details see *False Consciousness* (Basil Blackwell Publishers, 1975), p. 228 (an abstract of Mrs. Pankow's theory).
20. Igor A. Caruso, "Notes sur la "réification" et la sexualité," in *Psyché* (Paris) 74, (Dec., 1972), p. 778.
21. Raymond Ruyer, *L'Utopie, les utopies* (Paris: P.U.F., 1950), (Minkowski quoted, p. 41); J-J. Wunenburger, *L'Utopie ou la crise de l'imaginaire* (Paris: Editions Universitaires, 1979), p. 181 (chapter on "morbid rationalism").
22. Simone de Beauvoir, *Pour une morale de l'ambiguité* (Paris, 1947), p. 165.
23. Jean Marie Delassus, *Contribution à l'étude des délires schizophréniques: L'oeuvre et l'utopie de "G"*. M.D. Doctoral dissertaton at the Medical Faculty of Nancy (France) Nov. 12, 1965.
24. A virtually identical case was published in 1952 by the present author, "Délire politique chez un paranoide *L'Evolution Psychiatrique* (April-June 1952), reprinted under a different title (*Rêveries utopiques chez un schizophréne*) in the volume *Ideologies*, (Paris: Ed. Anthropos, 1974), p. 313 ff, and in

Gabel, *Formen der Entfremdung* (Frankfurt: Fischer Verlag, 1964), pp. 38–52.
25. Ideology is a form of morbid *rationalism*, while utopia is first and foremost akin to morbid *geometrism*. The patent kinship of these concepts in Minkowski's work serves as a corrective to the weaker kinship implied by Mannheim in *Ideology and Utopia*.
26. Victor Zoltowski, "La fonction sociale du temps et de l'espace: Contribution à la théorie expérimentale de la connaissance," *Revue d'Histoire économique et sociale*, vol. XXVI:2 (1940–1941).
27. The "Hungaro-Marxist" Paul Szende pointed to an alternation between periods of mystification and demystification in history (*Verhüllungsperioden und Enthüllungsperioden*). This alternation corresponds to that pointed out by Zoltowski.
28. The atmosphere of *1984* is very close to that of Minkowski's "morbid rationalism." The unquestionable de-alienating tendency of Orwell's novel confirms that of Minkowski's work and of Bergson's philosophy. The Hungarian left-wing readers of Bergson's in the period prior to 1919, who saw Bergsonism as a doctrine of de-alienation (Valeria Dienes among others), were quite correct in their insights.

11

Effet Pervers and False Consciousness

Although of Marxist origin, the theory of false consciousness (*falsches Bewusstsein*) was marginalized for a long time, both by "official" Marxism, which feared its possible use in a critique of left-wing totalitarianism, and by Western scholars because of its Marxist origins. In spite of the strong preference displayed by French intellectuals of the same period for the concept of alienation—closely connected theoretically with the notion of false consciousness—it was only in 1962 that a book appeared on that subject.[1] In fact, the very few references to Lukács's essential work, *History and Class Consciousness*, in philosophical and political writings, can be associated with this phenomenon. This work of the gifted Hungarian thinker represents a seminal contribution to the general theory of false consciousness, and an anticipated criticism of Stalinist bureaucracy, both mediated by a critical analysis of reification.

A renewed interest in this problem can now be observed in France and, even paradoxically, in liberal circles. The French liberal daily *Le Figaro* (more or less close to the political ideas of Raymond Aron) published an article about "the dangers of false consciousness."[2] In January 1982, in the same daily, B. Bonilauri, wrote about "the false consciousness which underlies the perception of Soviet realities."[3] This once marginalized component of Marxist philosophy is slowly regaining prominence, and is no longer exclusively associated with Marxist analysis. Critical

---

Prepared for the Congress of Sociology; translated from French by Zoltan Tar.

references to it are found in the works of several French philosophers such as Raymond Ruyer, Paul Ricoeur, and Raymond Boudon.[4] This chapter seeks to demonstrate that the notion of false consciousness is part of causal connections in some determinate relations. It can thus operate as an explanatory principle in historical research.

The concept of explanation is particularly complex in sociology as Gurvitch[5] repeatedly warned concerning the epistemological difficulties peculiar to it. However, a critical analysis of these difficulties would divert us from our present goal. Instead, what I want to show here is that, for instance, racism as a form of false consciousness can be considered one of the main causes of the German defeat in 1945. Of course, I am not the first to advance such a notion. It is well known that the expulsion of distinguished Jewish scientists from Nazi Germany was instrumental in its military defeat. While evident in this case, such a theoretical claim is less so in several other cases, becoming more difficult to legitimate as an explanatory principle in historical research.

As already stated, the notion of false consciousness that underlies our analysis has previously been analyzed under the influences of Lukács and Mannheim.[6] The main elements of this approach are the following: (1) Correlativity of the notion of false consciousness with that of ideology (Engels); that is, ideology is the theoretical expression of the egocentrical distortion of committed political consciousness. (2) Correlation of the notion of false consciousness with that of reification, whereby they become complementary. Reification is thus an inherent pitfall of all studies of human and historical reality and must be resisted in order to avoid the emergence of false consciousness concerning these areas of study. Between these Bergsonian speculations and the Marxian position, there is a much smaller gap than previously assumed. (3) Society-blindness and history-blindness of ideological thinking: "ideology is either an erroneous conception or an absolute abstraction of history," wrote the young Marx, anticipating the leitmotif of Orwell's *1984*.

The problem of false consciousness is closely connected with that of alienation in both its social and clinical aspects. Minkowski[7] detected, under the term *rationalisme et géométrisme morbides,* a psychopathological syndrome characterized by disequilibrium between spatial and temporal dimensions, but favoring the former. This syndrome can be interpreted in Marxist terms as a manifestation of reified consciousness. Thus interpreted, schizophrenia appears as a form of alienation in both the clinical and Marxist conceptions of the term.

The observations constitute the link with the hypothesis of the schizophrenic structure of political alienation (ideologization) just proposed. As Scott Warren pointed out:

> Gabel's unique contribution is that he goes beyond drawing a mere analogy between certain kinds of psychological disorders and the disorders of our social and political consciousness. Rather, he suggests an actual structural "identity" of schizophrenia and ideology—as two forms of reified, false consciousness. His work is replete with appeals to clinical and sociological data to support his particular claim. This suggestion of a schizophrenic structure of false consciousness and ideology has two major implications for Marxism. First, it shows how alienation as a schizophrenic form of consciousness is not determined by economic reification alone, but by reification as a total and independent mode of existence. This vitiates any overly materialist or economic Marxism, as well as any view that false consciousness is simply a matter of "content . . . " Second, in so far as Marxism, is a critique of ideology and of false social consciousness, it is also inherently a critical theory of deranged thought. Hence it can contribute to the development of psychopathology.[8]

An important consequence of the foregoing consideration is that false consciousness involves to some degree what Levy-Bruhl called *imperméabilité à l'expérience,* analogous to one symptom of schizophrenia, known as "autism." This viewpoint is important for political psychology since it explains that, in some circumstances, false consciousness may appear to be the source of repeated failures in life.

Recent political history offers two "identical" examples of false consciousness: Stalinism and racism. A critical analysis of the former is not our present purpose;[9] we shall limit ourselves instead to Orwell's famous literary work *1984.* In our view, Orwell's book is not simply a utopian novel but also a brilliant and complete critical analysis of a form of false consciousness, analogous to that which prevailed in the Moscow trials before the Second World War. We can find in this novel the three principal elements of false consciousness: (1) a "presentification" of historical duration (*durée historique*) characteristic of the schizophrenic spatialization of time, according to Minkowski's conceptions; (2) a repression of sexual relations,[10] and (3) political autism. As a result, no professional psychiatrist can deny that the world described in *1984* is a schizophrenic one.

Similarly, racist consciousness is also a typical form of false consciousness. In racist ideology, *le racial domine le social* ("the racial dominates the social"),[11] as a form of history-blindness in Lukács's terms,[12] and as a reified perception of presumably inferior ethnic groups. Adorno suggested that anti-Semitism involves the inability to experience Jews as individuals. Rather, each Jew is seen and reacted to as a sort of *sample specimen of the stereotyped reified image of the group*.[13] This statement holds true for all forms of racist perceptions of discriminated minorities.

Racist false consciousness within Nazi ideology was a factor of political and military maladjustment at four levels:

- as a cause for the exclusion of highly competent Jewish scientists from German scientific life;
- by casting suspicion on atomic physics, qualified by some Nazi scientist as "Jewish Physics";[14]
- by concealing the true historical significance of the German-Soviet pact of 1939;[15]
- by inducing German occupation authorities to discriminate racially against the minorities in the occupied areas of Soviet Russia which were at the beginning quite willing to collaborate. Considering in the present historical perspective the following course of events and, in particular, the participation of Jewish scientists in the war achievements of the anti-Nazi coalition, we may assert with some conviction that a militarist—but not racist—Germany (as the Hohenzollern Empire) would have won the Second World War. This is by no means an original statement. But it clearly shows the possibility of establishing a chain of comprehensive relations between reification of consciousness, ideological distortion and political maladjustment in an important historical event. The German defeat of 1945 may be considered as an *effet pervers*—that is, "an unanticipated consequence of purposive social action" (Merton) of Nazi racism.[16]

The example of racist consciousness as a form of false consciousness and a source of political maladjustment (*conduite d'échec*) is a telling example, since the rich literature on racism allows for a detailed analysis of the relations that exist between the different elements of the historical causal chain. Although a detailed and complete analysis of the two following instances—the influence of Japanese policies on decolonization and the murder in 1881 of Tsar Alexander II of Russia—is outside my competence. These events remain, however, particularly important for our thesis. The first clearly illustrates the correlativity of the *effet pervers* with false consciousness, while the second shows the importance of society-blindness at the origin of both. From 1905 until 1942, the Nippon Empire imposed a series of humiliations on Western "imperialistic" powers. However, in spite of its final failure, this policy was highly instrumental in triggering the historical process of decolonization. But the leading Japanese statesmen of that period, who acted in close partnership with imperialist Britain and, later, with racist Germany, certainly did not perceive their own political action as an antiimperialist expansion. Hegel would have appreciated this example as a fine illustration of his theory of the *List der Vernunft* (ruse of reason). We cannot enter here into the detailed analysis of the ideologies which underlay the Japanese expansion in that period. The only firm statement we can formulate is that, in this historical example, *effet pervers* and false consciousness go together. Marx stated very clearly the issue of false consciousness in these terms: We can no more judge a person according to the idea he or she holds of himself or herself, than we can judge a period of upheavals based purely on the idea that people have about it.

The objective of the members of the Narodnaya Volya (the People's Will), who killed Tsar Alexander II in 1881, was to alleviate the pressure of autocracy in Russia. However, this action resulted, on the contrary, in a palpable increase of this pressure under Alexander III and his minister Pobedonostsev. The political philosophy implicit in their action is akin to the methodological individualism advocated in France by Boudon. They associated the elimination of a man personifying autocracy with the fallacious hope of destroying autocracy itself. Reflection on the sociological mechanisms of the autocratic institution would have shown the dangerous errors of this reasoning. Society-blindness in a bold political action thus resulted into an

180   Ideologies and the Corruption of Thought

effet pervers which for several decades influenced unfavorably the destiny of the Russian Empire. This aspect of the problem—role of society-blindness in the production of *effets pervers*—will be manifest in our analysis of relations between the latter and utopian consciousness.

In *Ideology and Utopia*, Mannheim states that utopian consciousness is a form of false consciousness. The decisive common denominator between ideology and utopia is that both involve the possibility of false consciousness. The approach of Raymond Ruyer is complementary to that of Mannheim[17] although Ruyer does not use the term false consciousness (which was accepted by academic circles in France a few decades later). And it is by no means fortuitous that Ruyer would later be one of the first non-Marxist theoreticians to be interested in this problem. Similarly, the notion of *effet pervers* is equally absent from Ruyer's vocabulary during that period, although we can detect in his description of utopian consciousness the principal elements which permit us to characterize it as a form of false consciousness:

- antihistoricism illustrated by his statement: "*L'histoire glisse sur l'espirit des utopistes comme l'eau sur les plumes d'un canard.*"[18]
- antidialectical orientation ("*L'utopie ... est aux antipodes par son academisme d'une conception dialectique des choses.*")[19]
- an illusion of unlimited power ("*illusion de toute puissance*," or a form of rationalism disconnected from life).

All these characteristics of utopian thinking are present in the clinical picture of the above-mentioned variant of schizophrenia detected by Minkowski.[20] But utopia is equally characterized by its tendency to neglect secondary and composite effects.[21] Using a different terminology, we have tried to describe here the composition of the *effet pervers*. Utopian consciousness appears in this light as a schizophrenic form of false consciousness characterized by history and society blindness, by an opposition to dialectical forms of thinking,[22] and by an inability to account for the *effet pervers*. The logical coherence of these factors is more evident here than in the foregoing example.

The *effets pervers* of egalitarian utopianism are well known. Extreme forms of egalitarian ideology result in practical applications that often lead to new, different and more severe forms of inequality. This is what happened among the different *nomenklaturas* of socialist countries.[23] But egalitarian utopias also operate at the level of an intermediary state between macrosociology and microsociology, that is, as reform attempts seeking to alleviate certain inequalities without pretending to reorganize society as a whole. In this case, the *perverse effects* generated by false consciousness consist either in a nonhistorical perception of the issue or in sociological Daltonism. The protection of tenants (*Mieterschutz*) by the socialist municipality in Vienna before the war aimed, in principle, at easing the hardships of poorer people so that property owners were discouraged to lend their flats. However, this measure resulted in an *effet pervers*, that is, a crisis whose characteristic was to encourage people with enough resources to buy their flat. This reform was also aimed at providing an equal pension to all beneficiaries regardless of the work performed during active life, while preserving nevertheless an inequality of salaries. It is, of course, legitimate that an eminent physician should receive a higher retribution than a school teacher on the basis of the fact that their respective contribution to collective prosperity had been unequal. But in retirement, their contribution to that social prosperity becomes null for both, which, in a sense, might justify the uniformity of pension pay received by all retired workers. This view can be defended in an extra-historical perspective. However, a more historical approach to the problem would bring to light the *effet pervers* which would inevitably result: competent people seduced by higher salaries in the private sector or in foreign countries would desert the public sector.

Such examples could be multiplied. It is sufficient to say that, according to the definition presented in this paper, false consciousness consists in the systematic ignorance of the historical or sociological dimension of facts; that is, in a nondialectical approach to a problem. This also applies to most *effets pervers*, and is the reason why the more adequate approach to a phenomenon is not, as emphasized by Boudon, methodological individualism, but *dialectical sociologism* (in Marx's or Durkheim's analyses). The notion *effet de composition* mostly used as synonymous with *effet pervers* implicitly contains a reference to the notion of *totalité dialectique*.

False consciousness and *effet pervers* are therefore corollary notions. False consciousness can often be criticized for ignoring the resulting *effets pervers*, the consequences of an ahistorical, nondialectical perception of an historical and dialectical reality. This corollarity of dialectics, false consciousness and *effet pervers* is clearly illustrated in our example concerning Nazi racism. It is also exemplified by the analysis of utopian consciousness emerging out of the thesis developed by Mannheim, Bloch, and Ruyer.

If we agree with Boudon that the *effet pervers* is often, if not always, a motto of social change, we could also assume that false consciousness plays the same role. It has been said that history advances in a mask. *Effet pervers* and false consciousness are two aspects of the mask it bears when it advances and, more often, when it regresses.

Notes

1. H. Lefevbre and N. Guterman, *La Conscience Mystifiee* (Paris: NRF, 1936), reprinted in 1979, by Sycamore Publishers.
2. Written by Pascal Salin (October 28, 1982).
3. "*La fausse conscience qui préside dans les pays occidentaux à la perception des réalitiés soviétiques.*"
4. For instance, Professor Boudon finds the theory of false consciousness "confused"; *La place du désordre* (Paris, 1984), p. 61.
5. Georges Gurvitch, "La Crise de L'Explication en Sociologie" in his *Vocation actuelle de la sociology* (Paris: PUF, 1969), vol II, p. 62 ff.
6. Elaborated in my *Fausse Conscience*, (Paris: Editions Minuit, 1962).
7. In his classic book, *La Schizophrénie*, published in 1927.
8. See Scott Warren, "Gabel" in Robert Gorman (ed), *Biographical Dictionary of Neo-Marxism* (Westport, CT: Greenwood Press, 1985), p. 157.
9. See chapter 8 of present volume.
10. This can also be found in both Wilhelm Reich's and Herbert Marcuse's analysis.
11. Colette Guillaumin, "Characteres Specifiques de l'Ideologie raciste," *Cahiers Internationaux de Sociologie*, vol.III (1972), p. 265.
12. G. Lukacs, *Die Zerstorung der Vernunft* (Berlin, 1955), p. 342., translated as *Destruction of Reason*.
13. Theodor Adorno, et al., *The Authoritarian Personality* (New York: Harper, 1951), p. 94.
14. See the memoirs of Albert Speer, *Au Coeur du IIIe Reich* (Paris: Fayard, 1975), p. 324.
15. See Burnham, *The Managerial Revolution*.
16. The problem of the *effet pervers*, brilliantly analyzed in 1981 by Raymond Boudon, appears inseparable from that of false consciousness. See Raymond

Boudon, *Effet Pervers et Ordre Social* (Paris: PUF, 1979).
17. Raymond Ruyer, *L'utopie et les utopies* (Paris: PUF, 1950).
18. "History slides over the minds of utopians like water over the feathers of a duck"; Ruyer, *L'utopie*, p. 227.
19. "Utopia ... belongs to the antipodes of a dialectical conception of things, by its academicism," ibid. p. 98.
20. Minkowski's contribution is acknowledged by Ruyer, ibid., p. 41.
21. "Tendance à méconnaître les effets secondiares et composites," Ruyer, ibid., p. 80.
22. The term "composite effect" evokes the principle of *totality* in the sense given to it by Lukács and Goldmann.
23. "*Le progrés social considéré au long de l'histoire jusqu'à présent connue, peut être vu comme la série des manipulations de l'inégalité*" ("Social progress, when considered along the axis of history as we know it today, can be regarded as a series of manipulations of inequality"); G. Balandier, *Anthropo-logiques* (Paris: PUF, 1974).

12

Racist Consciousness as a Form of False Consciousness

In this paper, racism is examined exclusively in terms of its relationship with alienation and false consciousness. Both the scientific arguments against theories of racial inequality and the practical strategies in the struggle against racism are beyond the scope of this presentation. We think, however, that the link between racism and the Marxist concepts of alienation and false consciousness, can help illuminate a number of parasitic phenomena regarding pseudoracism. In particular, we have in mind the accusations of racism leveled against Israel and Jews in general. This "conceptual clarification" constitutes a contribution to the practical criticism of an ideology that is undoubtedly one of the plagues of our time.

We begin with the initial hypothesis that racism is an ideology in the Marxist sense of the word, underlaid by a *false consciousness*. However, the concept of racism has itself become an ideological concept. The term "ideological concept" refers to forms produced by the crystallization of egocentric "false identifications."[1] The presence of such concepts in political discourse is symptomatic of egocentric distortion. Since the privileged entity—such as the so-called "Aryan race"—is held to be the logical center of the political universe, all its opponents are presumed to be potentially identical to one another. In this sense, for a Nazi, all Jews are, at least potentially, communists, and all

---

Earlier version presented at the World Congress of Sociology (Mexico City, 1974), initially edited by Zoltàn Tar.

communists are, directly or indirectly, agents of world Jewry. Similarly, in the communist discourse of the Stalinist period, all opponents were indiscriminately branded as fascists. It seems to me that the role of egocentrism as the mechanism of ideological distortion has not been given due emphasis in the literature.

In a quite similar manner, the concept of racism became some time ago an ideological (egocentric) concept polemically surrounded by a halo of related definitions whereby all political opponents are indiscriminately branded as racists. It is therefore a practical as well as theoretical necessity to formulate a clear and unambiguous definition. The following definition can be suggested: racism is characterized by (a) unwarranted extrapolations ("All Negroes, or Jews, or Arabs are . . .); (b) the idea that some people are biologically superior to others; (c) the postulate that this supposed biological superiority confers specific rights (the principle of dissymmetry of rights); and (d) by the *demise of rationality* that underlies racism (referred to as the "eclipse of reason" by Max Horkheimer). By taking into account the importance of reification in this process (Adorno) and its fundamentally antihistoricist orientation (Lukács), we are entitled to speak of *racist false consciousness*. These four criteria are important, especially the last one. Otherwise, every conflict involving ethnically different opponents could be interpreted as a racial conflict.

A simple example may illustrate what is referred to as the *demise of rationality* inherent to genuine racism. During the Second World War, Americans of Japanese origin (the so-called Nisei) were subject to various restrictions for security reasons. And to some extent, therefore, one could compare their position to that of the German Jews after 1933. However, in the first case, "normal rationality" seems to operate for, in the given historical context, the Nisei certainly represented a higher security risk than Americans of other origins. The racist policies of Nazi Germany targeted a fully assimilated and patriotically minded minority, and, by expelling renowned German scientists of Jewish origin, Nazi Germany certainly contributed to its own defeat. We see here a typical phenomenon of false consciousness, with a consequent complete maladjustment to wartime necessities (*conduite d'échec*).

Max Weber distinguished between two kinds of rationality: a goal-determined rationality (*Zweckrationalität*) and a value-determined rationality (*Wertrationalität*). In the ideology of German racism, we observe a shift in emphasis from the first to the second form. In the darkest moments of the Second World War, Himmler wasted large sums of money on delusional racist "research-work" that had no military use (for instance, *Ahnenerbe*—ancestral inheritance, the Nazi attempt to establish "scientifically" the parameters of the "Aryan race"). So, even from the perspective of its own (criminal) war goals, Nazism exhibited a highly maladjusted type of behavior guided by a delusional (schizophrenic) rationality. Furthermore, the "value" of racial purity underlying Nazi rationality is rooted in biology, and is therefore independent from history. It is a value of pure consistency with no precariousness—in the sense of Dupréel—and is a nondialectical reified form of value. It is at the same time an *alienating value* since it is external to the individual . It is no more *Wertschaffer*, but merely *Wertträger* (a "heritage value" versus a "conquest value"). Hence, racism is linked to the problem of alienation. As the second criterion listed above (the principle of "unwarranted extrapolation") itself leads to a reified perception of human diversity. Thus, racism appears simultaneously as a form of antihistoricism and as a typical form of societal blindness. The convergence of these two elements is sufficient to call it an ideology in the original Marxist sense of the term. Sociologism—such as in the Durkheimian school—as well as the historicist-humanist variant of Marxism (Lukács-Mannheim-Goldmann), both structurally compatible with racism, possess an actual or at least a potentially disalienating tendency in this field. Hence, in contrast, one of the major grievances against the Althusser school, which claims to be a nonhistoricist variant of Marxism, is its highly inefficacious critical approach to this problem. Finally, this interpretation of racism stresses its structural analogies with *clinical alienation*, and particularly with schizophrenia. In my previous work, I have attempted to establish the fact that the concept of reification and of false consciousness, employed by classical Marxism only at the social (i.e., class) level, holds also at the individual dimension; and that schizophrenia—particularly a specific variant of this condition identified by Minkowski as "morbid rationalism"—may be interpreted as an *individual form of false consciousness* based on a reified logic.[2]

As Arieti suggested, racism is an autistic phenomenon for the racist individual and is confined to the inner world (*Eigenwelt*) of his stereotypes and phantasms. A genuine acquaintance with the object of his hatred is not necessary for the elaboration of his ideology. Shakespeare created his Shylock and Christopher Marlowe created his Barabas, "the Jew of Malta," most probably without ever having met a Jew in Elizabethan England, which was *Judenrein* for centuries. Personal contact often disrupts this reified "serial" perception of the discriminated minority, which therefore acts as a genuine psychotherapy for racist distortion. Furthermore, in the clinical sense of the term, racism is a projective attitude. The racist projects his own prejudices into the character of the discriminated minorities. Hitler, among others, blamed the Jews for their presumed domineering character as well as for both their endogamy and exogamy (Nüremberg Laws). This projective character appears with the utmost clarity in *racist caricatures*: an ideological equivalent of the "mirrors syndrome" (*syndrome de miroir*) that belongs to the clinical depiction of schizophrenia.

Hence, the assessment of racism as an eminently antidialectical and antihistoricist mental attitude, seems to hold true for the concept of alienation.[3] In Marxist circles, the theory of alienation is no longer universally accepted; some Marxists perceive this theory to be merely a useless theoretical construction in the daily class struggle. The attitude of Althusserians is most paradoxical as they exhibit a keen interest in the problem of ideology while they discard completely the link with the problem of reification and alienation, dismissing it as an obsolete legacy of the young Marx. Balibar even went so far as to reject, from the corpus of "genuine" Marxism, the theory of commodity fetishism.[4]

Thus it seems that the problem of racism offers a concrete possibility of testing the *practical* value of the theory of alienation. We have tried to show that racism, as a concept, risks degeneration into an omnivalent polemical category, instrumental for fighting political opponents, but useless in any scientific unmasking of racist ideology—unless we introduce the notion of false consciousness, and implicitly that of alienation, into our definition of racism.[5] The absence of any reference to alienation brings the debate down to the level of the former, that is, crudely speaking, from the level of scientific *ideologieforschung* to that of demagogy.

Notes

1. See Joseph Gabel, *False Consciousness* (New York: Harper Torchbooks, 1978), p. 92 and *passim*.
2. See the research of Silvano Arieti and of V. Domarus on the "paleologic" in schizophrenia.
3. Henri Lefebvre wrote that "le drame de l'aliénation est dialectique."
4. "Fetischcharakter der Waare" was included in the first chapter of the *Capital*.
5. Reference is made here to Mannheim's well-known typology of ideologies: the particular and partial concept of ideology versus its total and general concept.

13

Anti-Zionism as Ideology

The object of this paper is neither to defend nor criticize the political movement of Zionism. Its goal is exclusively scientific as it seeks to demonstrate that anti-Israeli political discourse incorporates certain typical features of ideological distortion curiously akin to those which underlie Stalinism, as analyzed in chapter 8 of the present volume.[1]

The two predominant features of ideological distortion brought to light by the related analysis of Stalinism are: (a) the negation or arbitrary reconstruction of historical facts (I suggest calling it the "Orwell phenomenon" or "Orwellization of the historical past"), and b) the dangers of identifying reasoning with "false identification" (Béla Fogarasi), "unwarranted extrapolation" (Whitehead) or "perverse equation" (Alain Dieckhoff). All these features, detected by different authors as symptoms of schizophrenia,[2] are also present in anti-Israeli political discourse.

Roger Garaudy, at the beginning of his career an outstanding French Marxist theorist who later converted to Islam, embraced the ideas of Béla Fogarasi on the danger of identification as a factor in (ideo)logical distortion. In one of his pre-Islamic (Marxist) works, one reads that "Identity is but an abstract moment of things. By setting up this abstraction in the absolute or in metaphysical reality, logic is distorted."[3] Strangely enough, concrete and vivid examples of this "distortion of logic" can be found in the post-Marxist (Islamic) work of Garaudy himself.

Earlier version presented at the World Congress of Sociology (Madrid, 1990), initially translated by Sarah Fine (Ben Gurion University).

In one of his polemical works, this author attacks without precise reference, the "Israeli obsession with *Lebensraum*."[4] Here, the destruction of the Egyptian Air Force in 1967 is compared to Pearl Harbor,[5] while the 1978 Camp David agreement is aligned with the tragic Münich agreement in 1938. Israel is thus cast in the role of the Third Reich and Egypt in that of the unfortunate Czechoslovakia.[6] Mr. Garaudy, then, critiques the Crusades as "Christian Zionism" and political Zionism as a "Jewish Crusade."[7]

Garaudy's distortions are a textbook case, and, thus, hardly unique. Anti-Israeli political discourse teems with such perverse equations. Their common denominator is the absurd statement that Israel's politics is in the spirit of that of the "Third Reich." "Israel is a semi-fascist country," claimed Chancellor Bruno Kreisky,[8] who, as a Marxist statesman, should have been more knowledgeable about his facts. No serious political scientist could agree with such a statement. Beginning with this basic "perverse equation," the mechanism of "chain reaction identification"[9] is set into motion: fascist political jargon is arbitrarily grafted onto the facts of Israeli political life. For instance, in an article of the Paris daily *Le Monde*, Gilles Deleuze evokes the "final solution" to the "Palestine Problem,"[10] despite the fact that no responsible Israeli has ever made use of such Hitlerian terminology to describe either the intentions or the capabilities of that government.

The accusation of racism directed against Israel (an accusation legitimized by the famous 1975 U.N. declaration) derives from the natural trajectory that precedes it: a "fascist" country, governed by Nazi politicians, cannot be but racist, according to the postulate concerning the "consistency of attributes."[11] Nevertheless, the appearance of Zionism on the historical stage was beyond doubt a defensive reaction in the face of anti-Jewish discrimination, which itself was often, if not invariably, racist. The concept of "defensive racism" denotes a moral absurdity, for the the aim of Israel's "founding fathers" was never to promote the imaginary "racial superiority" of the Jewish people, but to offer a sanctuary for a people victimized by a particular kind of racism.

It must be noted that if Zionism is by no means a racist movement, then the creation of a Jewish state is certainly one of the most provocative antiracist experiences of history. In the current political debate, the concept of "racism" is frequently the subject of confusion: it is generally the political opponent who, with or without good reason, is branded as racist. So, a scientific approach to racism necessarily involves the idea of biological fatality tantamount to "society-blindness,"[12] since for a genuine racist, a Jew (or a Negro) is supposed to remain the same regardless of the social circumstances. In creating a new basic Jewish personality different from the traditional stereotype, the Israeli state successfully challenged this biological fatality by presenting an experimental refutation of the basic postulate of racist ideology. Seen in this light, the equating of Zionism with racism, legitimized by the authority of an international organization, appears as a typical sample of a "perverse equation."

The same holds true for the equation "Zionism = Colonialism," which is a popular cliché frequently introjected (in the psychoanalytic sense of this term) in Jewish and even in Zionist circles. There is obviously no universally accepted definition of either colonialism or racism. However, the legitimization of the concept "colonialism without a parent country," may result in vicious extrapolations that lead to labeling refugees fleeing an oppressive regime as "colonialists." Colonialism is a sociohistorical "totality," in the terminology of Mauss and Lukács. It includes not only political, economic, and strategic dimensions but also a *moral* one, which gives its denunciation its full significance. It is morally inadmissible to equate the behavior of a German Jew in 1938 who resided illegally in Palestine in order to escape persecution, with that of a "Victorian" Englishman who legally installed himself in Calcutta in order to make his personal fortune. This ideological extrapolation of the concept of colonialism, as it appears in anti-Zionism, morally justifies the denial of asylum to political or racial refugees. It therefore challenges the principle of legitimate self-defense.

Anti-Zionism and Antihistoricism

Orwell's novel *1984* possibly offers the most important literary manifestation of historicism. Big Brother's totalitarian government habitually revises historical facts according to the ideological requirements of the present political situation.[13] One can state that the four major "Orwellian" elements of anti-Zionism are: (a) the protests again the archeological digs in Jerusalem; (b) the negation of genocide; (c) the idyllization of the common Jewish-Arab past before Zionism; and, finally, (d) a distortion of the anticolonialist dimension of the origins of the Israeli state.

The Problem of the Archaeological Digs at Jerusalem

It is a well-known historical reality, confirmed by archaeological digs, that Jerusalem was a Hebrew city under David, Solomon, and their successors. The attempts at precluding the evidence of these digs appear as a deliberate application of the technique of ideological rewriting of history as pointed out by Orwell. Accordingly, Caliph Omar conquered Jerusalem in 637 so that consequently the Holy City has never been Jewish, but Moslem and Arab "since the beginning of history." The archaeological digs that seek to prove the contrary—that is, to confirm historical reality—are considered illegal and have to be forbidden. O'Brien in Orwell's novel would have certainly endorsed such a procedure.

"Revisionism"—Denial of the Genocide of Jews During the Second World War

Much has already been said about the "revisionist" campaign promulgated by Professor Robert Faurisson in France. This campaign is first and foremost anti-Zionist in so far as it challenges the historical necessity and, consequently, the moral justification for the creation of an independent Jewish state. In their protests against the archaeological digs in Jerusalem, certain international organizations aim to erase a glorious chapter of the history of the Jewish people; while the "revisionist" campaign pretends to occlude a recent past of humiliation and of suffering. These two paths paradoxally converge in the same direction: to render the Jew into an "one-dimensional man" (Marcuse), deprived of any historical dimension and who, as such, cannot constitute a genuine people with a morally justifiable claim to statehood. I am also referring to the disdain of Engels, a historicist like all supporters of Marxism, towards *"geschichtslöse Völker"* (peoples without a history).[14]

The Idyllization of a Common Past Before Zionism

The third "Orwellian" theme in anti-Zionist literature is that of the idyllic co-existence of Jews and Arabs in Islamic countries before the rise of Zionism. This picture is not entirely inaccurate, especially if one draws a comparison between the situation of Jews in these countries with their condition in medieval Europe. It is nonetheless "hemiplegic" insofar as it merely glosses over all the discriminatory fiscal practices and humiliating vestimentary regulations passed under Islamic rule against the *dhimmi*.

The Anticolonialist Origin of the Israeli State

The "anticolonialist" dimension of the origins of the Israeli state constitutes a historical fact impossible to call into question. The final departure of the British—in other words, the real decolonization—was in large measure the result of the action of Jewish organizations in Palestine. The statement "Israel is a colonial reality" is thus doubly ideological: first, as a "false identity" (the concept of colonialism without a parent country is a false concept), and second as "an abstraction of history" in the words of the young Marx. From a doctrinal point of view, this example is interesting, since it clearly demonstrates the correlativity of the two basic structures of ideological discourse, those of "unwarranted identification" and antihistoricism.

Thus, this unwarranted correlation between the identificatory function and the antihistoricism of ideology are related phenomena, or are rather two aspects of the same basic phenomenon: the reification of political consciousness. According to Russell Jacoby, "the social loss of memory is a type of reification—better: it is *the* primal form of reification." And, Erica Sherover adds: "The reification which expresses itself in the forgetting of the past is simultaneously the mystification of the present."[15] Essentially Orwell made the same statement. The

French Marxist philosopher Henri Lefebvre also expresses the same idea in more florid language: "Ideology, culture ... and the struggle against time and evolution stand in league against the dialectic armed with a formalized logic. In order for logic to win and identity to triumph, *they must stop time*. Dialectics, being hounded, seeks refuge in dark corners."[16]

I sincerely hope that these two people, each with claims to a prodigious cultural past, will find a way to live in peace. Such an understanding would represent a step, every bit as important to the cultural and scientific future of humanity, as that of the postwar Franco-German reconciliation. However, a reconciliation worthy of this name, cannot be founded on the negation of historical reality and on "sociological partiality."[17] A reconciliation with a semifascist, racist and colonialist Israel is impossible for the mere reason that such an Israel not only does not exist today, but has never existed. This would be like attempting to establish a peace treaty with Atlantis. It is hence, a matter of greatest urgency to "de-ideologize" the historical perception of Jewish-Arab relations. As a model, we should follow the tragic hero of *1984* who haunts the decaying suburbs of the capital city of "Oceania," in search of lost time (*à la recherche du temps perdu*): that is, for a history confiscated by the power structure. This effort at historical disalienation is an effort towards peace and not towards war. It is in my view the ineluctable prerequisite for that "just and lasting peace" for which the international community is unanimously waiting.

Notes

1. See pp. 145–158 of the present volume.
2. As for the "hypertrophy of identification" within the logic of schizophrenia, see the research of A. Korzybski, Silvano Arieti and of the present author. The arbitrary reconstruction of the past has been detected by Honorio Delgado, and the notion of "unwarranted extrapolation" by G. Devereux. For details see pp. 132, 151 of the present volume.
3. "*L'identité n'est qu'un moment abstrait des choses. Eriger cette abstraction en absolu, en réalité métaphysique, c'est dévoyer la logique*"; Roger Garaudy, *La théorie matérialiste de la connaissance* (Paris: P.U.F. 1953), p. 263.
4. Roger Garaudy, *L'Affaire Israél-Le Sionisme politique* (Paris: Ed. Papyrus, 1983) p. 154. The concept of *Lebensraum* was, of course, one of the basic concepts of the expansionist ideology of the Third Reich.
5. R. Garaudy, ibid., p. 159.

6. R. Garaudy, ibid., p. 161.
7. R. Garaudy, ibid., p. 138.
8. Bruno Kreisky quoted in the Paris daily *France Soir* (June 16, 1982).
9. Term coined by Raymond Aron ("Identification en Chaîne") in *L'Opium des Intellectuels*, (Paris: Calmann Levy, 1955), p. 138 and *passim*.
10. Gilles Deleuze, "Les Gêneurs," *Le Monde* (April 7, 1978).
11. Formulated by the French epistemologist Emile Meyerson. See the chapter on the "consistency of attributes" in Emile Meyerson, *Le Cheminement de la Pensée* (Paris: Alcan, 1931), vol. 1, pp. 106–56.
12. According to Colette Guillaumin, an outstanding French specialist of this problem, in the racist ideology "le racial domine le social"; C. Guillaumin, "Caractères spécifiques de l'idéologie raciste," *Cahiers Internationaux de Sociologie*, vol. III (1972), p. 265.
13. The very same phenomenon has been detected in schizophrenia by the Peruvian psychopathologist Professor Honorio Delgado; see pp. 129ff. of the present volume.
14. See Roman Rosdolsky, "Friedrich Engels und das Problem der 'geschichtslösen' Völker," *Archiv für Sozialgeschichte* (1964).
15. Russell Jacoby, *Social Amnesia: A Critique of Conformist Psychology from Adler to Laing* (Boston: Beacon Press, 1975), p. 4. Also see Erica Sherover, "Review of the Work of Russell Jacoby," *Telos* No. 15 (1975), p. 196.
16. "*Se liguent contre la dialectique, avec la logique formalisée, l'idéologie, la culture, les actes visant la cohérence, la stabilité, l'équilibre, la lutte contre le temps et le devenir. Pour que le (la) logique l'emporte et que l'identité triomphe, elles devraient arrêter le temps. La dialectique traquée, se refuie dans les coins et les ombres*"; Henri Lefebvre, *Le retour de la dialectique* (Paris: Ed. Messidor, 1986), p. 28.
17. "*Partialité sociologique*" is Raymond Aron's term.

14

The Psychology of De-Stalinization and the Problem of Political Alienation

The Tactical Aspect of De-Stalinization

De-Stalinization surely constitutes the most significant political event of the 1950s in Russia. It also proved to be one of the least expected events in recent history. In the immense literature that grew up around the problem of the presumptive succession of the ageing dictator, nobody seems to have foreseen it very clearly. "The death of Stalin will not be the end of Stalinism" was the leitmotiv of the majority of the studies that appeared around 1953. Indeed, Marxist critics of Stalinism were naturally reluctant to attribute, in defiance of the principle of historic materialism, such far-reaching historico-sociological repercussions to the death of a mere individual. As for the right-wing detractors, they tended—no less naturally—to deny in principle any chances of lasting improvement for an abhorrent regime. For both groups, although for different reasons, Stalin himself had to be considered the *product* of Stalinism rather than its creator. As Isaac Deutscher has rightly remarked,[1] this is a matter of two different aspects of what social psychologists of the Kurt Lewin school call "resistance to change."

It seemed quite natural that a man who was the object of a quasi-divine cult during his lifetime should be elevated, after his death, to the Soviet pantheon, as though he were a Roman emperor. This was a "logical" development, politically speaking, and was more or less expected in the most varied circles, both friendly and hostile. With unfailing political intuition—blended with a very Stalinist sense of pure utility—Stalin's successors realized that this would have been a tactical error. Nothing prevented them from making a fetish out of the departed leader, but the advantages of this strategy would have been slender. A religion, even if it is *séculière*,[2] is not necessarily polytheistic, and moreover, the Communist pantheon is already very well stocked with deified personages. On the other hand, Stalin's disappearance afforded his successors a unique opportunity for getting rid of a weighty moral mortgage on their political futures (Stalin's pact with Hitler, anti-Semitism, police terrorism, etc.), without thereby renouncing one iota of the tactical advantages that accrued to Stalin's brilliant maneuvers for internal social control. This was the task which was tackled by his successors, in such a masterly fashion and with such an astute sense for the boldly-calculated risk—in a word, in such a *Stalinist* way—that one is bound to wonder whether they were not executing to the letter a genuinely secret will of the departed dictator.

The operation was not devoid of risks, although we now know that compared to the advantages, these risks proved rather small. The Communist electorate in the West was badly shaken, although comparatively little undermined, especially in Italy and France. Bearing in mind the psychological shock it suffered, the really surprising development is its durability. Its revolutionary ardor was no longer what it once was, but this fact is undoubtedly due less to de-Stalinization than to the slow sociopsychological action of the neocapitalist context. While the pro-Soviet zeal of the Western proletariat diminished, however, the anti-Soviet zeal of the Western bourgeoisie abated in similar proportion. Lastly, the relaxation of discipline in the socialist camp may be ascribed to de-Stalinization. Indeed, under Stalin, Albania would never have dared to raise its voice. But this is a cause rather than an effect of de-Stalinization, and it is no doubt an attenuated Eastern rejoinder to Western decolonization. De-Stalinization may therefore be regarded, by and large, as an historical necessity, coupled with an intelligent and rewarding form of tactics.

This fact must not be overlooked, especially when examining

the psychology of the de-Stalinization process. Deutscher was the first to demonstrate the presence of an objective sociohistorical process behind something that one was tempted at the time to consider a political accident. Once having admitted this, care must be taken not to go to the other extreme. The very way in which the dictator's undeniable political merits were straightaway hidden from view in 1953 seems to us to be highly symptomatic of a conscious strategy conceived in the highest circles of leadership. In *Gesellschaft und Gemeinschaft*, Tönnies distinguishes between the "essential will" *(Wesenswille)* and the "decisory [rational] will" *(Kurwille)* in political matters. In our view, the process of de-Stalinization owes something to both. From the tactical point of view, it is in the most authentic Machiavellian tradition. In chapter 7 of *The Prince*, Machiavelli recounts the tragic story of the Messire Remiro d'Orco, "a cruel and clever man," who was made responsible by Cesare Borgia for the definitive suppression of banditry in Romagna, and who, once his task was accomplished, was himself sacrificed on the altar of popular will. This lesson was not lost on posterity.

The Historical Role of Stalin and the Antihistoricism of Those Responsible for De-Stalinization

The success of "tactical de-Stalinization" points unequivocally to the persistance, in the full flush of Khrushchevism, of one of the fundamental characteristics of the totalitarian mentality, that is, its lack of historicist sensibility. Radical revisions and "rereadings" of history are a necessary component of totalitarianism. An attempt of this kind aimed, for example, at Clemenceau's role in 1917, would encounter insurmountable obstacles in France.[3] Totalitarian truth, unassailable in the present, is without "consistency"[4] with regard to the past; the slave of the present, it is incapable of understanding history. Conversely, democratic truth accepts present criticism, and by this very means, it acquires a consistency which transcends the immediate future. Historicist truth is therefore inseparable from a democratic way of thinking. It was because the historical greatness of a Clemenceau could be discussed during his lifetime that the same greatness—which was nevertheless very genuine—of Stalin was protected from any criticism during his rise to power, which prevented it from acquiring a genuine consistency in an historical sense. Thus, it happens that de-Stalinization is able to launch an attack on actual facts. It is characteristic that the same process which has been used in the past to deny the merits of Trotsky is re-employed to call in question those, no less undeniable, of Stalin. The intellectual climate of de-Stalinization therefore remains a totalitarian one.

Indeed, those who obstinately insist on placing the problem of Stalin against a historicist background are now getting rather more than they bargained for. Stalin was no doubt a ruthless dictator who did not hesitate to employ police terrorism. The fact that he was neither a "luminary" of science, nor a "leading light in human thought" has been recognized even in Moscow (if only later in Beijing). As for Stalin's "errors" and his historical role, this is quite a different question, and an analysis that aims to be scientific would need to take into account the objective balance sheet of his stewardship.

What might this balance sheet show? In 1930, Russia ranked sixth among the seven great powers, whereas in 1953, it was one of the first two. The Communist International was everywhere dominated by its socialist rival at the beginning of the Stalinist era; after a quarter of a century, the situation had been reversed. Lastly, Stalinist diplomacy achieved what seemed almost unthinkable in 1930. Thanks to it, socialist Russia weathered the storm of World War II with allies in the capitalist camp; by hoisting Hitler to power, Stalin succeeded in disequilibrating the capitalist world. I leave out of account for the moment the question of whether these successes were *socialist* or *Russian* successes, even though these two points of view seem to conflate the principal protagonists of de-Stalinization. In any case, they are unquestionable successes, the fruits of a far-reaching strategy. To neglect them systematically is symptomatic of a genuine *"imperméabilité à l'expérience"* (Lévy-Bruhl), in the same way that Trotsky's merits are systematically denied. Put another way, Stalin's interment took place in accordance with Stalinist ritual.

Hence, it might be said that de-Stalinization is the blend of a propagandistic artifact intended for export, plus a primitive *abreaction of guilt* craftily shaped for internal consumption. Much could be said about the psychoanalytical dimension of this latter aspect. In an article published in 1907, Robert Hertz described the phenomenon of the second funeral as practiced by the natives of Borneo.[5] Only important persons are entitled to this type of funeral. The period separating the provisional burial from the final funeral is proportional to the social importance of the deceased, and it may amount to several years. This rite is linked to the notion of *mourning work*, which in turn can be connected, through the intermediary of psychoanalytical theories, with melancholy and guilt psychosis. Insofar as these two aspects—tactical and expiatory—of de-Stalinization imply the tenacious persistence of the antihistoricist spirit, they refer us back to one of the essential dimensions of the totalitarian false consciousness. In a remarkable (and remarkably little-quoted) text, Marx points out that *"almost the whole of ideology may be reduced either to a mistaken conception of this human history, or to a complete abstraction of this history."*[6] In my Ph.D. thesis,[7] an attempt is made to interpret the phenomenon of false consciousness in politics as one of *schizophrenic* structure. In support of this thesis, consider the excellent article by the South American psychiatrist Honorio Delgado, who, under the term "invalidation of past events," describes the psychiatric equivalent of the deterioration of historicist sensitivity within ideology.[8] The attempted revision of the historical role of Stalin was certainly marked by an ahistorical or even antihistorical move, that is, by false consciousness. It should therefore not be interpreted purely as a process of political disalienation within the socialist world.

Technical Progress and Disalienation

As pointed out above, Deutscher considers Stalinism as a system of "magical thought," determined sociologically by the technological backwardness of the Russian economy. Indeed, "technique, planning, urbanization and industrial expansion are the mortal enemies of the primitive magic of Stalinism" (*La Russie*, p. 59). It is this development which, according to Deutscher, emerged at the time of Stalin's death. Technical progress, together with planning, would thus have played an irresistably disalienating role. The example of Hitler's Germany proves, nevertheless, that a planned economy based on an advanced technology can indeed function in the presence of what can properly be called "magical thought." The solution to the problem has to be found elsewhere. Deutscher has glimpsed a genuine yet secondary mechanism of the process of de-Stalinization, which he mistakenly took to be its essential motive force. The process of de-Stalinization, as we have seen, is deeply ambivalent. It does, indeed, entail the superimposing of two distinct processes, the significance of which, from the point of view of the problem of political alienation, is not the same.

Voluntary and concerted de-Stalinization utilized the (allegedly natural) death of Stalin as an occasion for abreaction of collective guilt and, at the same time, as a means of propaganda. This de-Stalinization shows no radical break with the prelogical tradition of the Stalinist era. On the contrary, without speaking of the *magical* character of the technique employed (double funeral, etc.), which may be traced back to precise data of ethnography, we have seen that the ex post facto reevaluation of the historical role of Stalin involves the same deterioration of historical time as that of the political past of Trotsky, Rajk, or other victims, now rehabilitated, of the purges. To a large extent, therefore, it is situated in the very trajectory of Stalinist ideology, as we have tried to show.

The objective sociohistorical process which underlies the first takes on the significance, on the other hand, of an authentic process of disalienation. Unlike Deutscher, who ascribes the merit for this to technological progress, I see in it the "ideological" reflection of a deconcentration of power, played out for many years on the stage of the Eastern Europe.

Indeed, a few words may be said about the social-psychological incidences of the advent of "polycentric" socialism.[9] Stalinism was a monolithic, monocentrist, and consequently Manichean doctrine. It postulated and maintained by force, the uniform and invariable nature of the communist world. It also maintained, at least at the propaganda level, that the noncommunist world was itself of a monolithic and invariable nature. For the Stalinist of the 1950s, Truman was an authentic successor (or rather, a scarcely modified new edition) of Hitler. His famous anti-racist sentiments were, it was claimed, merely a ruse intended to "dupe the masses." Diptychs in the style of "antiimperialist camp against imperialist camp" or "peace camp—war camp" became the public vocabulary of this Manichean essence. Egocentrism and a Manichean vision are diametrically opposed to real dialectics. One of the distinctive features of Stalinism was, consequently, its unconscious rejection of all genuinely dialectical social processes, in flagrant contradiction to its program which remained, in principle, a dialectical one.[10] From the point of view of the sociology of knowledge, this rejection of dialectics stemmed essentially from the central and logically privileged position of the USSR, which, while encouraging egocentrism, set in motion a process of regression to what might be termed a pre-dialectical state of awareness. This is a complex gnoseo-sociological and psychological mechanism, the details of which I have pursued elsewhere.[11]

The central process of this "dedialectization" is the establishment of *false identities*, to the detriment of a totalizing, dialectical grasp of empirical reality. An expression such like "Hitlero-Trotskyism" indicates that for sociocentric thought, all the adversaries of the party are fundamentally equivalent—are, in fact, *identical to one another*. Moreover, their common hostility with regard to the "privileged system" of power/knowledge is a concerted hostility, or in other words, the expression of a plot (what Sperber has called the "police conception of history").

This fundamental rejection of dialectics naturally had dire repercussions on the aggregate of the ideological and scientific attitudes adopted by sociocentrism, for example, Stalinism's systematic elimination of genuine dialectics in scientific matters on the pretext that they were tainted with idealism or irrationalism. One only has to think of the criticisms of psychoanalysis, relativity, or Gestalt (in the work of R. Garaudy, *inter alia*). It is understandable that the emergence of polycentric socialism provoked a complete upheaval in this epistemological field.

The advent and success of the Tito schism broke up the Manichean arrangement within the constrained universe of Stalinism. It undermined the basis of egocentric logic. Stalinism defended itself against this wind of change by what might be termed the "technique of efficient delusion." Titoism was cold-bloodedly identified with extreme forms of right-wing reaction

(Franco), accused of actions and gratuitous humiliations that would transform these accusations into reality, thus obliging Tito either to lose any possibility of return to the fold, to side with the capitalist camp, or to capitulate. The skillfulness of the Truman administration coupled with the courage of Tito and his comrades, led to the defeat of this plan, which was at points close to success.[12] One of the first gestures by Khrushchev was to liquidate this "reaction of delirious defense" by authorizing the revision of the Rajk trial and to readmitting Tito, who had renounced none of his autonomy, into the socialist camp. This gesture was pregnant with consequences. From that time on, as Fejtö has explained, "the dichotomic vision of the world, peculiar to traditional Marxism-Leninism and to orthodox communism, is tending to give way to a vision which is both *unitarian and pluralist*"[13]—in other words, dialectical. The sociological bases for a partial redialectization of the super-structures are thus created. This process might be designated by the term *intellectual thaw*.

China and the Future of De-Stalinization

The uncertainities of the future of de-Stalinization are inherent in the fundamental ambiguity of the processes described above. I have long tended to consider de-Stalinization from the exclusive point of view of various tactical hypotheses, and to see it as nothing more than eyewash intended for the Western world.[14] The strange spectacle of Khrushchev's report to the 20th Congress—a "secret" report, yet those who divulged its contents were not taken to task—appeared to authorize this interpretation, which in fact regarded Russian policy after 1953 as a kind of moderate Stalinism without Stalin. Over time, it is the sociohistorical interpretation of de-Stalinization that remains interesting, yet in this matter, as in so many others, one must be careful to avoid the pitfalls of what Aron referred to as the "temptation of extrapolation": that is, to consider a process as irreversible solely by virtue of the fact that it has lasted for a substantial amount of time. The future of thoroughgoing and lasting de-Stalinization depends upon the complex interplay of a great many elements, among which the Chinese factor looms as first among equals.

The Psychology of De-Stalinization 207

No-one could any longer minimize its importance. We shall confine our attention, therefore, to identifying its effects on the psychology—or more precisely, on the forms of political consciousness—of the great rival powers. Indeed, China's noisy appearance on the historical scene deals another, and perhaps final, blow to communist (and even American) Manicheism, thus rendering a return to Stalinism (or some form of McCarthyism) infinitely more difficult. In actual fact, the Beijing leaders committed only one rather harmless, largely symbolic act of aggression. But the immense weight of the new China now makes itself felt in all international deliberations.

From the military point of view, the promotion of China marks the beginning of a new phase, calling for a military revaluation of the mass of humanity. Before the industrial era, the size of the population was an essential factor of power. And it was thanks to this factor, plus the vastness of her territory, that Russia was able to play the role she played in the period from Peter the Great to Alexander I. The successive defeats of Russia and the more or less contemporary defeats of China,[15] correspond to the beginnings of the industrial age in the course of which the industrial and scientific potential of countries will, naturally, be of greater military significance than their human potential. But the advent of atomic weapons—those media of mass destruction—consecrates the *passive* military revaluation of the bulk of humanity, which, although a factor of no value for forcing victory, is nevertheless a sovereign element in sidestepping defeat. When faced with the prospect of a conflict from which no victors could emerge, but only the more or less vanquished, this "buffer effect" of the mass recovers much of its historical importance. China was the first to understand the significance of this new arrangment, which will also perhaps tempt India. China, then, stands a chance of emerging the sole "victor" from an atomic conflict between the two great powers.

This has given rise to a paradoxical situation. Both Chinese and Russian political thinking remain tributaries off the same utopian stream: that of the achievement, on the basis of an underdeveloped economy, of an industrialised and planned society, arbitrarily described as *socialist*. This common utopia took the form, for many years, of a political alliance which, although not untroubled, was on the whole stable. It is now more than offset by the difference in the approach of the two great powers of the socialist camp to the problem of war, which accelerates history for China, and a factor of its possible cessation for the Soviets.[16]

The fact is that, on this question of capital importance, the Russian and American approaches tend to coincide. At the time of the Cuba crisis, China fanned the flame; by contrast, the attitude of "the two K's" was characterized by moderation. The "war camp—peace camp" diptych is thus restored to its deserved place in the museum of outdated ideologies. On the question of atomic war, which is infinitely more urgent than that of economic utopias, the USSR and the United States share a distinct point of view. By reverting to a political tradition which is more Asian than her own,[17] will China contribute to making Russia more Western in the future? Historial providence—or Hegel's *cunning of reason*—sometimes follows circuitous paths.

Notes

1. Cf. I. Deutscher, *La Russie après Staline* (Paris: Seuil, 1954), p. 14 and *passim*.
2. The usage is J. Monnerot's in his *Sociologie du Communisme*, pp. 265ff.
3. An attempt was indeed made in 1944 to revaluate Petain's military activity in World War I as a function of his political attitude during World War II. This attempt, which was half-hearted, in practice failed to achieve its goal.
4. We use the word in the sense of Dupréel's axiology; for the author of *Esquisse d'une philosophie des valeurs*, all values are a synthesis of *consistency* and *precariousness*.
5. *L'Année Sociologique* 1907, pp. 48–137. We follow closely the (unpublished) article of Robert Paris, "Politique et Anthropologie: Travail du deuil en U.R.S.S." Cf. also the article by Robert Conquest, "Les morts successives de Staline," *Le Contrat Social* (March-April, 1962), 91ff, and the study by D. Lagache, "Le travail du deuil (Ethnologie et Psychanalyse), *Revue Française de Psychanalyse*, 1938, no. 1, who moreover quotes the study by R. Hertz.
6. Karl Marx, *Oeuvres philosophiques* (Costes Edition), vol. VI, pp. 153–54. We should recall that for Marx and Engels, ideology and false consciousness are strongly correlated conceptually.
7. *La Fausse Conscience* (Paris: Editions de Minuit, 1962), pp. 68ff.
8. H. Delgado, "Anormalidades de la conciencia del tiempo," *Revista de Psiquiatria y Psicologia Medica de Europa y America Latin* (1953, no. 1), p. 17, refers to "*reificación del tiempo y doble cronologia*" and on p. 14 to "*frustracion del presente e invalidacion de lo acaedio*" in schizophrenia.
9. The expression "polycentrism" is Togliatti's. Cf. F. Fejtö, "*Reflexions en marge de l'actualité*," *Arguments*, 27/28, p. 42.

10. The first theoretician who brought to our attention the antidialectical aspects of official Marxism was Karl Korsch in his *Marxismus und Philosophie* (Leipzig: Hirschfeld Verlag, 1930). This work, long out of print in its original form, has during the last two decades finally appeared in both French and English language versions.
11. The central idea of these studies is that collective ego-centrism (sociocentrism) involves a deterioration of a dialectical purchase on the world, by virtue of mechanisms which are in ways analogous and homologous to those described by Jean Piaget in his studies of child psychology.
12. Cf. the article by M. Djilas in *Le Monde* (May 20–21, 1962), p. 8, emphasizing that one of the leitmotifs of Stalinist policy was its desire to prevent the emergence of Titoism, Stalinist policy was in fact anti-Titoist. A social revolution in the Germany of 1933 involved the risk of causing the leadership of the socialist world to fall into the hands of socialist Germany, which was more industrialized than Russia at that time and which had at its disposal a Marxist theoretical tradition of quite another statute. By pushing Hitler to power, Stalinist policy thus attained a double goal: the prevention of the possible "Titoization" of Soviet Germany and the preparation of the 1945 victory that divided the capitalist adversary. The realistic political genius of Stalin had rarely manifested itself so strikingly.
13. *Arguments* 1962, no. 27–28, p. 44, emphases added. It is significant that the themes of ideological criticism (problems of alienation and false consciousness), which were strictly prohibited—quite understandably—under Stalinism, made a surprising comeback, particularly in Polish Marxist circles.
14. Cf. Joseph Gabel, "Tournant communiste?" *La Revue Socialiste* (January, 1953), no. 68.
15. The Crimean War, the war against Japan, and World War I, in the case of Russia; the Opium War, the war against France and against Japan, in the case of China. The Russian "victory" over Turkey in 1877–78, achieved with difficulty against an opponent far gone in decadence, may, from the point of view of the question at issue, be considered as the equivalent of a defeat.
16. Marx was perhaps personally nearer the present Chinese point of view, but the meaning of war has changed since his time, owing to technical progress. The economist Fritz Sternberg contemplated, as long ago as 1927 (in *Der Imperialismus und seine Kritiker*, Malik Verlag), the hypothesis of a cessation of history as a result of wholesale destruction, even though at that time atomic war was not yet a topical question. In 1927, and *a fortiori* in 1962 (when an earlier version of this essay was published), Marx would likely endorse Sternberg's opinion.
17. Tito's allusion to Genghis Khan was a far-reaching one, yet although he founded a Chinese dynasty, Genghis Khan was not Chinese, but Mongol. The Chinese intelligentsia was constantly anti-imperialist and pacifist; its opposition to the expansionist policy of the Han emperors is a notorious fact of Chinese history. Its pacifism was tainted with xenophobia, for example, "The barbarians are unworthy of our attention." For the Mongol, human life, both is own and that of his enemies, was of slight importance. It is this tradition to which the present-day Chinese ideology seems to be reverting. Such a position might well contribute, by recoil, to leading the Russians back to a more Western sense of human values.

Epilogue

From Schizophrenia to False Consciousness: Joseph Gabel and Theories of Psychopathology

David F. Allen

This essay sketches the relationship between Joseph Gabel's theorizing and the concept of schizophrenia as more generally defined. I will not deal with Gabel's sociology of knowledge, but shall instead consider some of the psychopathological theories to which he referred while constructing his unique bridge between individual and collective delusions.

The concept of "schizophrenia" was at its birth unsound—a ragbag concerning neurosis (twilight hysteria), manic-depression, and other forms of psychosis. The current medical use of the term (DSM IIIr or VI) reduces the condition to a vague disorder of affect and ideas. Gabel, however, fashioned his particular notion of schizophrenia by synthesizing the work of thinkers who aimed at a precise, limited concept that could not easily be confused with hysterical insanity.

In pursuing this goal, Gabel was strongly influenced by the philosopher-psychiatrist Eugene Minkowski (1885–1972), himself an intellectual follower of Henri Bergson. Minkowski had spent some months working with Bleuler (1857–1939), who

---

Edited by Alan Sica. David F. Allen teaches at the Conservatoire national des arts et métiers in Paris.

coined the term schizophrenia some time before 1908. Minkowski was also responsible for bringing his personalized vision of the concept into France. The Minkowski-Gabel connection is interesting not only because the former shaped Gabel's view of schizophrenia, but also because he adopted some of Gabel's ideas in his *Treatise of Psychopathology* (Paris 1966). This book was widely read by philosophers interested in mental derangement. Minkowski was also part of the committee before which Gabel defended *False Consciousness* as his "state thesis."

Beginning in 1923 Minkowski argued for a pure form of schizophrenia called *morbid rationalism*, a condition known by its symptom of antithetical attitudes. The patient sees the world in terms of black and white or in rigid, nearly totalitarian systems, and the relationship between time and space may be disturbed, broken, or absent. The patient perceives himself to be in space (houses, stations of the area, etc.), as if time had become, or could only be lived as, a form of space. The orientation systems used by such people often possess mathematical or pseudoscientific structure. These would appear to Freudians as an attempt at delusional reconstruction of self, but for Gabel they seemed more an individualized false consciousness.

Minkowski concludes his French thesis (1926) by stating that: "In certain cases of schizophrenia the failure of dynamic factors is accompanied by a veritable hypertrophy of the rational and spatial factors of thought. This hypertrophy then conditions the behavior of the patients.... It would appear justified in such cases to speak of morbid rationalism and geometrism."[1] It should also be noted that Minkowski was not proposing a biological condition (as Bleuler had). He was attempting to capture the modification that occurs in the structure of thought when the ability to reason abstractly assumes a sort of frightening independence, or internal "para-logic," of its own.

In 1927 Minkowski published his book on schizophrenia, the first significant French study of the problem. As an examination of schizophrenia per se, it is still valuable. Minkowski theorized a *morbid preoccupation with geometry* as characteristic of the schizophrenic. In 1933 he published *Lived Time*, redefining schizophrenia as transformation of time into space, with melancholia understood as the nonperception of space coupled with the predominance of a stagnant, infinite sensation of time. Since psychiatrists of Minkowski's generation were trained in the art of exacting, meticulous clinical observation, his analyses revealed precise syndromes that could be used as a clinical compass in the trying business of diagnosis. One such syndrome was formulated by the great Jules Cotard (1840–1889). In Cotard's "end of the world psychosis," the melancholic patient feels that his body is empty, he lacks innards, he feels himself to be immortal, time is lived as an ocean without movement or end, and the world and his family cease to exist. In short, there is time without space. Thus, Minkowski's theory is borne out by more than a century of clinical observation.

Gabel adopted Minkowski's dialectical understanding of schizophrenia because it was compatible with the concept of reification: antithetical attitudes correspond to reified logic. Both the strict separation of time and space, along with the emergence of paralogical systems based on unwarranted or illegitimate extrapolation, confirmed the destruction of dialectical capacities in schizophrenics. Morbid rationalism was the clinical proof that a key to understanding schizophrenics, as well as nonpsychotic mental life, lay in the general area of dialectics. While trying to formulate a pure definition of schizophrenia, Minkowski insisted on a specifiable structure of disturbed thought, whereas Gabel advanced this concept from the clinical format into the broader delusions of the collective.

Schizophrenic Logic

Although Gabel was not always aware of it, his theorizing grouped him with a small coterie of unusually creative specialists who had realized, independently of each other, that true schizophrenia arose from a form of logic by identity, leading unavoidably to reified thought. For example, in the early 1930s Korzybski observed that "in heavy cases of dementia praecox [schizophrenia] we find the most highly developed 'identification.'"[2]

Arieti, the noted American specialist on schizophrenia, confirmed the nature of the problem: "Any person who has a characteristic in common with an alleged persecutor, like having a beard or red hair or wearing a special dress, may become the persecutor or a relative of the persecutor.... [I]t is easy to recognize that many patients ... indulge in what I have called an orgy of identifications. A French psychiatrist, Gabel (1948), independently discovered the same phenomenon in schizophrenia and called it a hypertrophy of the sense of identification."[3]

Schizophrenics and absolutist ideologists share a systematic recourse to intellectually indefensible logical categories. This is one of the key points that undergirds the concept of false consciousness as understood by Gabel, and is easily clarified by a clinical illustration. A young schizophrenic claims that a pretty girl, a cigar, and the virgin Mary are all "the same." What explains this apparent nonsense is the victims' observation that the cigar is surrounded by a tax band, the pretty girl by the amorous gaze of the young man, and the virgin Mary by her halo. Thus, a secondary quality is allowed to stand in for the primary object or person within this heterogeneous mixture. Here the quizzical "logical" category amounts to "things surrounded by things." When fanatical groups treat the alleged "Jewish-Masonic" plot to take over the world as real, their logic is of similar nature and design. They see, for example, that certain famous Jews are influential in government, the arts, or the media, and conclude from this that all Jews harbor designs on world domination.

Another clinical problem known as "the mirror sign," though now seldom recalled, can also illuminate false consciousness, and remains central to the interpretation of schizophrenia. In the late 1920s Paul Abely (1897–1979) observed that young male schizophrenics, particularly during the onset of the disorder, engaged in long, amorous discussions with their mirror image, but perceived as a girlfriend. Thus, self is expressed and conceived as "other." Those mechanisms that allow the self to be perceived *as such* have failed to develop; *me* is perceived as *not me*. There is evidence here for a strong, Minkowskian argument in assessing schizophrenia as the destruction or absence of a capacity for dialectics. Also, the mirror sign provides clinical support for the necessity of a mirror phase. We can theorize the young babies' capture of identity via the mirror image, something sadly missing in the schizophrenic consciousness. In other words the mirror *sign* confirms the necessity of the mirror *phase*. Thus, schizophrenia and ideology can legitimately be analyzed in terms of the logic by identity rather than a logic of differentiation.

This phenomenon relates to Gabel's realization that nonpathological perception of the world must be, in axiological terms, dialectical perception. One could add that pure schizophrenia experiences atomized values and a world bereft of an anchor point that could stabilize values, language, and sense of self.

If reified logic predominates in both totalitarian (public) and schizophrenic (private) worlds, then surely one could find examples in recent history and literature. China has a population of around 20 million "political criminals," and Nazism or Stalinism are in a sense "ideal types" (Weber) of morbid rationalism. Orwell's *Animal Farm* is a sociopathic world run according to the logic defined by Minkowski many years ago; the slogan "two legs good, four legs bad" shows that the ideological and the pathological often walk hand in hand. In *Animal Farm* and *1984*, the reader observes a constant corruption of the knowable past. Life is carried out exclusively within the space of a permanent present. The concept of historical past, of temporal continuity, is killed off; only an atomized space of "now" remains. What Minkowski theorized at the individual level again becomes obvious in its collective manifestation.

Conceptual Confusions

Having briefly illustrated some elements that Gabel borrowed from psychopathology and incorporated in his sociology of political knowledge, it must be understood that the development of schizophrenia as a concept is itself part of the history of false consciousness within psychiatry. Bleuler's original formulation was notably unscientific, and is partly responsible for the international confusion that surrounds the conceptual problem even today.

In 1897 and 1902 Dr. S. J. M. Ganser of Dresden (1851–1931) identified a particular form of "twilight hysteria," the features of which were:

216   Ideologies and the Corruption of Thought

- A disorganized sense of environment and time.
- The production of "I don't know" answers even to simple questions, implying the temporary loss of information normally at the person's disposal.
- A clouding of awareness.
- An ability to understand questions matched by a psychogenic inability to give correct answers.
- Answers to questions are, however, in the correct semantic sphere, for example, "How many ears do you have?"/"Three." Or, a ticket agent does not give a customer a bucket of water or a lizard.[4]
- Hallucinations and hallucinatory reenactments of certain traumatic experiences.
- General or partial analgesia in the body (mouth area included), which may change location according to time of day or day of the week.
- Patients are not offended by the childish nature of questions; even questions like what is your name or what is this (watch, money, etc.) cause difficulty and stimulate idiosyncratic answers.
- Eventually the symptoms of "twilight hysteria," which appear simultaneously, give way to a mode of being similar to the personality which predated the attack.
- The patient is surprised when informed post facto of his behavior during the twilight period.
- Ganser also observed that the period of twilight hysteria was covered by a veil of amnesia.
- No mnemic loss occurred for the period of time before the appearance en masse of symptoms.
- Many patients had also suffered some physical trauma, for example, blows to the head.
- At least one confessed to imaginary crimes.
- Sometimes the ability to comment on reading material is disturbed under questioning.
- Many patients were awaiting trial.
- The cases were not simulated: one would require a profound knowledge of psychopathology, Ganser argued, to fake such a congeries of symptoms.
- Simple counting may become difficult: W.H. (OBS/35 1902) counted his fingers as follows: "1, 3, 7, 5, 10, 12, 14, 16, yes so 14."
- Answers peculiar to the locality of the questions were common to all cases.
- Patients put a great deal of effort in attempts to concentrate and thereby try (but often fail) to overcome their distraction (*zerstreutheit*).

- The transition from the pathological to ordinary field of awareness was gradual but relatively rapid.
- Some people complained of difficulty in thinking (*Erschwerung im Denke*)
- Many found themselves in a dreamlike state.
- The "mistakes" were not consistent.
- One patient joked: when asked how many ears he had, he replied "four," and when asked to explain said "outside ears" and, with his fingers in his ears, said "These are the inside ears" (Oct. 25, 1902).
- These symptoms constitute in sum a *form of twilight hysteria.*

Bleuler's thinking and terminology, however, won the day over Ganser's, and, analogously, Minkowski had to wait almost until he died for *Lived Time* to be translated in the U.S.A.

Along similar lines, one might ask about Bleuler's handling of hysteria. In 1908 under the subheading "Distinction between primary and secondary symptoms," he wrote:

> In analysing the power of individual symptoms to determine outcome, I lay great weight on a distinction between the primary symptoms which are part of the disease process, and the secondary symptoms, which arise as reactions of the ailing psyche to environmental influences and to its own strivings. To take an analogy, it is possible for osteoporosis to reach a very advanced state without obvious symptoms, until the patient suffers a physical trauma. The real disease, and with it the prognosis, lies in the brittleness of the bones which can, depending on external circumstances, produce symptoms or not. . . .
> To find analogous differences in the phenomena that manifest themselves in schizophrenia, there is already a point of reference, namely the symptoms which are triggered by external influences, even when they last a long time and begin with hallucinations. *The same significance can be attached to states of altered consciousness, including the Ganser syndrome.*[5]

In 1911, often cited as the birthdate of schizophrenia, Bleuler went a step further: "The twilight states can show a good deal of variability. In some cases we find a consistently carried out dream-activity. The twilight state is then essentially the reaction of a mildly schizophrenic personality to a psychic trauma."[6]

Bleuler's portrait of schizophrenia can be considered ideological to the extent that it blocks the path to any alternative understanding of the neurosis/psychosis problem. Both Ganser and Minkowski created their analytic apparatuses in terms of specific clinical data and favored a dialectical understanding of syndromes as a basis for modern psychopathology. One must recall that Gabel constructed his typology on the basis of Minkowski's viewpoint, and not on Bleuler's, a psychiatrist whose thinking was flawed, as I have tried to illustrate, by his recourse to logic by identity.

In conclusion we should remember that Gabel trained as a psychiatrist before becoming a sociologist of knowledge. Problems of dedialectization, the pathological divorce of time and space, reified logic and unwarranted extrapolation were all clinically exemplified for him prior to being merged with his study of ideology. It was the clarity of Minkowski's thinking—the pivotal idea that schizophrenia could profitably and reasonably be viewed as the fruit of a de-dialectized condition—which to a significant degree allowed Gabel to conceive of false consciousness as the crossroads of individual and collective delusions which sociologists have since known it to be. The French "alienist," F. Leuret (1797–1851), claimed in 1834, that there was as much madness in worldly systems as in his psychotic patients. Gabel is one of very few to have enlarged this remarkable insight systematically.

Notes

1. E. Minkowski, *La Notion de perte de contact vital avec la réalité et ses applications en pyschopathologie* (thesis) (Paris: Jouve & Cie, 1926), p. 76.
2. A. Korzybski, *Science and Sanity* [1933] 4th ed. (Lakeville, CT: The International Non-Aristotelian Publishing Company, 1958), p 568. *Nota bene:* "Identification" is not used in the Freudian sense here, but rather implies a disturbance of causality, meaning, and logical categories.
3. Silvano Arieti, *Interpretation of Schizophrenia*, 2nd ed. (New York: Basic Books, 1955/1974), p. 232.
4. In other words Ganser is not theorizing *"coq-à-l'âne."*
5. E. Bleuler, "The prognosis of dementia praecox: The group of schizophrenias," in *The Clinical Roots of the Schizophrenia Concept* [1908], J. Cutting and M. Sheperd (eds.) (Cambridge: Cambridge University Press, 1987), pp. 65–66 (emphases added).
6. E. Bleuler, *Dementia praecox or the group of schizophrenias* [1911], 10th ed. (Madison, CT, International Universities Press, 1987), p. 220.

References

Abely, P. "État schizophrénique et tendances homosexuelles." *Annales médico-psychologiques*, 2 (1927), 251–57.

———. "Le signe du miroir dans les psychoses et plus spécialement dans la démence précoce." *Annales médico-psychologiques*, 1 (1930), 28–36.
Allen D. F. & Postel J., "For S. J. M. Ganser of Dresden." *History of Psychiatry*, 5:3 (1994), 289–319.
———. Eugeniusz Minkowski ou une vision de la schizophrénie. *Évolution psychiatrique*, 60:4 (1995), 961–80.
Arieti, S. *Interpretation of Schizophrenia*, 2nd ed. New York, Basic Books, 1974.
Bannister, D. "The Logical Requirements of Research into Schizophrenia." *British Journal of Psychiatry*, 114 (1968), 181–88.
Bleuler, E. "Affectivity, Suggestibility, Paranoia." *New York State Hospital Bulletin* (February 1912), 481–601.
———. "The Prognosis of Dementia Præcox: the Group of Schizophrenias." In J. Cutting and M. Sheperd (eds.), *The Clinical Roots of the Schizophrenia Concept*. Cambridge: Cambridge University Press, 1987.
———. *Dementia Praecox or the Group of Schizophrenias*. Madison, CT: International Universities Press, 1950.
———. *Textbook of Psychiatry*. New York: Macmillan, 1924.
———. "La schizophrénie." In Congrès des aliénistes et neurologistes de France et des pays de langue française XXX session (Masson, 1926) 1–23; reprinted in J. Postel (ed.), *La Psychiatrie*, Paris: Larousse, 1994.
———. "The Physiogenic and Psychogenic in Schizophrenia." *American Journal of Psychiatry*, 10:2 (September 1930), 203–11.
Fullinwider, S. P. *Technicians of the Finite: The Rise and Decline of the Schizophrenic in American Thought, 1840–1960*. Westport, CT & London: Greenwood Press, 1982.
Gabel, Joseph. "Symbolisme et schizophrénie." *Revue suisse de psychologie et de psychologie appliquée*, 7:4 (1948), 268–86.
———. *La Fausse Conscience*. Paris: Éd. de Minuit, 1962.
———. "Dialectique, théorie de la valeur et critique idéologique," in J. Gabel, *Idéologies II*, Paris: Anthropos, 1978.
———. *Etudes dialectiques*. Paris: Méridiens/Klincksieck, 1990. "L'œuvre d'Eugène Minkowski et la philosophie de la culture." *L'Évolution psychiatrique*, 56:2 (1991), 429–34.
———. "La fausse conscience politique." *Prétentaine*, nos. 2 & 3 (1994), 63–69.
Leuret, F. *Fragments psychologiques sur la folie*. Paris: Crochard, 1834.
Lewis, N. *Research in Dementia Precox (Past, Attainments, Present Trends and Future Possibilities)* [1936]. New York: Arno, 1980.
Minkowski, Eugene. *La Notion de perte de contact vital avec la réalité et ses applications en psychopathologie* (thèse). Paris: Jouve & Cie, 1926.
———. "Bergson's Conceptions as Applied to Psychopathology." *The Journal of Nervous and Mental Diseases*, 63:6 (1926), 553–68.
———. *La Schizophrénie*. Paris: Payot, 1927. (A translation of chapter two is to be found in J. Cutting and M. Shepherd, (eds.), *The Clinical Roots of the Schizophrenia Concept*, Cambridge: Cambridge University Press, 1987: 188–212.)
———. *Le Temps vécu*. Paris: D'Artrey, 1933 (reprinted, Paris: PUF, 1995).
———. *Traité de Psychopathologie*. Paris: PUF, 1966.
———. *Structure des dépressions*. Paris: Nouvel Objet, 1993.
Minkowski, Eugene, and J. Rogues de Fursac. "Le rationalisme morbide." *Encéphale*, 18:4 (1923), 217–28.
J. Postel and D. F. Allen (eds.). *La Psychiatrie*. Paris: Larousse, 1994.

Name Index

Abely, Paul, 214
Acheson, Dean, 160, 161
Adorno, Theodor, 1, 8, 92, 96, 133, 135, 150, 151, 168, 186
Alexander I, Czar, 207
Alexander II, Czar, 179
Alexander III, Czar, 179
Alleau, Rene, 97
Althusser, Louis, 3, 8, 67, 89, 97, 103, 117–118, 124–125, 130, 134, 136, 152, 187, 188
Antoninus Pius, Emperor, 165
Arieti, Silvano, 27–28, 94, 131, 151, 168–169, 188
Aristophanes, 66
Aron, Raymond, 66, 89, 118, 129, 132, 134, 168, 206
Aubin, H., 46
Auriol, Vincent, 76
Auschwitz, 1, 35
Axelos, Kastos, 11

Bacon, Francis, 114, 117, 130
Balibar, Etienne, 188
Barnes, Harry Elmer, 106
Barthelemy, Joseph, 123
Baruk, Henri, 95, 165, 169
Beauvoir, Simone de, 96, 169
Bender, Lauretta, 94
Bentley, Elizabeth, 158
Berger, Peter, 10, 96
Bergson, Henri, 3, 13–14, 17, 21–22, 26, 28, 37, 40, 80, 90–91, 94, 131, 167–168, 211

Berze, J., 94
Beuchat, H., 109
Binswanger, Ludwig, 3, 11–14, 16, 22, 27–34, 38, 65, 94, 170
Bleuler, Eugen, 72, 80, 120, 168, 211, 212, 215, 217, 218
Bloch, Ernst, 62, 64, 182
Bonilauri, B., 175
Borgia, Cesare, 201
Bossuet, Jacques, 91
Boudon, Raymond, 135–136, 176, 179, 181–182
Bouthoul, Gaston, 68
Brown, Norman O., 4, 8
Buridan, Jean, 94–95
Butler, Samuel, 117

Carnot, Lazare, 161
Caruso, Igor A., 95, 169
Cassirer, Ernst, 50
Chambers, Whittaker, 157, 159
Charlemagne, 91
Chiang Kai-Shek, 157
Chronos, 94
Citrome, Paul, 166
Clemenceau, Georges, 201
Comte, Auguste, 123
Cotard, Jules, 213
Courtade, Pierre, 148
Cuvillier, Armand, 106

d'Orco, Messire Remiro, 201
Daudet, Leon, 103
David (King), 194

Delassus, Jean-Marie 72, 169
Deleuze, Gilles, 192
Delgado, Honorio 120, 132, 203
Derrida, Jacques, 3
Deutscher, Isaac, 199, 201, 203–204
Devereux, Georges 151
Dexter-White, Harry, 158
Dieckhoff, Alain 147, 191
Dilthey, Wilhelm, 22, 28, 117
Döblin, Alfred, 65
Dupréel, Eugene, 3, 11–12, 33–37, 39–40, 46, 91–94, 97, 187
Durkheim, Emile, 3, 101–102, 104–105, 107–108, 136, 181

Eddington, Arthur, 91, 120
Einstein, Albert, 39, 40, 102
Engels, Friedrich, 63, 90, 92, 130, 133, 136, 176, 195
Epictetus, 165
Ey, Henry, 81, 166

Fauconnet, Paul, 105–106
Faurisson, Robert, 194
Fenichel, Otto, 5
Fichte, Johann Gottlieb, 16
Flaubert, Gustave, 30
Fogarasi, Béla, 12, 147–148, 191
Fougeyrollas, Pierre, 11
Franco, Francisco, 206
Frankfurt School, 3, 8, 42
Freeman, Walter, 149
Freud, Anna, 65
Freud, Sigmund, 3, 5–6, 8–9, 22, 25, 28–29, 38, 93–94, 169
Freudo-Marxism, 3
Fromm, Erich, 5, 7

Ganser, S. J. M., 215, 217
Garaudy, Roger, 89–90, 191–192, 205
Gebsattel, Viktor, 95
Godelier, Maurice, 9
Goldmann, Lucien, 61–62, 89–90, 103, 135, 187
Goldwater, Barry, 121
Gramsci, Antonio, 118
Gumplowicz, Ludwig, 103
Gurvitch, Georges, 176

Habermas, Jürgen, 27

Hamelin, Octave, 167
Hamsun, Knut, 148
Hegel, G.W.F., 13, 42, 90, 118, 168, 179, 208
Heidegger, Martin, 21–22, 28–31, 34
Helmholtz, Hermann, 40
Henry, Lucien, 106
Hertz, Robert 101, 203
Himmler, Heinrich, 187
Hiss, Alger, 157–158
Hitler, Adolph, 97, 146, 148, 159–160, 188, 192, 200, 202–204
Hone, Joseph, 114
Horkheimer, Max, 186
Hsi, Tz'u, 125
Hudal, Alois, 149
Husserl, Edmund, 21–22, 28–30
Huxley, Aldous, 78, 117

Ibsen, Henrik, 29

Jacoby, Russell, 195
Jahweh, 94
Jaspers, Karl, 28, 38, 134
Jaszi, Oscar, 109
Jesus Christ, 94
Jowitt, Lord, 157
Jung, Carl G., 5–6, 22

Kafka, Franz, 39, 47, 49, 81, 121
Kahn, P., 132
Kai-Shek, Chang, 157
Kant, Immanual, 18, 40
Khrushchev, Nikita, 125, 206
Klausen (WWII spy), 162
Kluckhohn, Clyde, 129
Koestler, Arthur, 12, 162
Köhler, Wolfgang, 91–92
Korsch, Karl, 96
Korzybski, Alfred 151, 213
Kreisky, Bruno, 192
Kroeber, Alfred, 129
Lacan, Jacques, 9, 166

Lacroix, Jean, 135
Lagache, Daniel, 125
Lagneau, Jules, 106
Laing, R.D., 4
Lalo, Charles, 11–12, 33–34, 36
Lapassade, Georges, 68

Name Index

LaPiere, Richard, 6
Laplantine, Francois, 65
Lasch, Christopher, 7
Lattimore, Owen, 121, 157–159, 161
Leduc, Victor, 148
Lefebvre, Henri, 11–12, 45, 89, 103, 146, 196
Lenin, Vladimir, 96, 161
Leo III, Pope, 91
Leuret, Francois, 218
Levi-Strauss, Claude, 9, 104
Levy-Bruhl, Lucien, 101–102, 104, 107, 146, 177, 202
Lewy, Guenther, 121
Leys, Simon, 125
Luckmann, Thomas, 96
Lukács, Gyorgy, 3–4, 10–20, 23–27, 34–35, 37–38, 48, 61, 79–80, 89, 90–92, 97, 103–104, 107–108, 115, 117, 119, 121, 124, 131, 135, 150–151, 167, 175–176, 178, 186–187, 193
Luxemburg, Rosa, 125

MacArthur, Douglas, 139
Mach, Ernst, 40
Machiavelli, Niccolo, 201
MacIver, Robert, 138
Mannheim, Karl, 3–4, 9, 11–12, 17–21, 27, 35, 42–43, 62, 64, 67, 71, 103, 109, 117–118, 130, 132, 134, 151, 169–170, 176, 180, 182, 187
Marcuse, Herbert, 3–4, 7–8, 169, 194
Marshall, George C., 159
Marx, Karl, 3, 8–9, 13–15, 17–18, 38, 44, 63, 66, 101, 107–108, 120–121, 130, 133, 136–137, 147, 152, 160, 179, 181, 188, 195, 203
Maupassant, Guy de, 11
Mauss, Marcel, 109–110, 136–137, 193
May, Rollo, 21
McCarthy, Joseph, 158–159, 162
Mead, George Herbert, 3
Mennicke, Carl, 134
Merleau-Ponty, Maurice, 7, 9, 21, 89, 96
Merton, Robert K., 178
Meszaros, Istvan, 12
Meyerson, Emile, 3, 11–12, 26, 35, 39–44, 150, 168
Meynaud, Jean, 135, 136
Mill, John Stuart, 138
Minkowski, Eugene, 3, 9, 11–14, 17, 20–29, 37–38, 45, 50, 65, 72, 79–80, 91, 95, 111–113, 115, 120, 131–132, 151, 165–170, 176, 178, 180, 188, 211–213, 215, 217–218
Monnerot, Jules, 108, 134
Montesinos, Fernando, 123
More, Thomas, 63, 117
Morgenthau, Henry, Jr., 158
Morin, Edgar, 11
Morris, William, 117
Mussolini, Benito, 162

Nàdor, Georg (Gyorgy), 147
Napoleon, 130
Needleman, Jacob, 29
Nelson, Benjamin, 6
Newton, Isaac, 115
Nietzsche, Friedrich, 36, 64

Omar, Caliph, 194
Orwell, George, 66, 117–118, 120–126, 132, 136, 170, 176–177, 191, 193–195, 215
Osborn, Reuben, 7
Ostwald, Wilhelm, 40, 91–92

Pankow, Gisela, 121, 169
Pareto, Vilfredo, 3, 133
Parmenides, 41
Parsons, Talcott, 6
Pavlov, Ivan, 90
Petain, Philippe, 124
Peter the Great, 207
Piaget, Jean, 90, 95, 96, 98, 150
Pilsudsky, Joseph, 162
Pius XII, Pope 72, 75
Plotinus, 165
Pobedonostsev, Konstantine, 179
Poliakov, Leon, 102–103, 137
Polin, Raymond, 35, 37
Popper, Karl, 39, 118, 119, 137
Pucheu, Pierre, 123
Pullberg, Stanley, 10

Rank, Otto, 5
Ratzenhofer, Gustav, 103
Ravaisson, 106
Reich, Wilhelm, 5, 6, 7
Ricoeur, Paul, 176
Rieff, Philip, 6

Riesman, David, 6
Robin, Gilbert, 115
Rodinson, Maxime, 134, 135, 137
Roheim, Geza, 5, 13
Roosevelt, Franklin D., 157, 158
Rossi, Angelo, 145
Rossi, Mario, 114
Ruyer, Raymond, 65, 73, 91, 169, 176, 180, 182

Sartre, Jean-Paul, 9, 10
Scheler, Max, 21, 22, 28
Schlesinger, Rudolph, 149
Schneider, Michael, 8
Sebag, Lucien, 134, 136
Seeman, Melvin E., 97
Séve, Lucien, 9, 10
Shakespeare, William, 188
Sherover, Erica 195
Shils, Edward, 4
Simmel, Georg, 12
Solomon, King, 194
Solzhenitsyn, Aleksandr, 148
Sommer, Robert, 165
Sorokin, Pitirim, 3
Spencer, Herbert, 3, 103
Spengler, Oswald, 118
Sperber, Manes, 159, 205
Stalin, Joseph, 136, 199, 200, 202
Stark, Werner, 130
Stern, Alfred, 118
Strauss, Erwin, 95
Strindberg, August, 39
Swift, Jonathan, 78, 93–94, 111, 114–115

Szende, Peter Pal (Paul), 12, 170
Szondi, Leopold, 125, 169

Tarde, Gabriel, 103
Tatossian, Arthur, 166, 170
Theresa of Avila, Saint, 94
Tito, Josip Broz, 161, 206
Todd, Emmanuel, 98, 168
Tönnies, Ferdinand, 201
Trakl, Georg, 39
Troeltsch, Ernst, 117
Trotsky, Leon, 124, 145–146, 160–161, 202, 204
Truman, Harry S., 122, 148, 157, 159, 204, 206

Warren, Scott, 177
Watts, James W., 149
Weber, Alfred, 19
Weber, Max, 3, 7, 14, 16, 109, 145, 187, 215
Whitehead, Alfred North, 149
Wirth, Louis, 4
Wittfogel, Karl, 151
Wurmser, Andre, 146
Wyrsch, Jacob, 76

Yahweh, 43

Zhdanov, Andrei, 96, 136, 148
Zoltowski, Victor, 170
Zulliger, Hans, 81

Subject Index

affective coldness, 94
alienation, 20, 45, 47, 61, 64, 97, 107, 139, 176, 185, 187–188,
alienation, clinical, 187
Althusserian Marxism, 188
anaxiogenesis, 22
anaxiological consciousness, 45
Animal Farm, 215
anti-dialectics, 43
anti-Semitism, 3, 46, 97, 102, 139, 148, 159, 178, 188, 200
anti-Zionism, 191, 194–195
antidialectics, 137
antihistoricism, 67, 80, 121, 137, 160
antihumanism, 137
anxiety, 32, 114
Arguments, 11
Aryan race, 185
Aufenthalt, 31
autism, 25, 94, 114, 177, 188
axiogenesis, 15, 36, 91–92
axiogenic incapacity, 33
axiogenic totality, 92
axiological experience, 89
axiological bipolarity, 36, 37
axiological crisis, 42
axiological regression, 95
axiology, 5, 15, 34–35, 119

being-in-the-world, 25, 62
Bergsonism, 15, 165, 176
big lie, 35
blocked time, 22
Buridan's donkey, 94

Calvinism, 93, 97
Capital, 14
capitalism and the self, 10
catatonia, 94–95
Catholic doctrine, 75
causality, 102
causality, historical, 139
causality, Mills' definition, 138
China, politics of, 206–208
Christian personalism, 135
Christian theology, 93
collective consciousness, 106
collective ego, 159
colonialism, 193
commodity fetishism, 8, 9, 24
Communist party, French, 9
concentration camps, 81
concentrationary phantasms, 81
conduite d'échec, 178, 186
consciousness, 109
consistency, 93, 97–98
coprophagy, 114
Crusades, 103
cunning of reason, 208

Daltonism, 181
Darwinism, 103
Dasein, 31
Daseinsanalyse, 28, 34
de-Stalinization, 199–206
dead time, 21
dedialectization, 3, 12, 35, 45, 96, 125, 135, 151
delusion, 72, 205

delusional thought, 76
delusional utopianism, 72
democracy, 93
demonization, 135, 137
demystification, 152, 161
derealist thought, 47
dereification, 37
derivations, 133
detotalization, 95, 138
devalorization, 81, 95, 125
diabolic causality, 102
dialectical logic, 146
dialectical materialism, 96
dialectical totality, 104
dialectics, 12, 19, 43, 45, 89ff., 131, 136, 152, 167, 169
dialectics, historical, 206
dissociation, 80
dissymmetry of rights, 186
distorted communication, 27
diversity, 150
Division of Labor in Society, 104–106
Dolchstoss, 139, 159
double funerals, 101
doublethink, 66, 120
duration, 15
Durée bergsonienne, 123
Durkheimianism, 9, 103, 106, 109–110, 187
dystopias, 66

effet pervers, 175ff.
egalitarian nostalgia, 124
Elementary Forms of Religious Life, 107
endogmany and exogamy, 188
entropy, theory of, 91
epistemology, 39, 46
Eskimos, 109
espionage, WWII, 157–158, 162
eternal present, 33
ethics, 95
ethnocentrism, 30, 37, 133
ethnology, 101, 103
Eurocentrism, 102, 104, 108

false consciousness, 5, 18, 26, 39, 46, 61ff., 102, 108, 132, 147, 157, 175ff.
False Consciousness, reception of 4
false identification, 147–148, 160, 191
false identities, 205
fascism, 149, 186

fetishism, 95
fixism, 65
free-floating intelligentsia, 131
French academia, 166
Freudianism, 6
Freudo-Marxism, 7
futurology, 63

Gemeinschaft und Gesellschaft, 201
genetic structuralism, 90
genocide, 5
geometrism, 21, 25
geometrization of time, 161
Gestalt psychology, 89–91, 96, 205
Gestalt theory, 150
good (ethical), 49
grace (Calvinist), 93
Gulliver's Travels, 93–94, 111–115

Hegelianism, 38
hermeneutics of love, 29
heterophobia, 68
hiatus irrationalis, 16
hierarchy, 67
historicism, 97, 117–118, 136
history, rewriting of, 124
history-blindness, 175
Hitler-Trotsky "conspiracy," 146
Hitlero-Trotskyism, 205
hope, principle of, 125
Hungarian Marxism, 1, 2, 5, 11–12, 79, 119, 170

ideal-type, 129, 133, 145, 215
ideas, determination of, 130
Ideenflucht, 30
identification, 41, 43, 94, 132, 150, 168
identification, morbid hypertrophy of, 151
identificatory compulsion, 42
identificatory function, 26, 44
identity, 40, 68, 191
ideological causality, 137–138
ideological consciousness, 12
ideological thought, 67
ideology, 104, 113, 129ff., 132–133, 188
ideology, definitions of, 133–135
ideology, Gabel's definition, 136
ideology, Mannheim's definition of, 130–131
idols of the tribe, 131
imperialism, 179

Subject Index 227

imperialism, Soviet, 146
Incan state, 123
individualism, 105, 108
Irrationalitätsproblem, 16
irrationality, 16, 17, 25, 40
irreversibility, 40, 41, 91, 120, 206
Israeli politics, 195–196
Italian fascism, 105

Jerusalem, archaeology of, 194
Jews, 102–104
Judeo-bolshevism, 148
judgment by analogy, 149
Kampuchea, 105
Kantianism, 14
Khruchevism, 201
law, retroactive, 123
laws, Stalinist, 149
Lebensphilosophie, 14
liberalism, 109
lived time, 22
Lived Time, 212–213, 217

lobotomy, 149

macro-micro analysis, 181
magic, 137
magical thought, 203–204
maleficent space, 16
mana, 107
manic mourning, 125
Manichean thought, 62–63, 132, 135, 139, 151, 160, 204–205, 207
Maoism, 125
Marxism, French, 117
Marxism and psychoanalysis, 6
Marxism, 2, 5–9, 11–12, 14, 16–18, 20–21, 23–28, 48, 67, 89–90, 92, 96, 98, 102=1–3, 106–107, 109, 117–119, 124–125, 130, 132, 137, 152, 161, 175, 177, 187–188, 195, 206
Marxism and psychology, 9
Marxist psychopathology, 29
Marxist theory of ideology, 133
Marxists, 4–7, 10, 17–18, 26–27, 46, 48, 61, 67, 79, 89–90, 92, 94, 97, 103, 105–106, 108–109, 114, 118, 119, 124, 130, 136–137, 147, 152, 160, 167–168, 175–177, 185, 187–188, 191–192, 196, 199

McCarthyism, 3, 20, 121–122, 157, 161, 207
McCarthyist reasoning, 161
mechanical solidarity, 104, 108
methodological individualism, 181
mirror sign, 214
misoneism, 38
modesty, 166
morality, 165
morbid geometrism, 111, 113, 131, 170, 212
morbid rationalism, 9, 25, 41, 45, 65, 71, 94, 113–114, 132, 167–170, 212
Moscow "show trials," 121, 177
mourning work, 203
mundaniziation, 30

nationalism, 65
Nazism, 91, 97, 121, 145–146, 148–149, 176, 178, 182, 185–186, 192
neostructuration, 19, 25, 45
New Left, 7
1984, 177, 120–122, 193–194
noology, 18
normlessness, 97
nosology, 46, 80

objective morality, 96
organic solidarity, 104, 108
organogenesis, 44
Oriental Despotism, 106
Orwellization, 160, 191

parallelism, 98
paranoia, 47, 62, 98, 113
paranoia and history, 159
Pavlovism, 149
personality and social structure, 8
personality theory, 15, 48
perverse equations, 148, 192–193
perversion, 95
phenomenological compensation, 25
phenomenological psychiatry, 14
phenomenological psychopathology, 169
phenomenology, 21
phenomenology of love, 28
police conception of history, 205
poststructuralism, 8
Poverty of Historicism, 118–119
praxis, 26, 45

precariousness, 15, 33, 93, 97–98
presentification of history, 161
presentocentrism, 137
prevision, 39
primitivism, 110
principle of hope, 64
privileged knowledge, 42
privileged systems of thought, 43
pseudo-values, 98
psycho-structural theory, 27
psychopathology (summary table), 50
psychosis, 32
public sphere, 2

racism, 25, 43, 47–48, 91–92, 97, 101–103, 133, 148, 151, 159, 178, 185ff., 192–193
raison d'etat, 146
rationality, 29, 46, 111
rationality, demise of, 186
rationality, types of, 187
rationalization, 15–16, 19, 79
reasons of state, 95
reification, 5, 13–14, 19–20, 34, 39–41, 79, 92–93, 95, 107–108, 113, 139, 175–176
reification, logic of, 97
reification syndrome, 26, 80
reified consciousness, 15, 23, 47, 177
reified logic, 188
reified morality, 95
reified society, 108
religious alienation, 108
repression, 66
repressive desublimation, 3
requiredness, 92
residues, 133
revisionist view of WWII, 194–195

schizophrenia, 24, 26, 28, 38, 45, 47, 111, 151
schizophrenia, concept of, 211ff.
schizophrenia, definition of, 5
schizophrenia, logic of, 213–215
schizophrenia, political, 168
schizophrenic symptomatology, 80
Second Law of Thermodynamics, 36
secular religion, 108
seinsadäquat, 132
sexuality and paranoia, 77

social density, 104
social evolution, 106
social ontology, 23
social responsibility, 106
socialism, polycentric, 204–205
society-blindness, 103, 136, 179
socio-pathological parallelism, 46
sociocentrism, 42, 150
sociologism, 28, 34, 44, 103, 136
sociology of knowledge, 62, 96
sociology of morality, 146
sociology *vis a vis* psychoanalysis, 6
sociopathology, 5
Soviet ideology, 12
Soviet politics, 175
space, 38
space/time relations, 41, 120
spatiality, 26
spatialization, 25, 45, 120–121, 170, 178
species-being, 44
Stalinism, 4, 11, 96, 108, 118, 121–122, 125, 130, 132, 137, 139, 145, 147–149, 151–152, 160–161, 167–168, 175, 186, 191, 205, 207
Stalinization, 201, 202
stereotypes, 64
Stimmung, 30
subrealism, 63, 67
superstructure, 130
surrealism, 47, 63
surrealist utopia, 65
synthetic judgment, 40
syntony, 23

temporality, 17, 40
temporalization, 13, 32, 37, 121
time mastery, 122
Titoism, 205
total consistency, 97
total ideology, 18
totalism, 119
totalitarian truth, 201–202
totalitarianism, 65, 110
totalities, 92, 94
totality, 34–35, 37, 65, 150
totemism, 81, 101, 104
transcendence of being, 67
Tsadikim, 165–166
Tsedek, test, 165
twilight hysteria, features of, 215–217

unwarranted extrapolation, 149, 151
utopian consciousness, 18, 62, 180
utopias, 169

valorization, 98
value consistency, 47
values, 36, 49
Verstehen, 28
Verstiegenheit, 29

Verweltlichung, 30, 32
vital contact, 22

Wahnstimmung, 47
white man's burden, 109
World War I, 139
WUE (*Weltuntergangserlebniss*), 38

Zionism, 64–65, 139, 148, 191–194

STAFFORD LIBRARY
COLUMBIA COLLEGE
1001 ROGERS STREET
COLUMBIA, MO 65216